CARIBBEAN BY CRUISE SHIP

Compliments of
Cruise Connoisseurs

DOCUMENTATION

Passenger Name_____

Ship Name_____

Date of Voyage_____

Stateroom_____

Trunk Bay, St. John, U.S. Virgin Islands

CARIBBEAN
By Cruise Ship

THE COMPLETE GUIDE TO CRUISING THE CARIBBEAN

ANNE VIPOND

THIRD EDITION

*YOUR PORTHOLE
COMPANION*

TM

**OCEAN
CRUISE
GUIDES**

Vancouver, Canada   Pt. Roberts, USA

Published by: Ocean Cruise Guides Ltd.
Canada: USA:
4844 Cedar Cres.   PO Box 2041
Delta, B.C. V4M 1J8   Pt. Roberts, WA 98281-2041

Editors: Mel-Lynda Andersen, Richard Rogers
Contributing Editors: William Kelly, Michael DeFreitas
Additional Photography: Michael DeFreitas, Gordon Persson
Artwork by Alan H. Nakano
Cartography: Reid Jopson, Doug Quiring, Cartesia, OCG
Design: Ocean Cruise Guides
Printed and bound in Canada.
Publisher: William Kelly
Visit our web site: oceancruiseguides.com
email:info@oceancruiseguides.com
National Library of Canada Cataloguing in Publication Data

Vipond, Anne, 1957-
  Caribbean by cruise ship

Includes index.
ISBN 0-9697991-9-5

1. Cruise ships--Caribbean Area--Guidebooks. 2. Caribbean Area--Guidebooks. I. Title.
F2165.V56 2001   917.2904'52   C2001-911145-2

Producing a travel guide that is both informative and entertaining is always a challenge, and such projects require the assistance of many people and organizations. We appreciate the help and direction on Caribbean history from Dr. Margaret Krigger at the University of Virgin Islands. We also received valuable help from Carol Wakefield of the St. Croix Landmarks Society. Others who generously shared their expertise were Dr. Alina Szmant, University of Miami, who specializes in marine life; Fred Wickstrom, a professor of music at the University of Miami; and Frank Lepore of the National Hurricane Center in Miami. We also appreciate the co-operation of George Brizan, leader of the National Democratic Congress of Grenada, and Robert McCoy of Rio Grande Press Inc., Glorieta, New Mexico.

We would like to acknowledge the cruise lines that provided photography and information. In particular, Holland America Line, Royal Caribbean International, Celebrity Cruises, Princess Cruises, Seabourn Cruise Line, Windstar Cruises, Carnival Cruise Lines and Norwegian Cruise Line. We also thank the port authorities at Miami, Fort Lauderdale, Port Canaveral, Tampa and Galveston. In addition, we thank the many tourism departments which were, without exception, generous with their time and resources. This includes the tourism staff in Florida, New Orleans, Antigua, Barbados, British Virgin Islands, Puerto Rico, St. Kitts and U.S. Virgin Islands, where Juel Anderson and her associates were especially helpful.

A special thank you to Nan Vipond and Joyce Kelly.

CONTENTS

Foreword..VIII

PART ONE

GENERAL INFORMATION

CHOOSING YOUR CRUISE 10

    Land Tours 15

    Shore Excursions 16

PORTS OF CALL...20

PREPARING FOR YOUR CRUISE..24

THE CRUISE SHIP 32

NATURAL PHENOMENA 40

HISTORY OF THE CARIBBEAN

    Overview 47

    Slavery 56

    Pirates! 64

    Shipwrecks...69

    Sugar & Rum..70

    Today's Caribbean...74

    Caribbean Music..80

ARCHITECTURE IN THE CARIBBEAN 84

PLANT & ANIMAL LIFE 88

PART TWO

THE VOYAGE & THE PORTS

OVERVIEW 106

Chapter 1 FLORIDA 108

Chapter 2 GULF OF MEXICO PORTS....................................134
(Includes New Orleans, Houston and Galveston)

Chapter 3 COZUMEL AND THE YUCATAN..............................142
(Includes Belize and Roatan Island)

Chapter 4 GRAND CAYMAN 156

Chapter 5 JAMAICA...164

Chapter 6 BAHAMAS...176

Chapter 7 SAN JUAN, PUERTO RICO.....................................188

Chapter 8 U.S. VIRGIN ISLANDS 204
(St. Thomas, St. John and St. Croix)

Chapter 9 BRITISH VIRGIN ISLANDS.....................................224

Chapter 10 ST. MAARTEN / ST. MARTIN 234
(Includes Anguilla and St. Barts)

Chapter 11 ST. KITTS (Includes Nevis, St. Eustatius, Saba) 246

Chapter 12 ANTIGUA (Includes Barbuda and Montserrat)..............258

Chapter 13 GUADELOUPE / MARTINIQUE...............................270

Chapter 14 DOMINICA / ST. LUCIA 282

Chapter 15 GRENADA (Includes St. Vincent & the Grenadines) 294

Chapter 16 BARBADOS...306

Chapter 17 ARUBA, CURACAO, BONAIRE 320

Chapter 18 VENEZUELA / TRINIDAD & TOBAGO 336
(Includes Caracas and Isla Margarita)

GLOSSARY OF CRUISE LINES 342

INDEX 348

COLOR PULL-OUT MAP 353
WITH PORT MAPS

The island-dotted Caribbean Sea is perfectly suited to a cruise vacation. Ever since the concept was pioneered in the 1960s, when jet planes became the new mode of transAtlantic travel and shipping companies sought alternate roles for their ocean liners, the Caribbean has been the most popular cruising area in the world. The beauty of its beaches is legendary and its turquoise waters remain warm year round – ideal conditions for swimming, snorkeling and other water sports.

The region is also rich in culture. The West Indies once formed the most important colonial region in the world, when sugarcane was widely cultivated here on plantations. Each island nation has its own history and local flavor, an exotic mix of Indian, African, European and Asian influences. The African influence is most evident in the people themselves – their love of rhythmic music and their bold use of color in everything from folk art and batik clothing to their colonial architecture, be it a canary yellow fort, a flamingo pink church or a lime green government building. West Indian homes boast bright wooden shutters and gingerbread fretwork, and the local fishermen paint their skiffs a combination of rainbow reds, yellows and blues, inspired no doubt by an aquamarine sea shimmering across the colorful corals and tropical fish.

Sailing vessels have long plied the Caribbean's warm waters, riding the constant trade winds that temper the region's heat and humidity. North Americans yearning to escape the gray grip of winter soon find their senses reawakened by the warm breezes, the fragrant flowers and the carefree mode of travel that a cruise vacation provides. The ships usually pull into port as dawn is breaking, treating their passengers to the magic of a seaborne arrival as the golden pink sun rises above a rippled sea and the verdant shores of a volcanic island draw ever nearer. The departure is equally special, the ship easing away from shore and heading out to sea as the setting sun casts its Caribbean colors across the sky. For a vacation of relaxation and romance, nothing surpasses a cruise among these islands of endless summer.

– Anne Vipond

PART I

General Information

CHOOSING YOUR CRUISE: WHICH ITINERARY?

The West Indies extend in a wide, 2,500-mile arc from Florida to Venezuela, separating the Atlantic Ocean from the Caribbean Sea. They are comprised of the Bahama Islands, the Greater Antilles – which are the larger islands of Cuba, Haiti/Dominican Republic, Jamaica and Puerto Rico – and the Lesser Antilles, which are the smaller islands to the east and south. The Lesser Antilles are further divided into the Leeward and Windward groups, terms from the days of sail in reference to the prevailing trade winds.

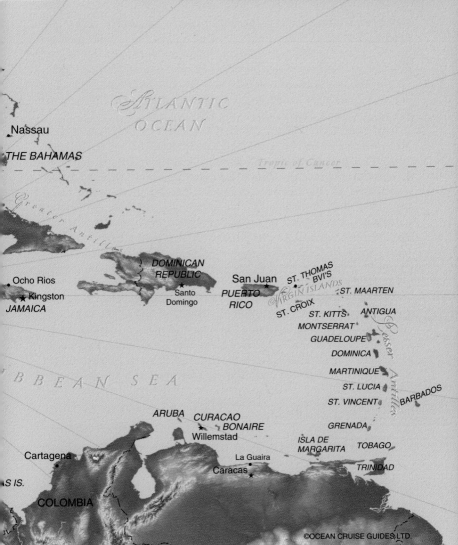

The many cruise ships plying the Caribbean can spread out and offer a variety of routes and combinations of ports. They use several base ports, the major ones being Florida's Miami and Fort Lauderdale, and Puerto Rico's San Juan. Other base ports include Port Canaveral (for cruises to the Bahamas), and Tampa, New Orleans, Houston and Galveston for cruises to the Western Caribbean.

The cruise lines arrange their itineraries to give passengers a good diversity of ports. Various European nations colonized the region and to this day a number of islands remain colonies of Britain, regions of France or members of the Kingdom of the Netherlands. The colonial architecture, customs, language and cuisine of each island reflect its Spanish, Danish, British, French or Dutch past. But the differences between islands are not only cultural. Some are flat and arid, others are lush and mountainous. Some are noted for their beautiful beaches, others for their excellent snorkelling and diving. One island might be included specifically for duty-free shopping, yet another for its natural beauty of volcanic mountains and tropical rainforests.

A **Western Caribbean** cruise includes such destinations as Key West, Jamaica, Grand Cayman, the Mexican island of Cozumel and the nearby Yucatan Peninsula with its famous Mayan ruins. An **Eastern Caribbean** cruise usually takes in the Bahamas, the U.S. Virgin Islands (specifically St. Thomas with its famous duty-free port) and the half-Dutch/half-French island of St. Maarten/St. Martin. **Southern Caribbean** cruises, many of which depart from San Juan, stop at a few Eastern ports but also proceed southward along the Lesser Antilles, often right to the Venezuelan coast, venturing into less-travelled waters and visiting quieter islands where tourism is not as highly developed and the authentic West Indian lifestyle is still predominant.

Caribbean cruises vary in length, from weekend getaways to extensive 16-day voyages. Seven-day itineraries remain as the standard cruise, with some lines offering the option of booking back-to-back cruises on alternate routes. Ten-day cruises are also popular, with a few more ports of call added and usually departing from Florida to the Southern Caribbean. The ideal itinerary for many is a 14-day cruise

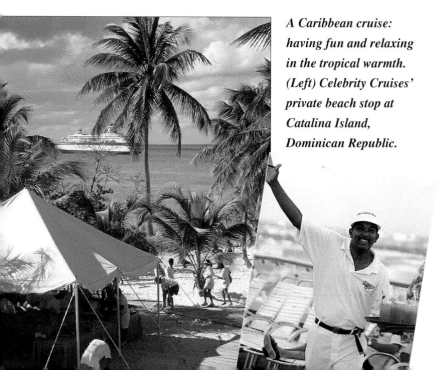

A Caribbean cruise: having fun and relaxing in the tropical warmth. (Left) Celebrity Cruises' private beach stop at Catalina Island, Dominican Republic.

(Above) Approaching St. Thomas, Royal Caribbean's Enchantment of the Seas is a good example of a large ship with all the amenities. (Below) Shown docking in Castries, a Seabourn mega-yacht is pure luxury.

deep into southern waters, stopping at a variety of islands. Simply put, the Caribbean is such a great destination, it warrants several visits.

WHICH SHIP?

The selection of ships cruising the Caribbean is exhaustive. Since this is the world's most popular cruise destination, every kind of ship – mega-ships, small luxury ships and sailing vessels – offers Caribbean itineraries. In recent years, the major cruise lines have been launching increasingly larger ships, and the array of onboard facilities has transformed them into impressive floating resorts, providing myriad activities for passengers. In addition to several swimming pools, a sports deck, health spa and fitness center, standard features also include a show lounge, movie theater, shopping arcade, library and youth center. And the traditional selection of intimate lounges has been joined by alternative restaurants for passengers who would rather not dine in the main dining room each evening. The passenger capacity on these large ships is generally about 2,000, with a few ships accommodating more than 3,000. Five- and six-star ships are generally more spacious than the mainstream ships and have a more refined atmosphere.

In contrast to the large ships are the small luxury ships carrying 100 to 300 passengers. Being aboard one of these upscale vessels is similar to being on board a billionaire's private yacht. The service is attentive and personalized and, although the onboard facilities are not as exten-

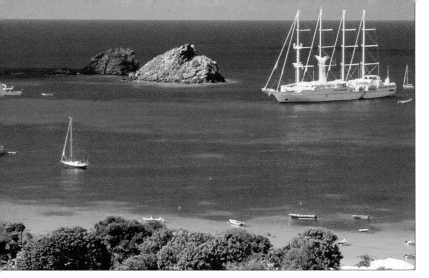

Windstar's luxury sailing ships anchor off secluded islands and pull into the less-visited ports of the Caribbean.

sive as on the large liners, all appointments are of the highest quality and some of the features are unique, such as a stern that folds out into a swimming platform, from which passengers can partake in various water sports while the ship is at anchor.

The romance of sail is a strong allure on the many sailing cruise ships, which range from small windjammers to large clipper-style ships carrying a few hundred passengers. While these ships use engines to help propel the vessel under most conditions, the sails are often raised in the trade winds of the Caribbean. Passengers can usually participate in sail handling through informal classes on board. Life on these vessels is unstructured, the cabins are compact and the meals less elaborate than on large ships, although some sailing vessels – such as the Windstar fleet – offer luxury accommodations and service.

The large ships pull into the popular ports while the small luxury ships and sailing vessels tend to visit quieter, less developed islands. Major cruise lines often include a private island stop in their itineraries, anchoring off a small undeveloped island (usually in the Bahamas) where passengers can spend a day on shore enjoying the cruise company's private beach, water sports equipment and snack bar facilities.

The **Glossary of Cruise Lines** at the back of this book provides a brief description of the various lines and ships servicing the Caribbean. To obtain more information on picking a cruise line, peruse the Internet or book stores, and visit a travel agent. In North America, look for an agency displaying the CLIA logo, indicating its agents have received training from the Cruise Lines International Association. Cruise agents are usually an excellent source of information, with personal knowledge of many ships. An experienced agent can provide important detail, including specific itineraries and cabin choices, and obtain the best deals available – both early-bird specials and last-minute promotions.

WHEN – AND HOW – TO GO

The weather varies little throughout the year in the Caribbean, due to the moderating effect of the surrounding water and steady breezes. The average temperature – about 80 degrees (26 Celsius) – fluctuates less than 10 degrees between the warmest and coldest months. The hottest, wettest months are in summer, marking the start of the hurricane season, which begins in July and continues through to November, the peak hurricane season being late August to early October. Cruise ships receive weather information from the National Hurricane Center and stay well away from the track of any approaching hurricane.

The topography of each island determines its local climate, with the low-lying islands receiving about half the rainfall of the mountainous ones, their leeward sides being dryer than their windward sides. On mountainous islands with many rivers, run-off during spells of heavy rain will send sediment into the water and reduce visibility for divers.

The most popular months for Caribbean cruising are mid-October to mid-April, with the peak season starting at Christmastime and lasting to the end of March, at which time the majority of ships leave the area to spend the summer in either Alaska or Europe. A few, however, remain in the Caribbean year-round.

Although air connections to and from your cruise can usually be arranged by the cruise line, there may be a premium for this convenience and the routing could be convoluted, with stopovers and plane changes. Paying the deviation fee ($50 and up) offered by most lines gives you some latitude in choosing the airline, routing and schedule. Cruise lines sometimes include transfers and hotel with their flights.

LAND TOURS

See Florida, Gulf of Mexico and San Juan chapters for more detail.
A cruise is a good opportunity to combine a vacation at sea with a land-based holiday. If time allows, fly to your port of embarkation at least a day before the cruise begins and avoid the stress of making same-day

Key West is an easy drive from Miami for passengers embarking on a pre- or post-cruise land tour of Florida.

A pre-cruise stay in Florida offers a chance to enjoy the state's fine beaches, good restaurants and wide selection of accommodation.

travel connections. Better yet, stay two or three nights at the base port and take the time to enjoy the local sights. Cities such as Fort Lauderdale, Miami, Tampa, New Orleans and San Juan, Puerto Rico are all tourist destinations in themselves and warrant a brief stay, either at the beginning or end of a Caribbean cruise. Most cruise lines offer hotel packages at these turn-around (home) ports, and several offer extended land tours.

The walled city of Old San Juan is especially fun to explore on foot, with its romantic setting of colonial buildings, excellent restaurants, fine beaches and some of the best shopping in the Caribbean. Florida also has numerous tour options and there is lots to explore in the Sunshine State between the John F. Kennedy Space Center near Port Canaveral and the highway leading south to the Everglades and Key West. Your travel agent should be able to sort through the hotel and tour options at any of these ports and arrange a complete cruise-tour package that suits your schedule and budget.

SHORE EXCURSIONS

See each chapter in Part II for more details.

In the Caribbean, many 'shore' activities actually take place in the water – swimming off soft sand beaches, snorkeling among coral gardens, scuba diving to shipwrecks inhabited by tropical fish, and skimming across the water on a windsurfer, catamaran or 12-meter racing yacht. For those who prefer to stay dry, submarine rides, semi-submersibles and glass-bottomed boats afford effortless views of the underwater world. Airborne excursions include helicopter

Racing a 12-meter yacht at St. Maarten.

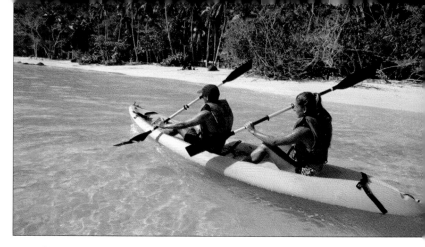

Kayaking is a popular shore activity at the ports of call and private beach stops. (Below) Island drives often include panoramic lookouts, such as this one at Estate St. Peter Greathouse on St. Thomas.

and seaplane flights for panoramic views of island-dotted waters, and parasailing off pristine beaches. There are also boat trips to secluded beaches, river rafting through mangrove forests, kayaking across tropical lagoons and hiking in tropical rainforests, where waterfalls, crater lakes and freshwater pools create a paradisal setting for the birds and animals living there.

In addition to the Caribbean's natural beauty, its colonial history can be explored on island drives to such points of interest as Nelson's Dockyard on Antigua and Brimstone Hill Fortress on St. Kitts. Some of the islands' former sugar plantation estates are open to the public, their grand mansions now museums and the grounds now parklands containing picnic tables and botanical gardens. The ports themselves often have numerous historical sites with colonial forts, churches and government buildings lining narrow cobblestone streets, where restored warehouses now contain shops and restaurants. A number of ports have local botanical gardens for easy viewing of the many indigenous and exotic plants that grow in the region.

Mullet Bay Resort, St. Maarten, is one of many golf courses open to cruise passengers. (Left) Atlantis submarine rides are offered at several Caribbean islands.

Most cruise lines offer organized shore excursions for the convenience of their passengers. These are described in a booklet enclosed with your cruise tickets. Onboard presentations are also given by the ship's shore excursion manager. There is a charge for these excursions, but they are usually fairly priced, and the tour operators are reliable, monitored by the cruise company to ensure they maintain the level of service promised to passengers, with the added advantage that the ship will wait for any of its overdue excursions, so there's no concern about missing the ship.

Ship-organized shore excursions cover a whole range of activities and are attractive for their convenience. You are transported to and from the ship, any needed equipment is provided and you know ahead of time how long the tour will last and how much it will cost. And while ship-organized shore excursions are not the only option, they are recommended for certain activities such as scuba diving. Several cruise lines offer scuba certification programs sanctioned by PADI (Professional Association of Diving Instructors), which include academic study, pool practice and open-water dives with professional guides.

Also recommended are ship-organized golf tours (some island courses limit play to residents and cruise passengers who purchase advance tee times). Tennis, on the other hand, is best arranged independently. Many Caribbean resorts let non-guests use their tennis courts for a fee, and the ship's shore excursion office can usually provide current information and recommendations for each port of call.

For independent sightseeing, renting a car is an option on most islands. However, driving is often on the left, the roads can be narrow and winding and a temporary driver's license is usually required in addition to the rental fee, bringing the total cost above that of hiring a taxi for a few hours. However, it's fun to strike out on your own, and the roads are often quiet once you get away from the port area. Just be sure to give yourself plenty of time to get back to the ship – distances can take longer to cover than anticipated on some of the islands' narrow and winding roads. Good islands to explore with a rented car include Barbados (with well-maintained roads, a scenic east coast and numerous countryside attractions), St. Kitts (with a new highway to the Southeast Peninsula) and the U.S. Virgin Islands. To save time and ensure the availability of a rental car, it's best to reserve ahead through your travel agent. Major car rental companies operate on most islands.

Hiring a taxi is another option. If you decide to take a taxi tour, chat with a few drivers and choose one who is friendly and shows promise as a tour guide. Most drivers are a wealth of information and represent an opportunity to learn more about the local people while seeing the island's natural and historical sights. Always agree beforehand on the price of the tour and exactly which stops are included. If you enjoyed the tour, a tip is appropriate. Fares to popular destinations are usually set by the local taxi association and posted near the cruise ship pier. At some ports a taxi director is stationed at the cruise pier to quote fares and direct passengers to qualified drivers. Other ports may provide pierside information booths.

Beaches are often within walking distance or a short taxi ride away and most are open to tourists, although it's not unusual for there to be a small admission charge. The beaches on volcanic islands can vary in color, while those on flat coral islands have white sand. Those on the Caribbean side of an island are sheltered; those on the Atlantic side will have a surf. Beachfront hotels often rent lounge chairs, beach umbrellas and the use of lockers and change facilities to the public as well as watersports equipment.

Professional taxi drivers operate well-maintained vehicles and are usually excellent tour guides.

(Above) A tree-lined street in Key West. (Right) Government House in Naussau, capital of Bahamas. (Below) Magnificent Mayan ruins overlook the Caribbean Sea at Tulum, on Mexico's Yucatan peninsula.

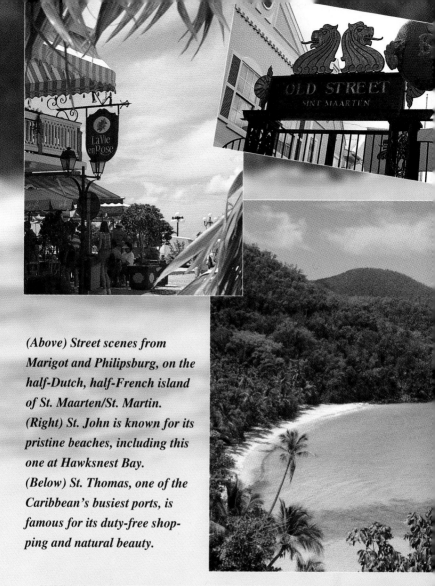

(Above) Street scenes from Marigot and Philipsburg, on the half-Dutch, half-French island of St. Maarten/St. Martin. (Right) St. John is known for its pristine beaches, including this one at Hawksnest Bay. (Below) St. Thomas, one of the Caribbean's busiest ports, is famous for its duty-free shopping and natural beauty.

(Above) Dutch colonial buildings line Willemstad's canal-like harbor on Curacao.
(Left) A ship docks at Fort-de-France, Martinique.
(Below) Snorkeling at Klein Bonaire.

(Above) The idyllic setting at St. Lucia's Marigot Bay. (Right) The British heritage of Barbados is preserved in plantation great houses like St. Nicholas Abbey. (Below) Grenada's Grand Anse beach is considered one of the most beautiful in the Caribbean.

DOCUMENTATION

A valid passport is the best proof of citizenship a traveller can carry, especially in these times of increased airport security. American and Canadian citizens are not required, however, to carry a passport when visiting most countries of the Caribbean, one exception being Venezuela. If you don't have a passport, you will need a birth certificate or a certified copy of one, accompanied by an official photo identification, such as a current driver's license. For American travellers, a U.S. naturalization certificate, accompanied by an official photo identification, is also acceptable. All non-U.S. and non-Canadian citizens must carry a valid passport or, in the case of a U.S. resident alien, an Alien Registration Receipt Card.

Before your departure, leave a detailed itinerary with a family member, friend or neighbor. Be sure to include the name of your ship, its phone number and the applicable ocean code, as well as your cabin number – all of which will be included in your cruise documentation. With this information, a person can place a satellite call to your ship in an emergency. Another precaution is to photocopy on a single sheet of paper the identification page of your passport, your driver's license and any credit cards you will be carrying in your wallet. Keep one copy of this sheet with you, separate from your passport and wallet, and leave another one at home.

Taking out a travel insurance policy at the time of booking is recommended. A comprehensive policy will cover travel cancellation, delayed departure, medical expenses, personal accident and liability, lost baggage and money, and legal expenses. You may already have supplementary health insurance through a credit card, automobile club policy or employment health plan, but you should check these carefully. Whatever policy you choose for your trip, carry details of it with you and documents showing that you are covered by a plan. If you plan on doing any scuba diving, be sure to bring your diving certification.

CURRENCY

Each island has its own legal tender, but American currency is accepted everywhere in the Caribbean, as are major credit cards and traveller's checks. Cab fares are usually paid in cash. It's a good idea to carry some small U.S. bills for minor purchases rather than receive large amounts of local currency in change. Traveller's checks should be cashed on board the ship unless you are planning a large purchase. Prices quoted in this book are in U.S. dollars, unless otherwise noted.

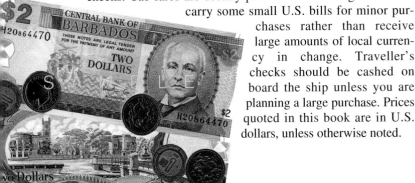

HEALTH PRECAUTIONS

No vaccinations are necessary for a Caribbean cruise, but if you are at risk of complications from the flu or other respiratory illnesses, you may want to get a flu shot. To avoid traveller's diarrhea, it's best to drink bottled water when ashore and never eat a piece of unfamiliar fruit you see hanging from a tree. The poisonous manchineel tree, which grows near beaches, bears fruit resembling small green apples. Contact with these or the tree's leaves, sap or bark will cause a chemical burning. Signs usually identify these trees but the best approach is to stay on designated paths to avoid potentially harmful vegetation. Insects are not a problem, although some of the Central American ports and Mayan jungle sites can have mosquitos.

All large ships have a fully equipped medical center with a doctor and nurses. Passengers needing medical attention are billed at private rates, which are added to their shipboard account. This invoice can be submitted to your insurance company upon your return home.

Modern cruise ships use stabilizers to reduce rolling motion when underway, so seasickness is not a widespread or prolonged problem with most passengers. However, there are several remedies for people susceptible to this affliction. One is to wear special wrist bands, the balls of which rest on an acupressure point. Another option is to chew Meclizine tablets (often available at the ship's front office) or take Dramamine pills. It's best to take these pills ahead of time, before you feel nauseous, and they may make you feel drowsy. Check with your doctor when deciding on medication. Fresh air is one of the best antidotes to motion sickness, so stepping out on deck is often all that's needed to counter any queasiness. Other simple remedies include sipping on ginger ale and nibbling on dry crackers and an apple. Lying down also helps. Should you become concerned about your condition, simply visit the medical center on board for professional attention.

WHAT TO PACK

Pack casual attire for daytime wear – both on board the ship and in port. Cool, loose cottons are best. Include sunglasses, a wide-brimmed straw or cotton hat, and comfortable rubber-soled shoes or sandals. Sunscreen is also important, one with a protection factor of 15 or higher, to shield your skin from the sun's burning rays. Apply generously before going outside and reapply frequently if you are spending time at the beach, even when the sky is overcast. A light sweater will come in handy, as the air conditioning in dining rooms, stores and museums is much cooler than the temperature outside. Your evening wear should include something suitable for the two or three formal nights held on board most ships. Women wear gowns or cocktail dresses and men favor suits. For informal evenings, women wear dresses, skirts or slacks, and men wear sports jackets with either a shirt and tie or an open-necked sports shirt. Shops on board often sell formal and casual wear, and colorful tops and shorts can be purchased at good prices at ports along the way.

Many ships have coin-operated launderettes with an iron and ironing board, or you can pay to have your laundry done, as well as steam pressing and dry cleaning. Basic toiletries, such as soap, shampoo and hand lotion, are usually provided, and other toiletries can be purchased in the onboard shops. A hair dryer may be installed in the stateroom. (Details about a particular ship's amenities can be confirmed with your travel agent.) Beach towels are supplied for use on shore, and it's not necessary to pack snorkelling or diving gear, or golf clubs, because this equipment is usually included in ship-organized shore excursions or can be rented. For boat excursions, deck shoes or light-colored rubber-soled sneakers are needed.

Keep prescribed medication in original, labeled containers and carry a doctor's prescription for any controlled drug. If you wear prescription eyeglasses or contact lenses, consider packing a spare pair. And keep all valuables (traveller's checks, camera, expensive jewelry) in your carry-on luggage, as well as all prescription medicines and documentation (passport, tickets, insurance policy). It's also prudent to pack in your carry-on bag any other essentials you would need in the event that your luggage is late arriving. Last but not least, be sure to leave room in one of your suitcases for souvenirs.

Good walking shoes are imperative for exploring the brick-and-stone walks common in many Caribbean ports of call.

LIFE ABOARD

Cabins – also called staterooms – vary in size but all are clean and comfortable. Telephones and televisions are standard features on most ships, and storage space includes a closet for hanging dresses and suits, and drawers to hold your other clothes and miscellaneous items.

Breakfast and lunch on a cruise ship are usually open seating, with meals served between set times. For dinner you will be asked, when booking your cruise, to indicate your preference for first or second sitting. Some people prefer first sitting as it leaves an entire evening afterwards to enjoy the stage shows and other venues. On the other hand, the second sitting allows plenty of time, after a full day in port, to freshen up and relax before dinner. Many ships now offer alternative restaurants (no set time or table for dinner) for passengers who prefer a less structured approach to dining, and room service is also available for all meals and in-between snacks.

On most ships, passengers are issued a personalized cruise card that is used for charging onboard expenses and also serves as an identity card when leaving or boarding the ship while in port, at which time it is shown to security personnel monitoring the movement of passengers on and off the ship.

SECURITY

While security is not a major concern when on the ship, you should take some precautions when venturing ashore. Property crime can occur anywhere, but tourists are especially vulnerable. Keep all credit cards and most of your cash securely stowed in an inside pocket of your clothes or shoulder bag, and keep a few small bills in a readily accessible pocket so you're not pulling out your wallet to pay for small impromptu purchases from street vendors. Don't wear expensive jewelry ashore, and leave your passport and other valuables in your cabin safe when going ashore. Do not leave valuables unattended on a beach, and never leave anything of value in a rented car.

EXTRA EXPENSES & TIPPING

There are few additional expenses once you board a cruise ship. All meals (including room service) are included, as are any stage shows, lectures, movies, lounge acts, exercise

Tipping is expected on most ships and usually is well earned.

classes and other activities held in the ship's public areas. Personal services and shore excursions, however, are not covered in the basic price of a cruise, nor are alcoholic drinks ordered in a lounge or with a meal. Most ships are cashless societies in which passengers sign for incidental expenses which are itemized on a final statement and settled by credit card, personal check or cash.

Although tipping is a cruising tradition, no passenger is obligated to give out tips at the end of a cruise. However, most passengers do tip because cruise ship service is usually worth rewarding. Cruise lines normally provide guidelines on how much to tip various staff, but a general rule is to tip the cabin steward about US$3 per passenger per day, your waiter the same amount, and your busboy half that amount. The maître d' and head waiter also can be tipped, if you decide the service and attention warrant a reward and the tips are about $1.50 per passenger a day. Tips are usually given the last night of the cruise and envelopes for this are often left conspicuously in your cabin. And, just because each is labeled, it doesn't necessarily follow each needs to be filled with cash. Tipping your cabin steward a partial amount at the onset of the cruise can be a good tack to ensure prompt service for any special requests that may come up during the cruise.

PHONING HOME

Passengers can phone home from the ship, either through the ship's radio office or by placing a direct satellite telephone call. This is expensive, however, and unless the call is urgent, you may want to wait and place it from a land-based phone. The pre-paid telephone calling card is an easy way for passengers to place long-distance calls while in port. Sold on board some ships, these cards allow the user to make international and domestic calls from any touchtone phone. Pre-paid Caribbean calling cards are sold at most ports of call, and public phones are usually located at or near the cruise pier. AT&T calling centers are also found at major ports of call.

The Caribbean spreads across three time zones. Islands east of Dominican Republic are on Atlantic time while those extending westward to the Cayman Islands are in the Eastern time zone. Cozumel, lying off the Yucatan peninsula, falls within the Central time zone.

VACATION PHOTOS

Photographs are often the most cherished souvenirs we have of our vacation, and even casual photographers will enjoy capturing the vibrant colors of the Caribbean on film. If you are taking a brand new camera on your trip, shoot and develop a roll of film at home beforehand to make sure the camera works properly and that you understand all of its features. The lighting conditions will range from brilliant beach scenes to dim light in the rainforest. For automatic cameras, 200-ASA print film is your best choice for all-around lighting conditions, although you may want to pack a few rolls of 400-ASA film for rainforest hikes.

Pack plenty of film and make sure you've got fresh batteries in the camera. When framing a shot, the subject matter should fill the frame, so move in closer if there's a lot of superfluous space in your viewfinder. If you're shooting underwater photos, be aware that water absorbs light, with red and orange colors reaching only a short distance below the surface, which is why the color blue dominates underwater photos (see example at right) unless special lighting is used. To protect your exposed film from airport X-ray machines when returning home, either pack the rolls inside a lead-lined pouch or keep them in your carry-on bag and ask for a hand inspection.

SHOPPING

The Caribbean is famous for its 'free ports' where the selection and savings on luxury goods are among the world's best. With few local manufacturing industries to protect, most Caribbean countries charge no duty on imports, nor is there sales tax, resulting in savings of up to 50%. These savings are passed on to visitors who, in turn, are allowed a duty-free allowance on goods they take home. Special permits are required to bring home restricted animal products made from certain species, including sea turtles and corals.

Before you embark on your cruise, you may want to visit your local customs office and register any valuables you plan to take with you (i.e. cameras, jewelry) so that you have no problem reimporting them duty- and tax-free. Separate from

(Below) A shopping street in Philipsburg, St. Maarten.

(Above) Clothings stalls at Needhams Point, Barbados. (Below) Jewellers line the streets of Charlotte Amalie.

goods bought at duty-free prices are those that are duty-exempt. Any item purchased in its country of manufacture is duty-exempt such as locally made handicrafts. Loose gems – emeralds, diamonds, rubies and sapphires – are also duty-exempt.

Your ship's port lecturer will offer valuable advice on what to look for and where to shop at each port of call. Although recommended merchants often pay a promotional fee to the cruise line, they must guarantee the integrity of goods they are selling to the line's passengers. If you are considering an expensive purchase, it's prudent to shop at stores known or recommended by the cruise line.

When buying a piece of jewelry, its quality grades, carat weight, gold content and purchase price should all be noted on the receipt, an important document for insuring the item when you return home. Gold content is measured in karats, with one karat equalling 1/24 part gold. Pure gold is 24 karats while an alloy containing, for example, 75% gold is 18 karats. Precious stones are weighed in carats, one carat equalling 200 milligrams.

Diamonds are graded for clarity and color. Only trained gemologists can accurately determine a diamond's grade, but there are a few features you can look for. If, for instance, you are buying a cluster ring or tennis bracelet, look to see if all stones are fairly well matched without any one being a different color than the rest. To test for brilliance, stand back from the bright lights of the showcase and see if the gems maintain their sparkle. Good buys in the Caribbean include large single diamonds and tennis bracelets.

(Above) At St. John's, Antigua, the cruise ships dock adjacent to Redcliffe Quay, its upscale shops housed in heritage buildings.

The world's finest emeralds are mined in Colombia and many of these stones are brought directly to the Caribbean, where jewellers sell them at impressively low prices. Emeralds, like diamonds, are sold by weight but the cut of the stone is less important than its color. The darker the emerald, the higher its value, yet shoppers should buy the color they personally prefer. All emeralds are flawed so be suspicious of someone offering you a dark green stone with no visible flaws at a low price, for it might be a fake. Also, a green oil is sometimes rubbed on an emerald to hide its flaws and deepen its color – until the oil wears off – so it's important to buy an emerald from a reputable dealer.

While the selection of brand-name luxury goods, including leather, linen, perfumes, cameras and electronics is truly tantalizing, not to be overlooked are locally made goods. Look for Caribbean clothing made of high-quality, sea island cotton. Batik and tie-dye processes are often used to color the clothing with bright floral patterns. Colorful Caribbean artwork, widely influenced by Haitian primitive art, ranges from folk art to fine art. Wood crafts, basket weaving, pottery and doll-making are practiced throughout the islands and these unique souvenirs can be bought at local markets and craft shops. Crafts tables are often set up near the cruise pier and some terminals contain shopping malls with a selection of duty-free goods and locally made arts, crafts and clothing.

A resident of Dominica sells flowers near Trafalgar Falls.

Holland America Line's Zaandam (63,000 tons, 2000) is a good example of the wood and warm colors seen in today's ship interiors.

Cruising the Caribbean provides many opportunities to ponder the complex workings of a modern cruise ship. Where once a voyage took months from South America to Florida, now it takes only days. Even a modern yacht, equipped with highly efficient sails, an auxiliary engine and satellite navigation equipment, can transit the Caribbean with a fraction of the effort required during Columbus's time.

The complexities of ships prompted mariners to develop their own nomenclature. A colorful vocabulary has been adapted with lyrical precision to describe each task. As quoted in Smythe's *Sailor's Word-Book*, "How could the whereabouts of an aching tooth be better pointed out to an operative dentist than Jack's, 'Tis the aftermost grinder aloft, on the starboard quarter.'"

During the 15th century, when commerce with distant lands became increasingly profitable, trading countries began investing in improvements to ship design. This resulted in stronger, faster ships with better sailing characteristics. Chart-making was also improved, as were navigational instruments, all of which resulted in greater confidence in ocean travel and exploration. It is this legacy of discovery, combined with tales of daring and adventure, that has given shipboard travel an aura of romance and mystique.

Sea travel attained elegance in the 20th century when grand transatlantic ocean liners were introduced. Opulent and breathtaking inside, graceful and inspiring to view from shore, these ships usually had an extended bow, rounded stern and raked funnels. Although design aspects have changed, today's cruise ships retain the ocean liner tradition of building attractive ships with well-appointed interiors.

Stern — Telecommunication Domes — Funnel — Navigation Bridge — Anchoring gear — Rudder — Propeller — Engine Room — Stabilizer — Thrusters — Bow Bulb — Bow

HOW SHIPS MOVE

Ships are pushed through the water with the turning of propellers, two of which are usually used on cruise ships. A propeller is like a screw threading its way through the sea, pushing water away from its pitched blades. Props can be 15 to 20 feet in diameter on large cruise ships and normally turn at 100 to 150 revolutions per minute. It takes a lot of horsepower – about 30,000 on a large ship – to make these propellers push a ship along and almost all cruise ships use diesel engines to do the work. It's the job of the chief engineer and his crew to keep these engines running efficiently. In addition to propelling the ship, the engines generate electrical power for the rest of the ship. Gauges, meters and control panels monitor the various systems that keep hot and cold water flowing to your cabin, lights working, the radio and television playing, and the heat and air conditioning functioning. Computer technology has transformed the workings of a ship's engine room which, in addition to improving engine efficiency, also gives more control and information to the crew on the bridge. The bridge crew can tap into any amount of engine power by moving small levers which adjust the angle (or pitch) of the propeller blades. The angle at which the blades are set determines the speed of the ship.

The amount of soot smoke from today's ships is a fraction of that produced by ships earlier in the century. Up to the end of the First World War, most ships used vast amounts of coal to heat large boilers along the length of the lower part of the ship. As a result, ocean liners of the past usually had two and sometimes three funnels to dispel the exhaust. More efficient steam turbine engines, introduced after the Second World War, replaced coal with diesel oil to generate the needed steam. Normally only one large funnel near the middle of the ship was needed to collect and disperse the gases. Diesel engines on modern ships transmit the power, either directly through a transmission, which can result in some vibration felt throughout the ship, or by supplying electricity to motors that smoothly turn the prop shafts or, more recently, to motors mounted on pods hung from the stern of the ship like huge outboard motors, which can swivel 360 degrees.

One or two rudders are used to turn a ship, in much the same way a paddle is held at an angle in the water to turn a canoe. A hydraulic arm connects the ship's rudder(s) to the helm, a small steering wheel located on the bridge. The bridge, positioned near the bow (the front of the ship), is where the captain and his officers oversee the safe operation of the ship. Almost all aspects of the ship can be monitored here.

A modern ship's underwater appendages include stabilizers, which are small wings located near the middle of the ship about 10 feet below the water's surface. The angle of the wings is constantly adjusted to minimize any rolling motion of the ship. Another innovation is the use of bow and stern thrusters, which have almost entirely replaced the need for tugboats when a ship is being maneuvered. In most situations, a captain can dock his ship using one of three unidirectional joysticks located on the bridge and on both bridge wings. These link the propellers and thrusters to one control center. A symbol, which looks like an upside-down question mark with two small circles inside, is painted on the hull near the bow to indicate the location of the bow thrusters in relation to the bow bulb. The bow bulb reduces the bow wave, allowing a ship's hull to move more efficiently through the water.

NAVIGATIONAL CHALLENGES
IN THE CARIBBEAN

The Caribbean poses a number of challenges for cruise ship officers, not the least of which are hurricanes from June to November. However, weather information has become very accurate in the last few decades and officers are aware of approaching storms well in advance. If necessary, cruise ships will take evasive action and, with the speed and power to avoid serious threat, will alter course for other ports. Ships are usually safer at sea than near land, where wind strengths can increase dramatically, and there is the danger of a ship being blown onto a reef or suffering damage while moored to a dock.

Pinpoint navigation is lesson number one for all junior officers on a cruise ship, who must always be aware of local hazards, such as reefs or strong ocean currents. Specifically, currents are strong in the Straits of Florida (between Florida and Cuba) where the Gulf Stream flows north at speeds up to five miles per hour. Old Bahama Channel and the Windward Passage (between Haiti and Cuba) also have north-flowing currents, as does Cozumel Channel, where currents can reach four m.p.h. If undetected, a strong current can slowly push a ship off course and lead to danger. During the days of the Spanish Main in the Caribbean, a number of galleons came to ruin when pushed by currents onto sandbars or reefs.

The Caribbean is now well charted and the numerous reefs and submerged hazards are known and indicated on nautical charts. Ships also use sophisticated depth sounders, which give the officers an accurate picture of the seabed to ensure there is ample water below the keel. A pilot is usually aboard to guide a ship into and out of each port, drawing on his local knowledge to advise the captain .

A few Caribbean ports present special challenges during docking. The most difficult ports are: Cozumel for strong currents and afternoon wind, Ocho Rios for strong winds that start early in the evening, and Barbados for the port's twisting, narrow entrance and strong afternoon winds. Grand Cayman also gets a mention by various captains for the swell that rolls into the bay where cruise ships anchor. Curacao can also present difficulties with its narrow entrance and cross winds that develop in the evening. Tampa is a beautiful harbor to exit or enter, with a long entrance to Hillsboro Bay and narrow channels leading to Garrison Seaport, but it can be a navigational challenge during bouts of fog, which occur from January to April.

SHIP SIZE AND REGISTRY

A ship's size is determined by measurements that result in a figure called tonnage. There are approximately 100 cubic feet to a measured ton. Cruise ships used to be called large if they exceeded 30,000 tons and, while that's still a big ship, most new ships are well over 50,000 tons. At the stern of every ship, below its name, is the ship's country of registry. It may be surprising to note that your ship is registered in Monrovia, Liberia, Panama or the Bahamas. Certain countries grant registry to ships for a flat fee, with few restrictions or onerous charges, and ships often fly these 'flags of convenience' for tax reasons.

Small ships (up to about 20,000 tons) will roll around a bit more in a bad sea, but are able to visit smaller remote ports. They also offer a more intimate onboard atmosphere, especially on the luxury ships which have the ability to cater to an individual's every need. Luxury ships in the small-size range include Seabourn Cruise Line's *Pride*, *Spirit* and *Legend*.

Medium-sized ships, up to about 60,000 tons, are a good compromise for cruisers wanting a range of amenities and entertainment yet not wanting to feel they are lost in a hotel complex. Ships of this size are easy to find one's way around on and often have a small-ship, relaxed atmosphere. Good examples include the *Zenith* (Celebrity Cruises), *Royal Princess* (Princess Cruises), *Crystal Symphony* (Crystal Cruises) and *Statendam* (Holland America Line).

Large ships (above 60,000 tons) will have an easier motion at sea and will certainly have more public areas with an amazing array of facilities. Spacious and beautifully appointed, some of these new ships have been extremely well thought-out, conveying both grandeur and a sense of intimacy in their small lounges and bistros. Good examples of this size of ship include the *Sun Princess* (Princess Cruises), *Splendour of the Seas* (Royal Caribbean International), *Galaxy* (Celebrity Cruises), and *Rotterdam* (Holland America Line).

A senior officer and two junior officers, shown plotting the ship's course, are always on the bridge when the ship is underway.

OFFICERS AND CREW

The captain, the highest-ranking officer on a ship, is ultimately responsible for running the ship. He also acts as host to the passengers. Reporting directly to the captain are his officers (ranked 1st to 4th), with the chief officer overseeing the physical condition of the ship. In charge of all technical operations is the chief engineer.

The captain, chief engineer, and their officers and crew, make up only a small portion of total staff on board a ship. The majority of employees are engaged in transforming the ship into a floating resort. Managing this extensive service staff is the hotel manager, who is second in rank only to the captain. Reporting to the hotel manager are various managers in charge of departments ranging from food service to housekeeping. Most visible is the cruise director, who oversees the ship's entertainment and onboard passenger events. He or she usually has a background in show business.

Dining, of course, is a very important aspect of cruising, and the quality and preparation of meals receives a great deal of attention.

Quality control begins on the dock as various food managers inspect shipments before they are delivered aboard. Inspection continues on a daily basis to ensure kitchen staff prepare meals to the standard most passengers expect on a cruise. If a problem with a particular item occurs, a fresh supply will be purchased locally or flown to the ship.

The ship's captain surveys the scene from the ship's bridge.

An inside cabin has all the amenities of a standard outside cabin except for a window.

STATEROOMS ON SHIPS

In a bad sea, the staterooms (cabins) with the least motion will be those in the center of the ship. This means if you are booking an inside cabin, see if your agent can get you in the middle and, if motion sickness is a concern, the lower the better. If you like to sleep in, avoid cabins under dining rooms, promenade decks or pool areas. The sound of scraping chairs could be your wake-up call. If you like to go to bed early, stay away from cabins near the ship's discos.

If experiencing the sea is important to you, then an outside cabin is definitely worth the additional expense. Verandah cabins are especially enjoyable on a Caribbean cruise for soaking up the tropical atmosphere. Also, for those who like to rise early, an outside cabin with the morning light coming in is a pleasant way to get started. Standard outside cabins (without a balcony) have a large fixed (non-opening) picture window and are normally situated on the lower passenger decks, providing a close view of the sea and any passing marine life.

The size of cabins can vary greatly, especially on new ships, ranging from inside cabins of 150 square feet to penthouse suites of over 1,000

An outside suite, such as the one shown here on Princess Cruises' Sun Princess, provides the ultimate in cruise ship accommodations.

square feet. Standard outside cabins will be around 200 square feet. Older ships generally have smaller cabins, some under 100 square feet which, surprisingly enough, can be quite cozy. The majority of new ships have good amenities with the accoutrements of a typical upscale hotel room (like 110 voltage outlets), but be sure to ask your agent if one specific facility, such as a bathtub, is important to you.

SOME REALITIES ON A CRUISE SHIP

Ships depart, almost always, on time. If you are late arriving at your embarkation port from a flight arranged by the cruise line or delayed on a ship-organized shore excursion, the ship will usually wait for you. Otherwise, you will probably be out of luck. Ships will not wait for a passenger or group of passengers who have arranged for their own flights or those who may still be strolling about in a port. There is no roll call or tabulation at each port – it is your responsibility to get back to the ship on time. The all-aboard call is usually half an hour before departure and the gangway is lifted a few minutes before the mooring lines are let go. Make sure you check the ship's departure time at each port, as these will vary. Should you miss your ship, you will have to find your own way to the next port of call, so it's prudent to take a least one credit card when venturing ashore on your own, just in case.

At some ports, the ship will anchor off a distance from the town and passengers are tendered ashore with the ship's launches. The organized shore excursions will be taken ashore first, so if you have booked a shore trip you will assemble with your group. Otherwise, wait an hour or so and the line ups will be shorter. Also, bear in mind that cruise lines reserve the right to change the itinerary of a cruise, which rarely happens and is almost always because of weather conditions.

Regular announcements over the ship's public address system, providing detail of the day's upcoming events, can be tiresome and some ships are more talkative with their passengers than others. Usually these announcements are broadcast in the public areas or over your TV, where you have some control. If they are being piped into your room you can ask your steward to turn down the volume. Anything really important, such as a fire alarm or other general emergency, will still make it into your cabin.

More and more, cruise lines are charging for small incidental items, such as premium-brand coffee and ice cream. Yield ratios, the revenue received from each passenger, have declined since the early 1990s as a result of lower fares, so the cruise lines look to other revenue sources to remain profitable. If the charges are an irritant, stay with the mainstream offering of the ship.

THINGS TO DO

There are so many things to do on a modern cruise ship, you would have to spend a few months on board to participate in every activity and enjoy all of the ship's facilities. A daily newsletter, slipped under your door, will keep you informed of all the ship's happenings. If exercise is a priority, you can swim in the pool, work out in the gym, jog around the promenade deck, join the aerobics and dance classes or join in the pingpong and volleyball tournaments. Perhaps you just want to soak in the jacuzzi, relax in the sauna or treat yourself to a massage and facial.

Stop by the library if you're looking for a good book, a board game or an informal hand of bridge with your fellow passengers. Check your newsletter to see which films are scheduled for the movie theater or just settle into a lounge chair and gaze at the beautiful scenery gliding past the picture windows. Your days on the ship can be as busy or as unstructured as you want. You can play the slot machines in the casino or relax in a deck chair, breathing the fresh sea air. You can stay up late every night, enjoying the varied entertainment in the ship's lounges, or you can retire early and rise at dawn to watch the ship pull into port.

There are usually two sittings for dinner on the large ships. Early sitting is about 6:00 p.m., late sitting about 8:00 p.m. You should indicate your preference when you book your cruise. If you're on a special diet, your needs can probably be accommodated. For those who are simply watching their calories, each night's menu will contain a number of low-calorie dishes in addition to the usual fare, all of which is excellent. There's no shortage of fresh fruit, salads and other healthy cuisine served on board, only a shortage of will power when confronted with so many delicacies.

Children and teenagers are welcome on most cruise ships and special, supervised activities are usually provided for them on a daily basis. Youth facilities and programs vary from line to line, and from ship to ship, so check with your travel agent for more detail.

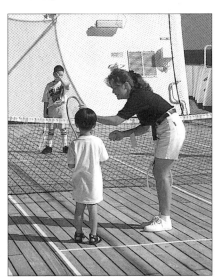

Daily shipboard activities and recommended shore excursions keep children and teenagers entertained when cruising the Caribbean.

TECTONIC BEGINNINGS

Volcanism, massive uplifting, fluctuating sea levels and large-scale erosion have all played a part in forming the West Indies. The earth's surface is divided into crustal plates, and most of the Caribbean islands lie close to the boundaries of the Caribbean Plate. Some 70 million years ago, the Caribbean Plate began pushing against the much larger American Plate, which encompasses the western half of the Atlantic Ocean. Tectonic pressures produced three volcanic mountain ranges, which now comprise the Greater Antilles and some of the Lesser Antilles, including the Virgin Islands, St. Maarten and Antigua. Meanwhile, volcanic forces were also forming the Andes Mountains of South America, branches of which extend to the north coast of South America where their partially submerged peaks are now islands, including the Dutch islands of Aruba, Bonaire and Curacao, and, to the east, the islands of Trinidad and Tobago.

All of this volcanic activity was followed by an era in which the sea temporarily covered the newly formed islands. Sediments of sandstone and limestone built up as the bodies of marine animals decayed, and some of the islands were flattened. Uplifting returned these islands to the sea's surface, and the Caribbean Plate began to move slowly eastward, creating a deep-sea subduction zone between it and the American Plate. As the spreading Atlantic floor was driven downward beneath the Caribbean plate, a new chain of volcanoes erupted along this boundary, their conical peaks now comprising an arc of mountainous islands that extends from Saba, at the top, to Grenada, at the bottom. Sea mounts (underwater volcanoes) also lie along this boundary.

Not all of the islands are volcanic in origin. Barbados began to form about 700,000 years ago, when tectonic forces slowly pushed a section of seabed to the surface. The eastern half of Guadeloupe also formed in a similar manner, whereas its western half is volcanic in origin. The Bahamas, some of which stand only a few feet above sea level, are elevated areas of the Bahamas Bank and were likely part of a large land mass before rising sea levels submerged all but the highest points.

DISASTER AT YUCATAN

Scientists have long agreed that the dinosaur, after roaming the Earth for 140 million years, suddenly faced worldwide extinction. Many theories have been proffered to explain the dinosaur's demise, one being that the formation of mountain ranges brought colder climates. A more recent theory, however, now points to a massive meteor or asteroid as the instigator. Some 65 million years ago this huge asteroid – estimated at six miles in diameter – apparently crashed into the Yucatan region of Mexico, its impact triggering the atmospheric and climactic effects that forever changed our planet's life forms.

San Francisco

San Andreas
Fault

Los Angeles

North
American
Plate

Pacific
Plate

Cabo San Lucas

Gulf of Mexico

Florida

Mexico

Yucatan
Peninsula

Middle America Trench

Cocos
Plate

Cuba

Gulf
Stream

North Atlantic
Ocean

Puerto Rico Trench
Atlantic Ocean's
deepest point (28,232 ft.)

Puerto
Rico

Hispaniola

Caribbean Plate

Mont
Pelee

Martinique

Trinidad

North
Equatorial
Current

South
American
Plate

Panama
Canal

Panama

Subduction Zone –

Transform Fault –

©OCEAN CRUISE GUIDES

VOLCANIC ERUPTIONS

Volcanoes form around an aperture in the earth's crust, through which gases, lava (molten rock) and solid fragments are ejected. A volcano's crater, its floor often covered with steam vents, is formed when the cone collapses during an eruption. A dormant volcano quickly loses its conical shape to erosion, so any mountain that is cone-shaped can be considered a potentially active volcano.

Numerous volcanoes in the Lesser Antilles are active, including St. Vincent's **La Soufriere,** which erupted in 1979, and Montserrat's **Soufriere Hills** volcano, which, after standing dormant for nearly 400 years, roared back to life in 1995, its most devastating eruption spewing forth an avalanche of scalding rock, ash and gas in June 1997. By then, two-thirds of Montserrat's 11,000 residents had already evacuated the island. Most of those who had chosen to remain were crowded into the north end of the island, but 19 people died when seven villages in an off-limits zone were engulfed by the pyroclastic flow which travels at speeds approaching 100 miles per hour. The island's abandoned capital of Plymouth was destroyed, and the southern two-thirds of this once verdant island lay in ash-covered ruins. In late 1999, vulcanologists reported a new lava dome growing in a crater left by a July 1998 eruption, and this dome collapsed in the summer of 2001, sending boiling rivers of ash and rock into the sea. By early 2002, the volcano's increase in rockfalls and levels of sulphur dioxide were warning of yet another eruption.

The Caribbean's most violent eruption in recent times was that of Martinique's **Mount Pelee** on May 8, 1902. Gases within the volcano reached such a critical pressure that masses of solid and liquid rock erupted into the air and a superheated cloud of burning gas and fine ash swept down the mountainside, blanketing the nearby town of St. Pierre and destroying all life in its path. Torrential rain, caused by the condensation of steam, often accompanies such an explosion. There had been warnings that Mount Pelee would erupt, but the 30,000 residents of St. Pierre chose to ignore the earth tremors, the rumbling sounds within the volcano, and its emissions of steam and light ash. The local wildlife, however, followed their instincts and evacuated the area. When the volcano finally erupted, all but one of St. Pierre's residents – a prisoner protected by the walls of his jail cell – died in the massive explosion.

EARTHQUAKES

Earthquakes are generated by blocks of rock passing one another along fault lines (fractures in the earth's crust). Their relative movements can be vertical, horizontal or oblique, and are usually measured in inches per year, except when a sudden release of stress along a fault triggers an earthquake. An earthquake begins with tremors, followed by more violent shocks that gradually diminish. The origin (focus of a quake) is underground or underwater, and the epicenter is a point on the surface directly above the focus. The magnitude and intensity of an earthquake is determined by the Richter scale, which measures ground motion to determine the amount of energy released at the quake's origin. A reading of 4.5 on the Richter scale indicates an earthquake causing light damage; a reading of 8.5 indicates an earthquake of devastating force.

The Caribbean Plate is no longer moving north, so volcanic activity has ceased in the Greater Antilles, but there is faulting and fracturing due to the plate's moving eastward. In 1692, **Port Royal** on the south coast of Jamaica was completely destroyed by an earthquake. The Lesser Antilles have also experienced earthquakes in historic times, with a number of ports suffering damage over the centuries, including Basseterre on St. Kitts, where a quake occurred in 1974.

HURRICANES

Of the natural phenomena affecting the Caribbean, hurricanes have been the most feared, causing widespread loss of life and billions of dollars in property damage. Leaves are stripped from trees, palms are toppled, roofs are peeled off buildings and flying debris is scattered island-wide. For the people huddled inside boarded-up homes, the noise is deafening. A storm surge – a wall of water pushed by the hurricane – may form and crash onto shore, and reefs lying offshore are often damaged by the pounding wave action. Even if an island is spared the winds, torrential rains from the tail of a hurricane often cause floods that wash out roads and swell rivers to dangerous levels. In a hurricane's wake, tens of thousands of residents are without electricity, running water or telephones. Some are missing a roof, or even an entire house if poorly built.

Scientists think the first human record of Atlantic tropical cyclones appears in Mayan hieroglyphics. By building their major settlements away from the hurricane-prone coastline, the Mayans practiced a method of disaster mitigation, which greatly reduced their losses. The word hurricane originated from the Arawak language and meant "evil spirits and big winds". The word was adopted by the Spaniards when they arrived in the Caribbean. In other parts of the world, terms such as typhoon and cyclone apply to the same sort of intense storm. Meteorologists in North America describe an intense tropical storm with winds exceeding 74 miles per hour as a hurricane.

Some storms left important marks on regional history. One hurricane was immortalized in 1609 when a fleet of ships carrying settlers from England to Virginia was struck by a hurricane. Several of the ships were damaged and part of the fleet grounded at Bermuda. The passengers became Bermuda's first inhabitants and their stories helped inspire Shakespeare's writing of *The Tempest*. The 1900 hurricane that struck Galveston severely damaged much of that city (with a loss of 8,000 lives) and, with it, the city's preeminence as the financial capital of southern Texas. The major Caribbean ports of San Juan and St. Thomas owe their existence to being excellent ports in a storm.

Hurricane season for the Caribbean and the eastern seaboard of the United States starts in June and lasts through November. The northward shift of the sun increases the temperatures of the Atlantic Ocean and the air mass lying between Africa and North America. In an average year, more than 100 disturbances (low-pressure systems) with hurricane potential are observed in the Atlantic Ocean, Gulf of Mexico and Caribbean Sea; on average only 10 of these reach the tropical-storm stage and about six mature into hurricanes. The 1950s and 1960s were active years for hurricanes in the Caribbean, and meteorologists think hurricane frequency may be related to rainfall over Africa's western Sahel, where hurricane seedlings originate. Rainfall in this area was above normal from 1949 to 1967, but since then has been generally below normal. A recent trend, however, seems to be one of normal rainfall and there is concern that hurricane activity may increase.

All storms in the northern hemisphere spin in a counter-clockwise direction at sea level and hurricanes are no exception. The wind speed is caused by heavy, cool air rushing to fill a low-pressure area where the warmer, lighter air is rising. If the low-pressure area is large and the pressure gradient (the rate of pressure change over distance) between it and adjacent pools of air is steep, it will attract larger amounts of cooler air. As the cooler air spins around the eye of the low-pressure system, it can begin to tighten the eye, making it smaller in diameter. This begins a cycle of increasing winds and an increase of air flowing upward. The warm, rising air loses heat and, as a result, water is condensed to form massive nimbostratus clouds. Heavy torrential rain is always a precursor of an approaching hurricane.

Although a hurricane's greatest wind strength (usually between 100 and 200 m.p.h.) is at the wall or edge of its eye where the winds cause very heavy seas and spray that reduces visibility to almost nil, the eye itself is very calm with little wind and a warmer air temperature. A hurricane can have a diameter of 500 miles or more, but the strength or intensity of a hurricane is unrelated to its overall size. Very strong hurricanes usually have relatively small eyes – less than 10 miles in diameter. Other factors come into play, such as the proximity of large, high-pressure systems and whether the storm track is over warm, shallow water.

Hurricanes often create large tidal surges, which are perhaps the biggest concern for coastal communities. These surges are sometimes referred to as domes and are caused by the low pressure of the hurricane lifting the ocean's water into a mound one-to-three feet higher than the surrounding surface. This mound can result in coastal surges, with the sea level rising 20 feet or more. Swells from a storm can pulse out along the water's surface for thousands of miles. Pacific surfers often ride the oceanic memory of distant typhoons.

Hurricanes are assigned different categories, depending on their storm surge, wind speed and other factors which provide a measure of the storm's destructive power. The United States National Oceanic and Atmospheric Administration (NOAA) uses five categories, beginning with category one. A hurricane of this strength will produce winds of 75 to 95 mph that can damage unanchored mobile homes and vegetation. A category-five hurricane is potentially catastrophic, packing winds in excess of 155 mph. Such winds can rip roofs off buildings, some of which may be completely blown away. Residential areas within 10 miles of the shoreline are evacuated.

The deadliest hurricane in the Caribbean occurred in the Lesser Antilles in mid-October 1780, and has become known as "The Great Hurricane". Estimates indicate that around 22,000 deaths occurred in that storm, with a total of about 9,000 lives lost in Martinique, 4,000-5,000 in St. Eustatius, and 4,300 in Barbados. Thousands of deaths also occurred offshore. The number of fatalities from this hurricane exceeds the cumulative loss in any year and, in fact, in all other decades. **Hurricane Mitch** is ranked as the next deadliest storm to pass through the Caribbean and did its greatest damage when it hit Central America in late October 1998. During its five-day rampage through the region the hurricane claimed over 9,000 lives and dumped several feet of rain, triggering floods and mudslides in Honduras and nearby countries.

In the past century up to 1998, there were just two category-five hurricanes – one in 1935 that hit the Florida Keys especially hard, and Hurricane Camille in 1969. **Hurricane Andrew** in 1992 was the third-strongest storm in history to hit the Carribbean and United States. With sustained winds of 145 mph and gusts over 175 mph, Andrew annihilated homes and businesses along a 30-mile swath through Dade County in Florida. When it was over, more than 60,000 homes were destroyed and 200,000 people left homeless. Insurance pay-outs and government recovery expenditures topped $29 billion – the costliest hurricane on record. Eleven insurance companies failed and 40 companies pulled out or curtailed underwriting property in Florida after Andrew. But it could have been even worse. The National Hurricane Center in Miami estimates

Devastating hurricanes can strike between June and early November.

that if Andrew had tracked only 20 miles further north when it hit Florida, losses would have topped $75 billion.

In 1988, **Hurricane Gilbert** – a category-three hurricane – pounded Jamaica, with the eye of the storm passing right over the capital of Kingston. In mid-September 1995, **Hurricane Marilyn** was a strengthening category-two, nearly category-three, hurricane when it passed over St. Thomas, and surface winds of 110 mph were recorded. Five people were killed and property damage was widespread, but the island quickly recovered. **Hurricane George** struck the eastern Caribbean and the Florida Keys in 1998, and the following year deadly **Hurricane Lenny**, a category-four hurricane, battered the region for three days before reaching the open Atlantic as it tracked in an unusual west-to-east direction.

Fortunately for the residents of the Caribbean, the prediction and surveillance of hurricanes has improved dramatically in the last 30 years. The National Hurricane Center in Miami successfully provided accurate advance warnings for Hurricanes Gilbert, Andrew and Marilyn, resulting in a relatively low loss of life. In addition to hurricane forecast centers in the United States, warning stations have been established throughout the West Indies.

Weather systems in the Atlantic are monitored 24 hours a day, with highly advanced radar and satellites to give hurricane forecasters the ability to detect and track storms long before they hit land. Island residents are warned of an approaching hurricane up to three days in advance – time enough to nail plywood over the windows or bolt the hurricane shutters. They also make sure they have survival kits that include flashlights, batteries, extra food and other essential items. Many retreat to public shelters, built of solid concrete, to wait out the storm.

The officers of cruise ships receive hurricane information from the National Hurricane Center and from NOAA. A cruise ship will sometimes forego a port if the captain decides conditions warrant such avoidance. The ship will either head to another port, or spend a day at sea, keeping well away from the track of the hurricane.

This spectacular view of the eye of Hurricane Diana in 1984, shot by NASA, shows the intense center of the storm.

The history of the West Indies is one of the richest stories ever to unfold. In less than a century, the islands ringing the Caribbean Sea went from tropical paradises to prizes of European imperialism, their fates determined by battles and revolutions staged on both sides of the Atlantic. Yet, the Caribbean was once an unimaginable place to Europeans, including Christopher Columbus who, to his dying day, believed he had found the Far East.

THE EARLY NATIVES

The Caribbean Islands were initially inhabited by three major Amerindian native groups – the **Ciboney** (the oldest and most primitive tribe), the **Arawak** and the **Carib**. All came from around the Amazon basin and migrated to the north coast of South America before travelling by canoe to the Caribbean. The Ciboney were first to ride winds and currents north along the island chain, followed by the Arawaks who settled first on the Lesser Antilles and then, pushed from these small islands by the warlike Caribs, moved to the Greater Antilles and the Bahamas.

By the time Columbus arrived in 1492, the aggressive and proud Caribs had settled most areas of the Caribbean, their largest populations located on the Lesser Antilles. The Ciboneys had been reduced to settlements on the northwest coasts of Cuba and Hispaniola, where they lived in small shelters and caves, surviving on shellfish, wild fruits, herbs and small game. They wore little clothing, painted their bodies and their only implements were stone tools.

More is known about the Arawaks, who lived in simple houses of brush and practiced conuco, a unique agricultural method of growing root plants by placing their cuttings in large mounds of ash and earth. Columbus described Arawak homes as '...simple and clean, very high with good chimneys.' Arawaks also rested on woven nets strung between trees and called these hammocks, an Arawak word.

A surplus of leisure time allowed them to develop skills for making pottery, baskets, woven cotton clothing, stone tools and jewelry including rings, necklaces and masks shaped

Well ventilated, easy to rebuild after hurricanes and providing good shelter from sun and rain, traditional Arawak houses were well suited to the Caribbean.

Pre-Columbian Arawak carving.

from gold found in local riverbeds. They also enjoyed games, including a form of soccer, and built rectangular playing courts similar to those of the Maya, whose influence was widespread.

The peaceful Arawaks, content with their simple housing needs and easily obtainable food, enjoyed a tropical paradise. Politically, they were organized as loose federations of provinces within an island, with the local village headman holding the greatest sway over his people. Women were equal to men in most areas.

Equality of the sexes was not the case with the Caribs. Tasks between genders were strictly defined and men treated their wives as servants. The Carib men excelled at boat building and navigation – useful skills for fishing and raiding other islands. The Caribs, who had little difficulty pushing the Arawaks from desirable islands, were fearless in battle. They were one of the few native groups in the Caribbean region to defeat Europeans in battle and, unlike the Arawaks who welcomed the first Spaniards with open arms, the Caribs consistently resisted attempts to conquer or enslave them.

They also developed a reputation for cannibalism, a word derived from the Spanish word *caribal*, but human flesh was not part of their regular diet. They did occasionally eat parts of warriors taken in battle, and Columbus, who witnessed this ritualistic act, used it as a pretext for enslavement.

COLUMBUS DISCOVERS THE CARIBBEAN

Europe's discovery of the New World came as a result of the ambition and persistence of one man – Christopher Columbus. Born in Genoa, Italy in 1451, Columbus's first sea adventure took place in 1476 when he was sailing with a small fleet of cargo ships that was attacked by pirates. Over 500 men were killed, but Columbus managed to escape by swimming six miles to the Portuguese shore.

A replica of Columbus's favorite ship, the Nina.

He married a Portuguese woman of high birth whose father was governor of the Madeira Islands. While living there, Columbus formulated his audacious plan of reaching the Far East by sailing due west.

Finding no support in Portugal, Columbus turned to Spain. In 1486, he presented his plan to King Ferdinand and Queen Isabella, who were interested but preoccupied with driving the Moors from their country. For five years Columbus stayed near the court and campaigned the Queen for financial support. Finally, in January 1492, upon Spain's defeat of the Moors, an agreement in principle was reached.

With three ships – the Nina, the Pinta and the flagship Santa Maria – Columbus set out from Spain on August 3, 1492. This first voyage across the Atlantic was completed in 33 days when he arrived at an island at the south end of the Bahamas island group, which he named San Salvador (also know as Watling Island). Columbus promptly met some friendly local Arawaks (also known as Tainos) who saw the newcomers as protection against the Caribs. Columbus convinced a few to guide him further west and sailed on to discover Cuba, then Hispaniola, where he left the crew from the wrecked Santa Maria. After a few more adventures, and finding a small amount of gold, Columbus returned home to a hero's welcome.

Columbus completed three more voyages to the Caribbean, each less successful than the last. On his second voyage, Columbus had a skirmish with some Caribs at Salt River on St. Croix – the first fatal confrontation between Europeans and New World natives, which claimed the lives of two Caribs and one Spaniard. On his third voyage, Columbus and his brother were sent home in chains by the Governor of Hispaniola on charges of misrule.

By this point, relations with the natives had deteriorated dramatically and Columbus now saw Indians simply as a labor force for mining gold and gathering food. He introduced the dreaded system of *encomiendas,* which allotted to Spanish settlers the lands and lives of natives. This act marked the beginning of slavery in the New World. Columbus's last voyage (1502-04), with four ships, was along Panama and Central America in search of a strait leading to the Indian Ocean. He found no strait, no gold and lost all four ships. He returned to Spain near collapse and died in 1506 in obscurity.

A monument to Columbus stands in Barcelona, where the royal court bestowed him with honors upon his return in 1492.

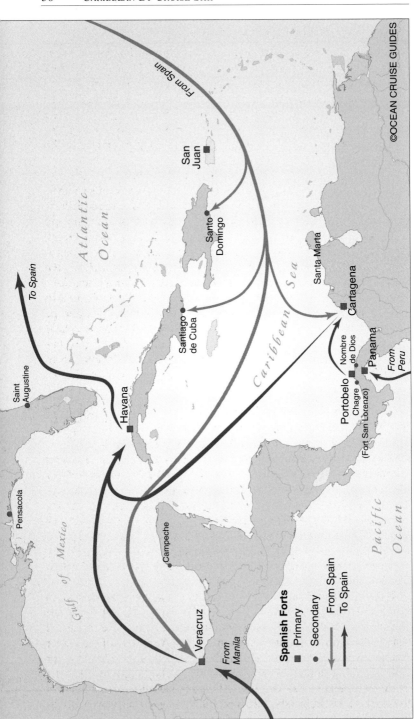

©OCEAN CRUISE GUIDES

THE EXTERMINATION OF THE ARAWAKS

The impact of Spanish commerce and culture on the indigenous population was rapid and devastating. Many natives perished from overwork and murder, but even more died from various European diseases, such as influenza and small pox. Isolated for thousands of years, the Arawak simply did not have the natural immunities needed to fight off even a common cold. By the end of 16th century, the friendly Arawaks, of whom Columbus said 'there is no better nor gentler people in the world', were extinct.

Population estimates of the Caribbean at Columbus's arrival range from half a million to as high as six million, but whatever the number, it was soon reduced to zero for the Arawaks. This unprecedented genocide was denounced by outspoken religious leaders living in the Caribbean. One of the most influential was a Dominican priest, **Bartolome de Las Casas**, who wrote a scathing critique of the Spanish conquerors in his book called *A Short Account of the Destruction of the Indies*. Las Casa's disturbing firsthand account of Spanish atrocities had a profound and lasting impact on European politics. Printed in 1552, it became a best-seller (and is still in print) throughout Europe and was translated into every major language. For 300 years it upheld an image of the cruel Spanish conquest of America. Protestant countries regarded the book as proof of the unholy greed of Catholic Spain and used it in support of an ongoing campaign to attack and plunder treasure ships returning to Seville.

COLONIZING THE CARIBBEAN

Fifty years of empire building followed Columbus's discovery of the New World, and from the mid-1500s to the mid-1700s, two armed convoys were sent annually from Spain to collect precious gems, gold and silver. The New Spain flotilla, bound for Mexico, sailed in April to Veracruz to load silver from Central Mexico. The Tierra Firme fleet would sail in August to Cartagena and wait for the gold and silver to arrive from Portobelo. Both fleets would rendezvous in Havana to reprovision for the long trip home through the Florida Straits and past the Bahamas. Although many vessels fell prey to pirates, storms and reefs, most ships made the journey safely back to Seville.

Following Columbus's last voyage, thousands of Spanish settlers had arrived in the Greater Antilles eager to find gold. Following the conquest of Mexico and Peru, many moved on, leaving the exhausted island mines to seek fortunes on the mainland. Almost all of the Lesser Antilles were abandoned once it was determined they were 'useless' for lack of gold. The natives were carted off as slaves and by 1570 the islands were empty and forgotten. All that remained was wild Spanish livestock which, ironically, sustained Dutch, English and French privateers while they preyed on Spanish fleets.

Sir Francis Drake.
From an Original in the Sydenham Family.

Sir Francis Drake (1540-1595)

By the late 16th century, English, French and Dutch interlopers had spent more than 50 years harassing Spanish treasure fleets. Exploits of various captains, most notably Sir Francis Drake, made pirating a romantic career option for young Englishmen. It was the Dutch, however, who first turned the West Indies into a viable trading zone, when a Spanish embargo in 1598 forced them to look elsewhere for salt and tobacco. At that time the Netherlands owned half of the world's merchant fleet and Amsterdam was the center of international trade. For a brief period, Dutch aggression against the Spanish resulted in their monopolizing the slave and sugar trade in the Caribbean. Their greatest victory against the Spanish came in 1628, when Piet Heyn captured the entire Mexican treasure fleet near Cuba. By 1630, the Dutch West India Company, operating as a commercial venture with shareholders in Amsterdam, had settled on St. Maarten, Curacao and Bonaire.

Dutch attempts to usurp Spanish control in the Caribbean and South America eventually failed, but the net gainers were adventurers from France and England who, encouraged by high tobacco prices, looked around the Lesser Antilles for suitable land. On January 28th, 1624, Thomas Warner, with 20 fellow adventurers from Guyana, landed on the beautiful island of St. Christopher (St. Kitts) and founded the first British settlement in the Caribbean. Some French sailors arrived about

Second largest fortress in the Caribbean, the British citadel and surrounding fortifications of Brimstone Hill on St. Kitts were known as the 'Gibraltar of the West Indies'.

the same time and the two groups divided the island, with local Caribs their mutual enemy. St. Kitts became the Caribbean mother colony for further settlements by the British and French. Warner's tobacco plantation was a huge success and news of the fortunes being made in tobacco prompted rapid settlement of other islands – Barbados, Montserrat, Nevis, Antigua and the British Virgin Islands by English farmers; Martinique, Guadeloupe and the western half of Hispaniola (Haiti) by French farmers. The Carib natives, after being pushed off St. Kitts, retained strongholds on Dominica, Grenada and St. Vincent.

Tobacco was still the crop of choice for settlers arriving at new islands, but it was soon observed tobacco, like most weeds, will grow almost anywhere. Supply soon outstripped demand, prices fell and the tobacco boom burst. Then settlers on Barbados began planting sugar-cane after visiting Brazil to learn of Dutch innovations in planting and harvesting. The first successful crop on Barbados set off a frenzied boom and by 1647 most planters had switched to sugar, a luxury commodity with far greater staying power than tobacco. Demand for labor soared and the population grew from 10,000 in 1640 to 43,000 by 1655. Sugar became the new gold of the Caribbean and thousands of English peasants signed themselves into years of indentured work.

The French colonies grew at a slower pace until the early 18th century, when sugar production lifted their prospects. Like the British, the French crown tried to enact trade restrictions that kept its colonies under exclusive control. The effort was unpopular and Caribbean planters – both British and French – soon got their own way in commercial matters as well as winning control of their local governments.

THE STRUGGLE FOR CARIBBEAN CONTROL

During the 17th century, Spain's influence declined significantly and the Dutch, with the greatest number of ships and least amount of regulatory baggage, succeeded in controlling trade. To the Dutch, free trade was almost a religion, and Dutch merchants provided the best service and highest profits for Caribbean farmers. But, during a determined effort in the latter half of the 17th century, England and France finally wrenched control from the Dutch who were left with six small islands – Sint Maarten, Sint Eustatius, Saba and the ABC's – Aruba, Bonaire and Curacao.

By this time, both English and French merchants had increased their Caribbean possessions. In 1655, a fleet under Cromwell's government took Jamaica, while the French solidified their hold on Martinique, Guadeloupe and Saint-Domingue (later renamed Haiti), and took possession of St. Barts, St. Croix and Grenada. The Caribs continued to suffer at the hands of Europeans. A massacre of natives was organized by the French on Grenada in 1653, where 40 desperate Caribs jumped to their deaths from a cliff that became known as Morne des Sauteurs (Leapers' Bluff).

In 1654, the French failed to eliminate the Caribs on St. Lucia and St. Vincent but did slaughter those remaining on Martinique. Finally, in 1660, a treaty was signed reserving Dominica and St. Vincent for the Caribs.

One other European country got into the act of taking and settling Caribbean islands. The Danish West India Company was the first to permanently settle St. Thomas when its sponsors, encouraged by the Dutch, believed they could make large profits by carrying slaves from Africa to St. Thomas for resale in the West Indies. The company went on to acquire St. John and St. Croix. However, like its Dutch and French rivals, the Danish West India Company rarely made a profit and went out of business in 1754, when the Danish crown purchased the islands. The Company had given up its monopoly rights at St. Thomas in 1724 and permitted ships of all nations to trade, charging only small customs taxes. Since then, St. Thomas has been known as a 'free port'. Throughout the 18th century, France and England engaged in a series of wars of which the Caribbean was a major theatre, with islands changing hands several times. St. Lucia, only 25 miles from Martinique, was considered an important strategic base and may hold the record for different owners.

Impressive forts were erected to protect the islands from enemy attack, but the battles were fought mainly by each country's navy. Britain permanently stationed squadrons of warships in the West Indies while France sent over fleets in response to specific issues or conflicts.

The first of these conflicts was the War of Jenkins Ear from 1739 to 1748, which ended inconclusively with both sides returning their conquests. The next war was the Seven Years War from 1756 to 1763,

Sugar was an important factor leading to the American War of Independence. (Below) Slaves push hogshead barrels of sugar out to a tender for loading onto ships.

which resulted in a huge gain for Britain in North America when they received Canada in exchange for Guadeloupe. The years from 1776 to 1783 proved to be one of the most historic periods throughout the Caribbean, when American colonists threw off the yoke of colonial rule and confronted Britain's oppressive trade laws.

In a direct way, Caribbean sugar helped push the United States to revolution. American merchants had been buying sugar from a number of Caribbean sources. To stem this illicit trade, Britain's Parliament in 1733 placed high duties on all sugar products imported from non-British islands. American merchants openly violated this act until the 1760s when Britain prohibited the American colonies from importing any foreign rum and molasses. Such restrictions infuriated American merchants and became a major grievance leading to revolution in 1776.

The American Revolution received support throughout the Caribbean, where the same conflict of interest between home countries and colonies existed. Troops from Saint-Domingue fought for George Washington under Lafayette. The Jamaica Assembly demanded equality with England and the Bahamas openly supported the mainland colonies. It seemed, without the British Navy to stop them, the islands of the British West Indies would have joined the Revolution. The Dutch island of St. Eustatius became the first territory in the New World to recognize the independence of the United States.

The Caribbean's sugar industry also gave the United States the very symbol of its independence, the Capitol. It was designed by a planter from Jost Van Dyke in the British Virgin Islands, Dr. William Thornton, a Quaker interested in architecture. After seeing an advertisement for a competition to design the Capitol, he presented his winning design to President Washington.

The after-effects of American independence were devastating for the Caribbean islands. Britain blockaded the mainland ports from West Indies trade and, with exports and imports suddenly cut off, food became a scarce commodity. Between 1780 and 1787, 15,000 slaves died of famine in Jamaica alone. In 1778, 300 white planters fled St. Kitts to escape court action for recovery of debts. And yet, England continued to enforce the archaic Navigation Act. Economist

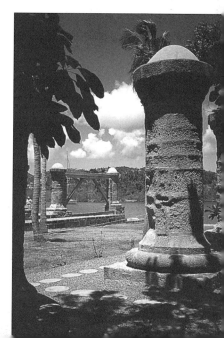

The sail loft pillars remain intact at Nelson's Dockyard in Antigua.

Adam Smith pleaded with the British government to allow resumption of trade between the United States and the British West Indies, and warned that continued interruption would hurt the islands more than America. Slowly, Britain reopened trade and relaxed the embargo.

In the meantime, however, the French West Indies enjoyed boom times as the main supplier of rum and sugar to America. But the sweet life was not to last, for the upheaval of the French Revolution eventually spread to the Caribbean. Saint-Domingue (Haiti) convulsed in a terrible civil war led by slaves yearning for freedom. Guadeloupe and Martinique were also caught in the struggle, enduring battles and a reign of terror after Jacobin republicans arrived to take control. In 1793, the local white planters on these islands sought protection from Britain, which quickly took advantage of the chaos to capture almost all French possessions in the Caribbean. This was reversed in the fall of 1794, when Victor Hugues, leading a squadron of troops, retook Guadeloupe and sent more than 1,200 white planters to the guillotine. Hugues went on to stir up rebellion on other islands and successfully expelled the British from St. Lucia. On Grenada, the British just managed to hang on to their main fort while fighting an insurrection led by the Creole planter Julien Fedon. In Saint-Domingue, Britain endured its most serious losses, both in money and men, during a conflict that dragged on until 1798 when a Creole slave named Toussaint L'Ouverture successfully repelled the British.

SLAVERY

In the early years of sugar planting, white indentured laborers, serving terms of three to five years, were far more common in the islands than black slaves. An important boost for planters came when Cromwell sent thousands of Scottish and Irish people to Barbados in the 1650s. However, Barbados was a death sentence for white laborers and as

West African tribes, sometimes hundreds of miles from the coast, were under continual onslaught by slave traders, who would march whole villages to a slave depot.

many as three out of four white workers perished soon after arrival. Many died from tropical diseases, introduced by Dutch-sold African slaves in the 1640s. Black workers generally fared better at adjusting to the climate with one out of three dying in the first two years. But survival meant a constant routine of hard work between cutting the cane or working in the sugar mill, where temperatures reached 120 degrees.

By 1650 it was clear a massive labor force was needed to grow sugar. Africa was already supplying slaves to Asia, the Middle East and Europe, and slave traders were quick to satisfy the labor needs of Caribbean planters. Trade in human cargo was underway and about to take place on a scale never before seen. Europe's acceptance of slave labor in the Americas for over 300 years is, today, difficult to understand. Slavery had virtually disappeared in Europe by the Middle Ages and had been replaced with the notion of semi-freedom under which most serfs labored. It was the Portuguese who first began the lucrative trade of transporting black labor from the west coast of Africa in the 15th century. By the middle of the 17th century, French, English and Dutch slavers were actively buying and selling from warlords along the African slave coast. From Senegal to Angola, forts were built to protect slave companies, and cities such as Luanda, Accra and Lagos existed for centuries as human warehouses.

The Atlantic triangle brought manufactured goods from Europe to Africa, slaves from Africa to the Caribbean, and sugar, cotton and tobacco back to Europe. It was a system that suited accepted economic dogma of the time and was so profitable it seemed providential. The triangle made the West Indies among the most valuable colonies the world has ever known. Scholars estimate over 15 million people were taken from Africa in the transatlantic slave trade. This massive depopulation had far-reaching negative effects on Africa, wrenching apart families and communities, and causing long-standing tribal animosities.

Slave huts still stand near Lacre Punt on Bonaire, where they once housed Africans brought to the island to work the nearby salt pans.

Cutting sugarcane from sunup to sundown during harvest (January to June) was backbreaking work. Women often outnumbered men in the fields.

England's Liverpool was transformed from a fishing village into a center of international commerce, becoming one of the largest ports in Europe devoted to the slave trade. The city's red brick Customs House, blazoned with Negro heads, bore mute testimony to the origins of the city's rise in the world. (Today Liverpool is home to Britain's first permanent gallery examining the transatlantic slave trade.)

After South America, the Caribbean was the most active buyer of black labor, importing over four million Africans from 1601 to 1870. (The United States, by comparison, imported about half a million slaves.) The biggest buyers of slaves in the Caribbean in the 18th century were Saint-Domingue (Haiti), Jamaica and Barbados. The appalling rate of mortality, both on the plantations and on the slave ships, kept the death rate far in excess of the birth rate, and new slaves for the islands were always in demand. For every 100 slaves put on a ship bound for the Caribbean, only 56 would be alive after three years.

Planters had complete control over their slaves, who had little recourse against injustices, although some – called Free Coloreds – earned their freedom through faithful service or bought it with money raised by selling handicrafts or garden produce. Desperate slaves simply ran away, and on most islands were quickly captured and severely punished. Runaway slaves stood a better chance on the Greater Antilles where they hid in the dense rainforests and rugged mountain areas. Jamaica was home to the best known and most successful group of runaways who became known as the Maroons. They successfully raided frontier plantations, established towns and beat off numerous attacks by British troops, finally gaining two homelands of more than 2,500 acres.

Eventually the importance of the Caribbean colonies diminished as other world sources for sugar were found, and slavery became an odious anachronism in the new era of enlightenment.

ABOLITION AND THE ROAD TO FREEDOM

In the latter part of the 18th century, the Age of Enlightenment resulted in new ideas about freedom and equality. Confidence in human reason and progress lent credibility to radical beliefs, and people were open to change. During this time, anti-slavery movements throughout Britain gained momentum and, led by a number of powerful parliamentarians, they won the support of the prime minister, William Pitt. The chief spokesman for abolitionists, William Wilberforce, initiated a series of parliamentary inquiries publicizing the horrors of the Middle Passage – from Africa to the colonies.

Armed with information to reveal the slave trade as a vast graveyard for African slaves and British sailors who died from various tropical diseases, the abolitionists spread their campaign across the country and found a receptive public willing to sign petitions. The result was a success and the British Parliament scheduled an abolition bill for 1796. However, revolutionary France's Reign of Terror discredited radical ideas, and not until May 1806 did the British government pass the Foreign Slave Bill prohibiting the shipping of slaves to foreign colonies. Two years later, it abolished the importing of

Abolitionist leader William Wilberforce at the age of 29.

Cover of abolitionist pamphlet in late 18th century. Millions of similar tracts were circulated in England before emancipation.

slaves into British colonies.

Convincing planters to accept abolition was a different matter. Transitional steps were attempted, with slave registration introduced in 1815 to prevent the illegal importing of slaves and provide evidence of maltreatment, but resistance from planters only stiffened the resolve of abolitionists, who were convinced stronger measures were needed to free Caribbean slaves.

While planters and politicians fretted about the method and consequences of changing the status of slaves, the slaves took matters in their own hands. The frequency of revolts increased dramatically from the end of the 18th century to emancipation, and in 1816 a revolt ravaged Barbados, which had not known a slave conspiracy since 1701. Ironically, the very measures enacted to end slavery made the situation worse. The labor force dwindled at the cessation of the slave trade in 1808 and masters forced their existing slaves to work harder, moving women, children and older domestic servants out to the fields to work.

By 1830, Caribbean slaves and British abolitionists were losing patience with the slow progress towards freedom. A large slave rebellion in Jamaica led by a Baptist lay preacher named Sam Sharpe brought events to a head when more than 60,000 slaves revolted by burning 200 sugar estates in the northwestern parishes. Over 500 slaves and 14 whites died. News of the revolt and its repression galvanized British abolitionist groups to organize a final drive to end slavery. More than one and a half million people signed petitions which were presented to Parliament early in 1833. The Abolition Act was passed in

After emancipation, many former slaves settled into a new life tending small plots of land to grow food for themselves and local markets. (Below) A scene from Christiansted, St. Croix, circa 1910.

Under the governorship of Peter von Scholten, slavery was abolished in the Danish West Indies (now the U.S. Virgin Islands) in 1848.

August, ordering the end of slavery by the following year, making Britain the first European power to abolish slavery. Parliament voted to pay planters about £25 per slave, which went a long way toward encouraging passage of the Emancipation Bill in colonial assemblies.

France, during its revolution, abolished slavery on Saint-Domingue in 1793 but, under Napoleon, slavery was restored in 1802. Britain forced the French government to outlaw the trade in 1818, but it was not until 1848, when French abolitionists gained power, that an emancipation decree was passed. The Dutch and Spanish islands were slow to free their slaves. The Netherlands ended slavery in the Caribbean in 1863 while the Spanish colonies, which were enjoying a boom in sugar production in the 19th century, took longer, eventually abolishing slavery in Puerto Rico in 1873 and in Cuba in 1886.

The Danish Virgin Islands introduced slavery reforms in 1839 and issued an emancipation decree in 1848.

Following emancipation, the freed slaves either moved off the plantations to form 'free villages' and grow their own food on small plots of land, or they continued working on the estates as wage earners. As labor costs climbed, sugar prices fell, due to the large quantities of beet sugar being successfully grown in Europe as well as cane sugar exports from countries, such as Brazil, that were still using slave labor. Jamaica, once the biggest producer of sugar in the Caribbean, saw its output plummet.

CARIBBEAN POLITICS IN THE 19TH AND 20TH CENTURIES

After emancipation, the Caribbean islands all beat to a different drum. The British islands became Crown colonies and remained thus until powerful labor movements in the late 1930s prompted several to seek full autonomy from Britain. Jamaica, Barbados and Trinidad and Tobago were led by forceful, populist leaders with socialist leanings, who borrowed ideals and slogans from Britain's Labour party. The 1940 Moyne Report recommended self government for the islands and, although the British government agreed, it wanted to hand over the reigns of power to moderate political leaders who enjoyed popular support. Jamaica and Trinidad and Tobago were the first colonies to gain independence in 1962, followed by Barbados in 1966 and the Bahamas Islands in 1973. Next was Grenada (1974), then Dominica (1978), St. Lucia (1979), St. Vincent and the Grenadines (1979), Antigua and Barbuda (1981), and St. Kitts and Nevis (1983). Most of these sovereign states are members of the British Commonwealth of Nations and, as recently as 1997, were allowing legal appeals to the judicial committee of Britain's Privy Council in London. A number of the smaller islands have chosen to remain British Crown colonies, these being Anguilla, the British Virgin Islands, the Cayman Islands and Montserrat.

Following a plebiscite in 1945, the French Antilles chose assimilation and political union with France. Both Martinique and Guadeloupe are overseas departments and administrative regions of France, the latter including the dependencies of St. Barthelemeny and St. Martin.

The Dutch islands of Aruba, Curacao, Bonaire, St. Eustatius, Saba and St. Maarten have also retained links with their home country, remaining part of the Kingdom of the Netherlands. In 1986 Aruba separated from the Netherlands Antilles, but remains part of the Kingdom. Curacao, the capital of the Netherlands Antilles, prospered during the oil boom of the 1960s and 1970s, but refining capacity has been cut since the 1980s and the state has taken over ownership.

Finally unburdened of trade restrictions in the late 18th century, the economies of Spain's colonies improved. Cuba became a huge sugar producer but resentment against Spanish rule and taxes continued, leading to civil wars in the latter part of the century. A separatist movement, with strong support in the United States, resulted in an open conflict between Spain and America, which lasted for 10 weeks in 1898. After two naval losses to the American fleet, Madrid surrendered. Cuba was granted independence and Puerto Rico and other possessions were ceded to the United States. The United States became the main economic and political force in the Caribbean. American capital provided the means to rebuild sugar, banana and coffee industries in the Greater Antilles and, by the 1920s, American-owned companies were producing most of the world's cane sugar.

To protect American shipping, the United States purchased the Danish West Indies during the First World War in 1917. Renamed the Virgin Islands of the United States, they are strategically positioned along the approach to the Panama Canal. America's presence in the Caribbean has brought stability to the region and such benefits as building roads, establishing institutions and improving communications.

THE CARIBBEAN TODAY

Any island, with its limited resources, is challenged to meet the economic needs of its citizens and this is especially true in the Caribbean. Tourism has been a bright spot for many islands and the cruise ship industry, with a total economic impact estimated at $4 billion annually, has created over 80,000 full-time jobs in the Caribbean region .

Notwithstanding Cuba, the Caribbean region's political determination is adherence to democracy. The acid test of this occurred in 1983 when countries of the Caribbean refused to tolerate the murder of Grenada's prime minister, Maurice Bishop, by an unelected military regime and backed intervention by the United States. Grenada has enjoyed democratic elections ever since.

The West Indies, physically isolated from one another by the Caribbean Sea, remain fragmented politically. A case in point is the secessionist movement in Nevis, the smaller member of the twin-island federation of St. Kitts-Nevis. The two islands, separated by a narrow channel, have a shared history, common language and much inter-island travel, yet the residents of Nevis – many of whom feel their union with St. Kitts was imposed upon them in 1871 by a British colonial government – voted 62 per cent in favor of secession in a 1998 referendum. However, the St. Kitts-Nevis constitution states that 66.6 percent of Nevisians must vote for secession before it can take place. With democracy a valued institution, peace and stability prevails.

A narrow channel of water but a wide gulf of politics divides the islands of St. Kitts (foreground) and Nevis (background).

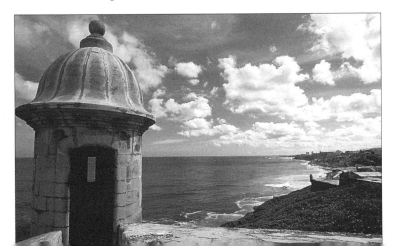

The immense wealth brought back to Spain from Mexico and Peru was a constant source of envy for other European countries, and resentment grew when Spanish claims were confirmed by papal decree. Without the resources to attack the Spanish empire directly, northern European nations relied on piracy to tap into the New World's gold supply.

Piracy was called privateering when it received tacit approval from British, French and Dutch crowns in the form of licensing or commissions. This subtle distinction gave captains latitude to pursue innocuous activities, such as collecting livestock on Caribbean islands, when the real purpose was to pillage Spanish towns and ships. The captains would return home to divide their spoils with the crown while receiving the royal pardon.

France, almost continuously at war with Spain until 1559, was the first to attack Spain's source of wealth. When news that French privateer **Jean d'Ango** seized four Spanish ships laden with treasure near the Azores in 1523, men throughout France boarded ships bound for the Caribbean to prey on Spanish vessels. As many as 30 French ships raided the West Indies annually, the climax of these efforts coming in 1555, when corsair Jacques de Sores took Havana and burned it to the ground.

The exploits of **Sir Francis Drake** fired the imagination of all Europe when he captured an entire year's production of Peruvian silver in 1572. With only two ships and 73 men he took the city of Nombre de Dios (near today's location of the Panama Canal) and captured three mule trains transporting 30 tons of silver. This voyage brought Drake wealth and fame, and inspired generations of adventurers to seek their fortune in the West Indies.

San Juan's El Morro fortress was Drake's undoing. The Spanish, unlike in earlier days, were ready for the much-feared privateer when he showed up in 1595.

Howard Pyle's illustrated "Book of Pirates" depicted pirates as a colorful and ruthless bunch taking big risks in small boats.

Drake made a number of sorties to the Caribbean and is also credited with being instrumental in the defeat of the Spanish Armada in 1588. Drake met his end during a siege of the newly built El Morro fortress in San Juan, Puerto Rico. After failing to penetrate the settlement, he sailed to other ports looking, without success, for treasure. Returning to his old haunt of Nombre de Dios, he met his fate when he died of dysentery and was buried at sea near Portobelo.

The struggling Spanish colonies, limited by crown decree to trade only with Spanish ships, were themselves participants in piracy. When ships from Seville were captured by pirates, the motley crew would sell the prized cargo to Spanish merchants in the Caribbean at prices well below the official tariffs.

The term 'buccaneer' derives from French colonists who, hiding out on Hispaniola, sold the meat and hides of cattle left by the Spanish. These buccaneers began setting up camps on various islands to repair their vessels and rest before venturing back onto the high seas. One of the first such camps was on Isla Tortuga off the north coast of Haiti. Established in the late 16th century, this multinational settlement was perhaps the earliest independent European community in the New World, owing allegiance to no crown and trading with every nation. The Bahamas, Turks and Virgin Islands were also excellent pirate hideouts, for they were windward of Spanish bases in the Greater Antilles and difficult for the lumbering galleons to approach.

One of the best harbors was **Charlotte Amalie** on St. Thomas, which became a haven for pirates who brought booty to sell to local merchants. Collusion with pirates became so blatant that an international incident unfolded at Charlotte Amalie in 1683, when the island's governor refused to hand over a pirate ship to a British man-of-war.

However it was Jamaica that had the most infamous reputation as a pirate enclave in the 17th century and for 30 years, from 1643, it offered hospitality to thousands of pirates from Europe and the Caribbean. The most celebrated of all pirates at Port Royal was **Henry Morgan**. A bold captain who knew the coasts of the Spanish Main well, Morgan's first great success was taking the rich city of Portobelo in 1666. This astounding achievement garnered Morgan a pardon from the Jamaican governor and earned him a reputation throughout the Caribbean as a shrewd and fearless leader.

More exploits followed, climaxed by the spectacular capture of Panama in 1671. When the pirates marched back across the isthmus, they took a string of 200 pack mules laden with gold, silver and other valuables, plus a large number of captives. While the crew quarreled over their share of the loot, Morgan slipped away in his ship with the greater part of the booty, leaving his followers without food or ships. Although Morgan was sent to England to stand trial (England and Spain had recently signed a treaty) he was exonerated as a hero, knighted by the king, and sent back to Jamaica not as a prisoner, but as Deputy Governor of the island. Sir Henry finished his days on his sugar plantation and, unlike others of his kind, died in his bed in 1688.

Pirates were often an unpredictable and contradictory bunch. Many a notorious captain would, upon sinking a ship and killing the survivors, call his crew together for prayer service. Some skippers forbade swearing, drinking and gambling, and some even displayed empathy for their hapless victims.

S.ʳ HEN. MORGAN
Part. 2. Chap. 7.

Sir Henry Morgan's life (1635-1688) as a pirate, living in luxury to his dying day, was the exception rather than the rule. After being knighted by Charles II, he was sent back to Jamaica as Deputy Governor to rid Port Royal of pirates. Morgan's Lookout, his famous retreat, is located near Ochos Rios on Noel Coward's Firefly estate.

Two female pirates, **Anne Bonny** and **Mary Read**, made the annals of pirate history in the early 18th century for their exploits and method of escaping the hangman's noose. Convicted of piracy in Jamaica, Bonny and Read successfully pleaded for their lives, claiming they were pregnant. On the day that Bonny's lover 'Calico' **Jack Rackam** was hanged, he obtained permission to see Anne for a farewell interview in which she apparently told him '...she was sorry to see him there, but if he had fought like a Man, he need not have been hang'd like a Dog.'

One of the most interesting pirates was **Major Thomas Bonnet**. He was not raised for a seafaring life and, before taking to piracy, he was apparently enjoying a quiet retirement on his large estate in Barbados. A married man, he lived in a fine house and was much respected by his neighbors and other gentry of the island.

But one day, something snapped. Bonnet decided to fit out a ship armed with ten guns and a crew of 70 men. To satisfy the curious, he said he intended to trade between the islands. Without so much as a word of good-bye to his wife, Bonnet slipped out of Bridgetown harbor at night and began looking for victims off the coast of Virginia, capturing half a dozen small ships.

His undoing was meeting the infamous **Edward Teach** (better known as Blackbeard) who had terrorized the Bahamas and American mainland for years. Teach attracted warships like flies to molasses and both he and

(Above) Piratess Anne Bonny was a tough pirate who fought bravely against being captured. (Below) Captain Thomas Bonnet is the only pirate actually known to make his victims walk the plank.

Bonnet were finally captured by armed sloops. Bonnet was found guilty and hanged in November 1718. When news of Bonnet's exploits and demise reached Barbados, his neighbors were shocked and found it difficult to imagine what had caused this sudden change in one of their own. It was suggested his mind had become unbalanced from the unbridled nagging of Mrs. Bonnet, whose husband was one of few known pirates, other than those in fiction, who actually made his prisoners walk the plank.

The archetypal pirate was **Blackbeard**. Notorious for his cruelty, he tortured victims and crew with equal enthusiasm. Once, after blowing out the candle in his cabin, he fired at his guests in the darkness, severely wounding one. He said afterwards that if he didn't shoot one or two, they would forget who he was. A great practitioner of psychological warfare, he would stick lighted candles in his bushy black beard to enhance his fearsome image. Blackbeard was successful for many years in the Caribbean and the U.S. eastern seaboard before being trapped by British warships off the North Carolina coast in 1718. A physical giant who wore 12 pistols and several cutlasses when heading into battle, he killed several Marines before falling to the pistol shots and sword wounds that finally killed him.

These were the dying days of piracy as Britain began stationing naval ships in the Caribbean and installing governors determined to clean up their islands. Some, like Henry Morgan of Jamaica and

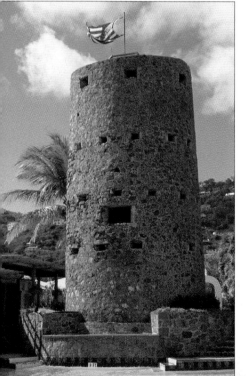

Pirates seeking island real estate were attracted to stone watchtowers, such as this one overlooking the harbor in Charlotte Amalie on St. Thomas. Built by Danes in 1678, Skytsborg is said to have been used as a hideout by the infamous pirate Blackbeard.

Nassau's Captain Woodes Rogers, were former pirates who knew where in the 'faggot heap to search for the ferret.' Woodes Rogers, who was an extraordinary navigator (he found Alexander Selkirk, a.k.a. Robinson Crusoe, on a small island in the Pacific) and a natural leader, rounded up 2,000 pirates in the Bahamas and convinced most to give up piracy.

SHIPWRECKS

Over the centuries, storms, reefs, sea battles and pirates have claimed many a ship plying the waters of the Caribbean. Those that foundered on shallow reefs kept wreckers employed in salvaging their contents, while those that settled in deeper water have, in many instances, become prime diving sites. It's estimated that some 700 ships lie wrecked on the bottom of the Caribbean Sea, and many are still being discovered. High-tech private salvagers, also known as treasure hunters, are often employed by the governments of developing countries to extract artifacts and treasures from sunken ships. This practice is opposed by archeologists, who believe historic shipwrecks should be protected from what they consider to be modern-day piracy. When the wreck of *Queen Anne's Revenge*, Blackbeard's flagship which sank off the North Carolina coast in 1718, was discovered by treasure hunters in 1996, the state claimed the wreck and its artifacts, imposing an exclusion zone around the site. The salvage company that discovered the wreck after years of research into historical documents, plans to recoup its costs by selling film and book rights.

Cartanser Sr., an encrusted World War II cargo ship, sits in 35 feet of water off St. Thomas.

Sugar, initially a luxury good, had a tremendous impact on the world economy in the 17th and 18th centuries, when it became a staple of the masses. British consumption in particular soared, and the Caribbean's highly prized 'sugar islands' were often used as bargaining chips at peace conferences between warring powers. Sugarcane grew so well in the Caribbean, and such huge profits were being made, that almost all the Lesser Antilles turned themselves completely over to its cultivation.

Cane cultivation usually took place from June to December, during the rainy season, when slaves planted cane cuttings and nurtured the growing plants. After 18 months, the cane was eight to 10 feet tall and ready for harvesting during the dry season from January to June. Early methods of extracting juice required an enormous amount of cane; about 20 pounds were needed to produce a pound of sugar. Heavy bales of cane stalks were brought from the fields to the mills where the juice was extracted. The cane was run through the mill's rollers at least twice to squeeze as much juice out of the stalk as possible. The juice would run by trough to the boiling house where it was boiled and clarified in a series of copper vats to remove excess water and impurities. Workers would skim off gross matter and strain the juice before finally allowing it to flow into cooling troughs. The resulting raw sugar, called muscovado or unfinished sugar, was put in huge barrels called hogsheads which weighed 1,600 pounds. The hogsheads were placed on racks and

The production of sugar began with the harvesting of cane, which was brought to the mill for crushing. Wind-powered mills were more common on low-lying islands such as Barbados and St. Croix.

left to stand for 12 to 16 hours when a plug at the bottom was removed and the molasses drained off. The barrels were then topped up with sugar and ready for export.

The refining of this raw sugar product was normally completed in Europe or North America but the production of rum, at least for domestic consumption, was usually carried out on the individual islands. Early rum was made by fermenting a mixture of water and molasses (five parts to one) in a vat with a measure of skimmings, oranges and herbs to taste. After fermentation, the mix was heated in a still through condensing coils, emerging as rum of 120 proof or stronger. It was sometimes rough, usually uneven, but it was rum.

RUM

Known as ron in Spanish and rhum in French, rum is a versatile spirit with a range of taste and characteristics unique to each producing island. The history of rum runs parallel with that of the Caribbean. Sir Henry Morgan glowingly described rum as, 'A friend and brother to one alone in the dark, a warm blanket on a chilly night, an excitement in the cheek and an inspirer of bold and brave deeds.' Many islands have a long history of producing rum. In the tropics, rum has long been the preferred drink, and not just for its taste. Alcohol dilates the peripheral blood vessels and actually has a cooling effect on the body, which makes rum more refreshing than ice water.

A distillery on St. Croix with pot stills shown at left . Workers roll a hogshead barrel filled with raw sugar along the loading dock.

Rum, which is produced from either molasses or cane juice, is unique in that it retains more natural taste factors from its product of origin than any other spirit. Starch-derived spirits, such as vodka (made from potatoes) or whisky (from grain), must be cooked or malted to produce a sugar for fermentation. Since rum is derived from sugar, it doesn't have to go through a cooking process, nor does it have to be distilled at very high proofs, so it receives the minimum of chemical treatment.

Production begins with the fermentation of either cane juice or molasses to make the originating product for the start of distillation. The method of distillation and aging, along with the strain of yeast used, and the type and amount of caramel used in coloring, are what differentiate the various rums. The traditional pot still (also known as batch production) and the more modern continuous column stills are both used in the distillation process, with some rums being a blend of each method. Like whiskey and brandy, rum needs to mature, and full bodied rum is normally aged three years or more while drier, lighter rums are generally aged only one year. Rum is naturally colorless but it will pick up some color if it is aged in charred casks (which also adds aroma) or, more usually, if sugar caramel is added. These darker rums are often used in hot drinks in cold damp climates while the drier light rum is popular as a chilled summer cocktail.

DIFFERENT TYPES OF RUM

Popular rum distilleries hold regular tours for visitors and are well worth the visit for rum aficionados. Most Caribbean rum is produced from local sugar cane products, although imports from Mexico and Central America are sometimes used. Here is a quick overview of various island rums.

Puerto Rico: The rums produced here are dry and light bodied. The molasses is fermented in gigantic vats using mash from a previous fermentation. If the rum is matured for only a year in uncharred oak casks,

it is light-bodied, neutral in flavor and white in color. Two years in charred barrels and the addition of caramel produces a somewhat darker rum with more body and a stronger aroma. Puerto Rico's best-known rum is Bacardi – the top selling rum in the world. Bacardi, using continuous stills which impart a remarkable consistency in taste, has a range of rums aged one to six years, including an excellent reserve rum (six years old) best savored neat. The bat on the logo is from the company's beginnings in 1862, when Don Facundo bought the distillery which was then home to a colony of fruit bats. The bat symbol was, at that time, an easily recognized trademark for illiterate customers.

Jamaica: The traditional Jamaican rum, full bodied with a pungent aroma, has in recent decades been blended lighter with the taste and aroma toned down. However, most Jamaican rum is still made using pot or batch stills and aged a lengthy three to five years. The molasses is allowed to ferment naturally, which can take up to three weeks but allows for greater saturation of cane flavor. A number of fine rums are produced on Jamaica and the major producer is Appleton, which makes an excellent range of rums from its own sugar cane, blending pot-still and continuous-still rums to make its popular brands. Appleton produces a 12-year-old rum, one of the oldest and finest available.

Barbados: Rums from this island are semi-light in body and color, with an almost smoky flavor. Distillation methods include pot and continuous stills, and most Bajan rums are a blend of the two. Cockspur, Mount Gay and Doorly's are popular brands. The world's oldest rum is claimed by Mount Gay, its production traced prior to 1703. Mount Gay rums are distilled from molasses using natural spring water from the island. Different aged rums are blended to make its final smooth-tasting Eclipse product.

French West Indies: A considerable amount of full-bodied rum is made on Martinique and Guadeloupe. On Martinique alone there are nearly a hundred cane growers and over a dozen large distillers. French West Indies rum is different from other islands in that the product is distilled from the concentrated juice of sugar cane rather than from molasses. It is produced by pot still and takes on a dark color.

Other Islands: The U.S. Virgin Islands produce a light-bodied rum, with Cruzan on St. Croix enjoying a very good reputation, while the British Virgin Islands are producers of Pusser's famous Royal Navy Rum, a dark rum which can be bought in a traditional clay jug. Antigua produces a decent and inexpensive rum called Cavilier, and Westerhall distillers on Grenada produce a limited pot-still rum from sugar cane juice aged in oak. Each bottle is numbered, which somehow makes the sipping of this rum all the more delightful.

The Caribbean is a sea of cultures, its people as diverse as the world itself. Their official languages include English, French, Spanish and Dutch, yet it's a Creole dialect, based on a French vocabulary and African grammar, which is used on many of the islands and is incomprehensible to most outsiders. Local customs and cuisine also vary from island to island, but what does prevail throughout the Caribbean is exuberance, especially during each island's Carnival.

Carnival is a celebration of life and no where is it displayed with more fervor than in Trinidad, where the music of Carnival – calypso and steel band – was born. Pulsating Afro-Caribbean rhythms provide the beat and the brilliant costumes worn by dancing paraders provide the color. A year of preparation produces elaborate, three-dimensional costumes, some up to 10 feet tall and weighing 300 pounds. Competition for prizes is fierce – not for the money, but for the honor.

Mocko jumbie stilt walkers – the traditional symbol of Carnival – originate from the traditions of West Africa. They parade atop 10-to-20-foot stilts, dressed in bright colors and covered in mirrors because these 'elevated spirits' are said to be invisible and onlookers see only themselves. Carnival celebrations vary from island to island, and not all are held in the days prior to Lent. In the Bahamas, a festival called Junkanoo is held right after Christmas, with people flocking to Nassau to participate in the parades. In Puerto Rico, fiestas honoring patron saints are held in central plazas and include religious and costumed processions. In the U.S. Virgin Islands, Carnival is celebrated on St. Thomas in April, on St. John over July 4th, and on St. Croix in

A girl on St. Vincent participates in the children's parade, a popular event at Carnival.
(Opposite page) Straw markets selling local handicrafts are a common sight in the Caribbean.

December. Crop Over Festival in Barbados – a revival of the traditional celebration of the end of the sugar harvest – is held each summer, as is Antigua's annual festival celebrating the abolition of slavery.

Whether it's called a 'jump-up' or a 'mas' (masquerade), the celebration is uninhibited and the mood joyful, with spontaneous street parties, reggae concerts, calypso competitions, food fairs and the crowning of a Carnival king and queen.

Each port has a bustling marketplace, located in a central square, where fresh produce is sold along with other wares. Traditionally a social gathering place as well as the town's commercial hub, with island farmers, fishermen and traders bringing their goods here to sell, the market reflects traditions long rooted in Africa. Matriarchs called 'market women' often control, through mutual understanding, a specific spot in the square and acquire goods to sell either by purchase or on consignment.

The fresh fruits, vegetables and spices on colorful display at the market are the mainstays of creole cooking. Root vegetables, including yams and sweet potatoes, are commonly used, as are breadfruits, tomatoes, peppers and ackee which, when removed from its ripened pod and cooked, resembles scrambled eggs. Rice, peas, beans and fried plantains (a type of banana) are served alongside a main dish of saltfish (salted cod), curried goat or conch fritters. Stews are also popular, such as kalaloo which consists of okra, spinach, goat, crab, fish and West Indian spices.

The flavorful dishes created in West Indian kitchens incorporate a number of local spices. Allspice, chives, curry, ginger, nutmeg, turmeric (the 'poor man's saffron') and thyme are all favored. Jerk, a popular Jamaican cooking technique introduced by African slaves, involves marinating pork, chicken, sausage or fish in a mixture containing Scotch Bonnet (a very hot chile pepper), thyme, allspice, scallions, garlic and nutmeg, then cooking the meat in an outdoor pit over a pimento wood fire. This traditional dish was likely introduced by African slaves,

(Above) Colorful batik clothing is made throughout the West Indies. Here, a worker applies wax to cloth at the Caribelle Batik factory on St. Kitts.
(Left) Bahamian wood carvings.
(Below) A fisherman mends his nets at the coastal village of Anse-la-Ray, St. Lucia.

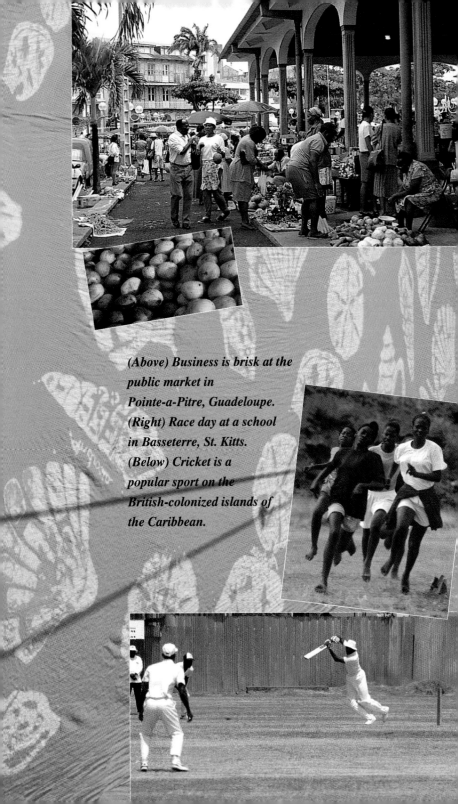

(Above) Business is brisk at the public market in Pointe-a-Pitre, Guadeloupe. (Right) Race day at a school in Basseterre, St. Kitts. (Below) Cricket is a popular sport on the British-colonized islands of the Caribbean.

but the Arawak natives before them were already grilling meats and fish. The Arawaks introduced many tropical fruits to the West Indies, as well as vegetables such as corn, callaloo (similar to spinach) and cassava (resembling sweet potatoes and the source of tapioca).

Rum is another important ingredient in Caribbean cooking, used widely in deserts featuring bananas and coconut. A typical Caribbean fruit punch, with or without rum, consists of orange and pineapple juice, with grenadine syrup and nutmeg added. Limes, mangos, pineapples and papayas are just some of the delicious fruits grown locally and served up Caribbean style.

In a region where self expression and creativity are evident in the dancing, singing and easygoing nature of the people, it's easy to forget there's a more serious side to Caribbean culture, one that has produced a number of critically acclaimed writers and poets. Nobel-winning writer Derek Walcott, born of mixed-race ancestry on St. Lucia in 1930, was educated in Jamaica where he immersed himself in classical literature. His poems draw both on the folklore of a West Indian childhood and the teachings of a higher education, a dichotomy that once caused him to complain that he felt more at ease describing an English cherry tree than the breadfruit tree under which he sat while writing.

Another famous West Indian writer is V. S. Naipaul, considered a master of English narrative, who was born in poverty to Indian parents in Trinidad in 1932. Apparently hating both his mother and his tiny country's provincialism, Naipaul moved to England at the age of 18 to study at Oxford. Knighted in 1990, Sir Vidiadhar Surajprasad Naipaul has written a sweeping selection of novels, travel books and documentary works, and in 2001 he was awarded the Nobel Prize in literature for his vivid portrayal of post-colonial society and his critical assessments of Muslim fundamentalism. A highly educated street fighter, Naipaul is unflinching in his opinions and his legendary brusqueness is described in Paul Theroux's unflattering book *Sir Vidia's Shadow: A Friendship Across Five Continents.*

Also making her mark on the world is Antigua-born Jamaica Kincaid, who ran away to New York City at age 17 to escape an unhappy childhood which, along with the bitter realities of her homeland, are frequent subjects of her writing.

Caribbean visual artists have been widely influenced by Haiti's primitive art, which developed in isolation among the peasantry until discovered by the outside

A Jamaican girl in her school uniform smiles for the camera.

world in the 1940s. Colorful and vivid, Haitian art often depicts voodoo images based on African tribal practises. African motifs – animal patterns and geometric designs – are often incorporated in Caribbean works, both fine art and folk art, and the works of local painters and artisans are widely displayed in island shops and galleries.

Prominent singers and songwriters who hail from the Caribbean include Cuban-born songstress Gloria Estefan, Puerto Rican pop star Ricky Martin, and the late reggae superstar Bob Marley of Jamaica, whose music was introduced to an international audience by record producer Chris Blackwell, the founder of Island Records (which he sold to Polygram in 1989). The actor Sidney Poitier was raised on Cat Island in the Bahamas, and fashion designer Oscar de la Renta was born in the Dominican Republic, his namesake perfume inspired by his mother's garden in Santo Domingo.

West Indian men and women are leaders in many fields. St. Lucian-born Sir Arthur Lewis won a Nobel prize for economics in 1979, and Dominican prime minister Eugenia Charles, dubbed the 'Iron Lady of the Caribbean' for her outspoken personality and political strength, led her country in the 1980s and 90s. Famous Caribbean athletes include Puerto Rico's baseball legend Roberto Clemente, and two of the world's fastest 100-metre sprinters – Donovan Bailey (winning Olympic gold for Canada in 1996) and Linford Christie (Britain's gold medalist in 1992) – are from Jamaica.

Churches are numerous and well-attended in the West Indies. (Below) Pews await Sunday worshipers in the 19th-century Cathedral of Our Lady of Fair Haven in Roseau, Dominica.

CARIBBEAN MUSIC

Caribbean music, drum laden and danceable, has direct connections with the music of West Africa. The Gankogui (or double African bell), which provides a steady repeating pattern and is the rhythmic basis to West African music, evolved from a 12-count rhythm into the eight-count 'clave' rhythm that is the foundation for most Caribbean music. Wooden concussion sticks, called claves, produce a beat that guides all other instruments in their rhythmic variations. The clave sticks may or may not be used in a particular piece of music, but their underlying rhythm is always present.

Many Caribbean songs are lyrically linked to the experience of slavery, both in style and subject matter, for although slaves were not allowed to speak to one another in the fields, they could sing. After emancipation, former slaves maintained their musical heritage at social events and church services, passing on rhythms, techniques and lyrical motifs to successive generations.

The main rhythm of reggae – in which the accent is put on the second and fourth beat of a four/four time signature – has been traced back to the Yela rhythm created by women in southern Senegal by alternating hand claps with the pounding of grain. The African wellspring from which Caribbean music evolved is also the source of jazz, which developed in New Orleans in the latter part of the 19th century and was based, in part, on black work songs and field shouts.

In an evolving tapestry of musical sounds, Caribbean music has been influenced by American jazz, along with other, less closely related musical forms, including European waltzes, quadrilles and mazurkas, as well as Latin styles such as the Cuban rumba. American Gospel,

Calypso is heard everywhere during Trinidad's famous Carnival.

rock and roll and rhythm and blues also have played a big part. The following is a compilation of the different styles you will hear when visiting ports of the Caribbean.

CALYPSO

Originally from Trinidad, calypso is popular throughout the Caribbean. The beauty of calypso is twofold: sophisticated lyrics with clever word play and driving rhythms for a festive unwinding. The music is thought to have progressed from the field songs of slaves employing allegory to pass along information and gossip. This interest in subtle lyrics, to hide meaning from slave masters, was turned into a source of entertainment and art. The game evolved with work crews fighting mock battles in song and the number of bon mot lyrical strikes determining the winner. Instruments were added to the sound in the 19th century, when calypso was first recorded. Today, driven by syncopated bass rhythm, calypso is filled in with drums, guitars and occasionally tenor and alto steel drums. Calypso, like its offspring soca, is a favorite at Carnival in Trinidad, where there are competitions for lyrical quality and party-pleasing rhythms. Popular artists include Chalk Dust, Mighty Sparrow, David Rudder, Roaring Lion (who at 89 years of age released a hit album) and Eddy Grant. Another recent offshot of calypso is "ring-bang" developed by Eddy Grant which marries a modern sound utilizing synthesizers and recording techniques with classical calypso lyrics and melody. A major record label for calypso (and soca) is Ice Records, which has a dazzling array of artists and releases a selection of Carnival competitors each year. *Hot and Sweet*, recorded by calypso king Mighty Sparrow in the 1970s, is a classic.

STEEL BAND

The steel pan, the only contemporary instrument created in the Caribbean, is made from a 55-gallon oil drum. The base of the drum is

Steel bands play calypso arrangements on drums called steel pans.

heated and stretched into a concave shape, and the surface is then pounded out in graduating rectangles to create different notes. Steel bands normally arrange popular calypso songs for their drums. The Rising Stars of St. Thomas are a popular steel pan band. Cruise lines often arrange for steel bands to play their music during arrival or departure of their ships

SOCA

A blend of soul and calypso, soca is jumped-up calypso with bawdier lyrics. The music of choice on Trinidad, soca is popular throughout the Caribbean and played non-stop at Carnival time when famous calypso and soca artists perform at competitions. Well-known artists include the versatile Mighty Sparrow (who has the longest straight number of wins at the Road March King competition in Trinidad) as well as Superblue, Fab 5 and ring bang artist Viking Tundah. Cuban percussionist Changuito, often referred to as the father of modern soca, developed the soca rhythm while playing with the group Los Van Van. One of the best known soca songs is Hot Hot Hot, recorded by Hot Hot Hot Arrow, a native of Montserrat.

GOOMBAY

Unique Bahamian music with a fast-paced tempo driven by a range of skin drums, goombay is directly linked with West African dances and drums. Nassau holds an annual Goombay Summer Festival featuring this and other Afro-Caribbean music.

REGGAE

Perhaps the biggest revolution in Caribbean music, reggae literally lifted Jamaica from a post-colonial funk in the late 1960s to an era of new confidence and hope. Born in the slums of Kingston, reggae quickly became popular around the world as mainstream artists such as Eric Clapton, Paul Simon and the Rolling Stones produced hits using the reggae beat. Evolved from ska (Jamaican dance-hall music) and a slow rock-steady beat, reggae was slower still with a greater emphasis on bass and, traditionally performed outdoors, was played loudly. Reggae's early lyrics were social, political and spiritual, exerting a real impact on Jamaican politics in the early 1970s. Its main artist was the late Bob Marley, whose songs of redemption, salvation and prophecy made him a leader for poor Jamaicans

Beres Hammond is a leading reggae artist.

(see profile in Jamaica chapter). Bob Marley and the Wailers produced a string of reggae hits with bestselling albums such as *Catch a Fire* and *Natty Dread* and became the leading reggae group of the 1970s. *Get Up, Stand Up*; *I Shot The Sheriff*, and *One Love* are some of Marley's well-known songs.

Although local DJs gave reggae its big push in the mid-to-late 60s, it was record producer Chris Blackwell's early support that gave reggae an audience in the markets of Europe and the United States. One of the first albums to become an international hit, now a classic, was Jimmy Cliff's *The Harder They Come* which was actually a soundtrack to a movie about the hardships of attaining success as a musician in Jamaica. Other reggae artists from this era include the Maytals, Desmond Dekker and Burning Spear. Marley's son Ziggy and wife Rita continue to record, and other popular artists include Beres Hammond, Buju Banton, Shabba Ranks and Maxi Priest.

SALSA

Hot, sensuous dance music with a distinct call-and-response singing style, salsa is popular in Puerto Rico. Its strong emphasis on brass and percussion is derived from the Cuban salsa which uses timbales, bongos and congas to carry the rhythm. Popular artists include Eddie Palmieri and Bobby Valentin.

OTHER MUSICAL STYLES

Merengue, created during the 19th century in the rural townships of the Dominican Republic, utilizes the cylindrical, double-headed tambora drums and brass instruments. Merengue is experiencing a comeback in its country of origin, and both it and Cuban salsa are currently the hip music rage in Madrid night clubs.

Cadence is popular in Martinique, Guadeloupe and Dominica. It began as a sort of Caribbean jazz fusion (featuring clarinet and trombone), which synthesized various Caribbean musical forms, including soca and reggae, with exuberant driving drum rhythms.

Zouk is popular French Caribbean music that grew from cadence and is very fast with lots of Latin influences. Vocal harmonies are featured in zouk music, which was originally used to describe parties on Martinique and Guadeloupe.

Jazz has become increasingly popular in the Caribbean on several islands, including St. Lucia, Jamaica, Grenada and Puerto Rico, which host annual festivals which feature local and international performers.

Gospel is American religious music that developed in the southern slave-holding states and can be heard in many a Caribbean church. A fusion of jazz, blues, reggae and calypso, gospel evolved from a combination of plantation work songs and Protestant hymns. When a West Indian congregation raises its unified voice in a jubilant gospel song, the spiritual inspiration of the music is a salve for tired ears.

(Above) The customs house in San Juan reflects the Plateresque style of contrasting bare walls and ornamental doorways.

(Below) Spanish and French colonial buildings featured overhanging grilled balconies, built over the sidewalk to provide shade, such as those lining a Marigot street in St. Martin.

The Caribbean is a showcase of colonial architecture, its various styles reflecting the Spanish, French, Dutch, British and Danish settlement of the area. The prevailing styles in Europe were adapted to the terrain and climate of the West Indies, and building techniques were modified to accommodate the availability of materials. Forts and other structures were built using brick brought across the Atlantic as ship's ballast, or of volcanic rock and limestone quarried on the islands.

The Spaniards were the first to introduce European architectural styles to the New World. Initial structures, including cathedrals and monasteries, were military in design and their style was massive and plain. This strain of simple, solid construction prevailed throughout the Spanish colonial period, although elaborate design elements were introduced as Spain's artists, and their colonial counterparts, made the stylistic transition from Gothic to Renaissance.

The sturdy West Indian house is both functional and visually pleasing. Its steep, gabled roof withstands strong winds, sheds rain quickly and, vented at both ends, allows hot air to escape. Hoods and louvered wooden blinds keep out the hot sun and driving rain while admitting light and fresh air. Solid wood shutters are another feature on islands, where hurricanes are an annual threat. Gingerbread fretwork, in a variety of patterns, is often added as decoration.

The Dutch colonial buildings found in the Netherlands Antilles are often baroque in style, their gabled roofs designed with fluid, curving lines and embellished with ornamental trim. Shown here, the Penha building in Willemstad, Curacao.

British plantation owners lived in 'great houses', their outer walls often built of large limestone blocks up to 20" thick which absorbed the sun's heat. St. Nicholas Abbey in Barbados, one of the oldest great houses in the West Indies, was built by a British colonel around 1650 in the Jacobean style, with gables and corner fireplaces – an unlikely feature for the tropics.

Barbadian chattel houses – moveable wooden homes built by freed slaves – were a miniature version of the Georgian-style manor house.

Features of West Indian neo-classical architecture included rows of arches running the length of arcaded sidewalks and upper-floor galleries designed to provide shade from the tropical sun and catch the breezes. (Above) Christiansted, St. Croix, has some of the best-preserved examples of this style.

(Above, right) The Sacred Heart Basilica in Balata, outside Fort-de-France, Martinique, is a smaller version of the famous Montmartre landmark in Paris, its design a revival of the Byzantine-Romanesque style.

European technological advances in the 19th century included the widespread use of metal, as evidenced in the Schoelcher Library (shipped in pieces from France) and the Saint-Louis Cathedral (shown at right), both located in Fort-de-France and designed by French architect Henri Pick (a contemporary of Gustav Eiffel, builder of the Eiffel Tower).

Bird of Paradise

Amazon Parrot

The Caribbean's plant and animal life is rich in diversity and beauty. Flowers, both indigenous and exotic, flourish here amid the lush, tropical greenery, as do nearly 300 species of butterflies and hundreds of species of birds.

Heliconius Ismenius butterfly

Hibiscus

Torch Lily

PLANT LIFE

The vegetation on a single island can vary considerably, with a jungle-like growth of dense foliage proliferating on its windward side, and stunted plants that tolerate arid soil growing on its leeward side. The vegetation zones occurring on mountainous islands are well defined. At the summits of the higher peaks is an elfin woodland of matted mosses, lichens and ferns, which can survive in wet and windy conditions. A montane (mist) forest grows on the mountains' upper slopes and ridges, and consists of small trees and ground vegetation of grasses and ferns.

At lower elevations is the rain forest, its tall trees and interlaced foliage forming a dense canopy, through which little sunlight can penetrate. **Bromeliads** (air plants) sprout from massive tree trunks and ferns grow at their bases. A secondary forest will grow in areas previously cleared through natural disaster or cultivation for crops, its open canopy allowing the growth of shrubs and small plants at ground level. Often intermingled with secondary forests are seasonal formations, which contain many of the flowering trees that blossom during the dry season.

In addition to being sources of food and material for handicrafts and construction, a number of island plants and trees are also used for bush medicines and herbal remedies, their leaves boiled to make therapeutic teas and soothing baths for treating such ailments as rheumatism and the common cold. Children use young green fruits for playing marble games and a broad leaf on a stick can serve as a parasol.

Many of the tropical hardwoods, such as mahogany, are deciduous but are considered evergreen because, rather than shed all their leaves

at once, they do so sporadically throughout the year. In addition to supplying oxygen, tropical trees support vines and air plants, an example being the banyan tree, which sprouts roots that hang between the tallest branches and the ground. Tree roots supply nutrients to the soil and prevent soil erosion during heavy rains.

Forests are important watersheds, with almost all fresh water originating in forest rivers and lakes. The widespread cutting of tropical rain forests has become a controversial practice due to its destruction of freshwater sources as well as its

The massive trunk of this tropical tree is supported by buttress roots.

destabilization of the earth's temperature, humidity and carbon dioxide levels. Island rainforests, being self-contained ecosystems, are much more susceptible to extinction than those on a continental land mass. On some Caribbean islands, the removal of vegetation around watersheds has caused rivers to dry up, and fresh water must be imported or produced by desalinization plants.

The importance of forest preservation is recognized by a growing number of Caribbean nations that are countering development with the establishment of national parks, nature reserves and wildlife sanctuaries. Guided tours are offered throughout the islands, which allow visitors to see first hand such species of tree as the soapberry, fig and maho, its bark used for making rope. Limes, bananas, papayas and other fruits can be seen hanging from tree branches, as can cocoa tree pods containing cocoa beans. These and other species, such as the nutmeg tree, were introduced to the West Indies for cultivation. Banana plants are widely grown, their leafy, palm-like aspect a familiar sight. The overlapping bases of the banana plant form a false trunk, from which emerges the true stem of a mature plant, bearing the male and female flowers. The latter develop into clusters of upturned bananas, called 'hands', with each banana a 'finger'. The plant is cut down for harvesting, since it bears fruit only the once.

Exotic flowers blossom everywhere. Introduced to the islands during the colonial era, they provide brilliant splashes of color amid the green tropical foliage. Some of the popular flowers are

Rainforest conservation is critical to the survival of an island's watershed.

Three Palms Beach, Puerto Rico

bougainvillea, hibiscus, orchid, frangipani, flamboyant (royal poinciana) and the trumpet-shaped yellow cedar. Indigenous plant species include bamboo, guava trees, wild pineapple, dodder vines, century plant, soursop, tamarind and coconut palms.

Palm trees grow throughout the Caribbean, their flowing crowns of frond leaves swaying in the breeze and providing welcome shade. Palms grow to heights of 100 feet or more, their smooth cylindrical stems marked by ringlike scars left by former leaves. The towering royal palms, often seen lining avenues, reach heights of up to 120 feet and were traditionally used as boundary markers for sugar plantations.

The **coco palm**, from 60 to 100 feet tall, readily establishes itself on shorelines and small islands because its seeds, enclosed in a large buoyant pod, can float. Its fruit is the coconut, a hard woody shell encased in a brown fibrous husk, and a single coco palm can bear more than 200 nuts annually. A coconut has three round scars at one end, its embryo lying against the largest, which is easily punctured to drain the nutritious juice inside. Copra, from which oil is extracted to make soaps, cooking oil and suntan lotion, is produced when a ripened coconut is broken open and dried.

Every part of a coco palm has value, its leaves used for making fans, baskets and thatch, its coarse coconut husks turned into cordage, mats and stuffing, its nutshells polished and carved to make attractive cups and bowls. Even the fibrous center of old trunks can be used for rope. In addition to its fruit being a staple food, the young head of its tender leaves – called palm cabbage – is cooked as a vegetable.

Called 'trees of life' for the many functions they serve, coco palms are susceptible to lethal yellowing disease, caused when minute insects called planthoppers infect the palm leaflets with a mycoplasma-like

Found in the Caribbean, iguanas can weigh up to 400 pounds.

organism. The yellowed leaves soon die, as does the tree's trunk. This disease devastated Key West's coco palms in 1955, before spreading north to Miami where, by the mid-70s, the disease had eradicated 90% of the city's coco palms. In the early 80s Mexico's Yucatan Peninsula was hit by the disease. Although a palm infected with lethal yellowing can be treated with regular applications of tetracycline funneled through a hole that is bored into the trunk, the most workable solution is to replace the stricken palm with a resistant variety.

ANIMAL LIFE

Over the centuries various animal species have been introduced to the West Indies, such as the mongoose, a ferret-sized mammal imported from Asia to hunt rats and snakes but which also destroys much of the native fauna. Others are indigenous to the region, such as the **iguana**, a herbivorous lizard common to Mexico's Yucatan peninsula and a number of Caribbean islands. Being cold blooded, it derives body heat from the sun and basks on rocks and tree tops for much of the day to maintain a body temperature high enough to digest the leaves and fruits it consumes. Peaceful and harmless, iguanas grow to three feet in length and can weigh over 400 pounds. The larger males are gray with a tall crest on the back, while the females retain the bright green body of a young iguana. The female burrows a nest in sandy soil, laying her eggs at the end of a tunnel, which she then refills for concealment. When the young iguanas hatch, they dig their way to the surface where they are vulnerable to predators.

The American **crocodile**, found in South Florida, the West Indies and Central America, lives in both fresh and salt water and does not attack humans without provocation. Crocodiles are large, carnivorous reptiles that live in swamps or on river banks, slipping into the water to hunt for prey with their powerful jaws. Its eyes, ears and nostrils are on top of its head, with valves closing on the ears and nostrils when the crocodile submerges. The average length of a crocodile's flat body and tail is about 10 feet but the saltwater variety is often 14 feet long, sometimes growing to 20 feet.

Alligators, which are found in the southern United States, are generally less aggressive than crocodiles, have wider snouts and, unlike the crocodile, the lower fourth tooth does not protrude when the mouth is closed. Caimans are similar to alligators, growing to lengths of 15 feet, and are found in Central America.

Jaguars have a unique coat with rings surrounding spots, and it is this pattern of rosettes that distinguishes jaguars from leopards. Jaguars are good swimmers and can live in trees for months when the jungle floor is flooded. Belize has a world famous jaguar reserve.

BIRDS

The Caribbean's abundant bird life ranges from tiny hummingbirds to the high-flying frigate bird. Because the West Indies are close to both South and North America, there is some crossover of range between tropical birds and those commonly seen in the United States.

The magnificent **frigate bird**, also called man-o'-war bird, is the most aerial of the water birds with a wingspread of 7-1/2 feet – the largest in proportion to its body of any bird. Highly skilled fliers, frigate birds can be seen riding thermal updrafts along coastlines for extended periods of time. They feed mainly on fish they spot while in flight and they will harass other birds, such as pelicans, until they drop their catch, which is then snatched in midair or retrieved from the water

Frigate Bird

Brown Pelican

or beach. Its long tail, deeply forked and scissor-like, is opened only while maneuvering in flight. Although classed as a sea bird, it is awkward in the water.

The **brown pelican**, in contrast to the frigate bird, is heavy bodied with a long neck and large, flat bill. It too is a graceful flier, as well as a skilled swimmer, and it will glide in circles in the air before suddenly diving straight into the water to scoop a fish into the large, expandable pouch hanging from its lower jaw. Brown pelicans nest on shore and the young feed from their parents' pouch.

The **flamingo** is a tall, tropical wading bird related to the stork and heron. Now an infrequent visitor to southern Florida, the American flamingo nests chiefly in the West Indies, with sizeable breeding colonies located on Bonaire and on the southernmost Bahamian island of Inagua. Flamingos build conical mud nests, one to two feet high, with mates taking turns incubating one or two eggs. The flamingo feeds in the shallow water of marshes and lagoons, where it scoops water into its large bill, the serrated edges of which strain algae and shellfish from the water. The bird's pink color comes from its diet of shrimp and other crustaceans containing the pigment carotene.

Flamingo

The **Great Egret** (also called Common Egret) is a type of heron that feeds in shallow water on small aquatic life. Threatened in the early 20th century when its white, silky plumage was used to adorn ladies hats, the egret is now a protected species.

Parrots, with their brilliant plumage, longevity (up to 80 years in captivity) and ability to mimic human voices, have for centuries been popular cage birds. Their natural habitat is the tropical rainforest and the smaller species tend to be mostly green, a camouflage defense against predators. The best mimics are the Amazons, which are found in the West Indies.

Great Egret

CORAL REEFS

Some of the most unusual animal life in the Caribbean is found beneath the water's surface, where coral reefs, formed by living organisms, are home to a fascinating variety of fish and other sea creatures. These underwater habitats are formed by soft, saclike animals called polyps. Smaller than a pea, each polyp secretes an exoskeleton of limestone. A colony forms by polyps budding new polyps, with all the buds remaining connected. These tiny polyps, each living inside its own limestone cavity, feed mainly at night on floating plankton, which they trap with their extended tentacles. Microscopic algae grow within the polyp tissues and are collectively responsible for the coral colony's vivid colors. These symbiotic algae, called zooxanthellae, need sunlight and clear water to take up carbon dioxide and photosynthesize, thus providing an internal supply of oxygen and organic nutrients to the polyp.

Green Sea Turtle

Queen Angelfish

Moray Eel

Brain Coral

Sea Anemone

A Coral Reef Community

An abundance of life thrives in warm Caribbean waters, where coral reefs support schools of colorful fish and other aquatic creatures.

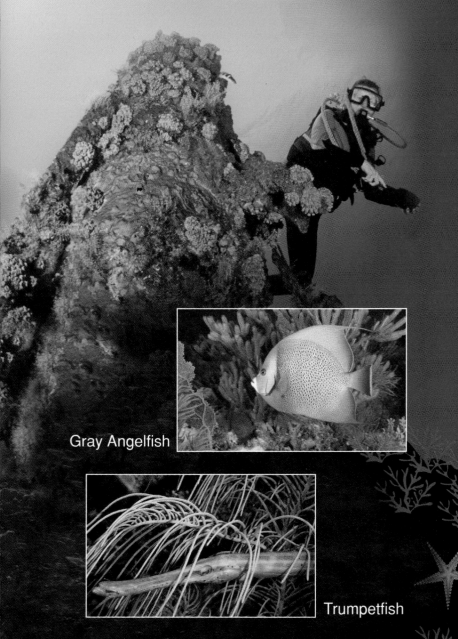

Gray Angelfish

Trumpetfish

When coral colonies die, their surfaces are recolonized by new corals or other types of invertebrates, such as sponges or soft corals. Layers of skeletal materials gradually accumulate over time to form a coral reef. Although corals live in temperate as well as tropical waters, coral reefs are found only in tropical waters, within 30 degrees of the equator, where the water temperature remains above 70 degrees Fahrenheit year round.

Coral reefs that extend from shore are called fringing reefs, and those separated from shore by a wide lagoon are called barrier reefs. Barrier reefs rise like fortress walls from the sea floor and are habitat for tropical fish and large ocean-going predators, which feed here on the smaller fish. Fringe reefs, often within a few yards of the water's surface, serve as nurseries for hundreds of small tropical fish, as do mangroves which grow along shorelines. Their tangled roots and dense branches are saltwater tolerant, and they help stabilize coastlines by absorbing wave action. Coral reefs also deflect incoming waves, their porous character allowing the absorption and dissipation of a pounding sea. In bays protected by strategically placed reefs, the steady shifting of particulate debris from the coral colony onto shore results in a beach of fine sand.

Adjacent to reefs are **seagrass beds**, where the sturdy stems and roots of underwater plants weave together to form a mat that stabilizes the shallow sandy bottom and provides food for sea turtles, manatees, conchs and reef fishes. A band of bare sand containing only the roots of seagrasses sometimes separates a reef from its adjacent seagrass bed. This is caused by grazing reef fishes which are reluctant to venture too far from the security of their reef, or by urchins which come off the reef

at night to feed along the edge of the seagrass bed.

Seagrass beds also anchor sediments, helping maintain the water clarity required for a healthy reef which needs sunlight to survive. Excessive nutrients in the water, often caused by sewage and agricultural run-off, can trigger algal blooms that cloud the water and prevent sunlight from penetrating and activating photosynthesis in the corals' symbiotic algae. These unwanted blooms of algae can also attach to the surfaces of corals and grow until portions of the reef are smothered.

The mangrove's roots and branches help stabilize a shoreline.

Protective measures are being taken in the Florida Keys and islands of the Caribbean, where environmental pressures in the form of coastal development, water pollution, overfishing and increased recreational use have all threatened the survival of coral reefs. Preservation measures include the installation of mooring buoys so that no anchors are dropped from boats, and prohibiting snorkelers and divers from touching and taking pieces of coral. A number of marine parks contain signposted underwater trails guiding visitors past the colorful corals while providing an appreciation of their fragile environment. Artificial reefs in the form of sunken ships encrusted with corals and inhabited by schools of fish are one way of luring divers and snorkelers away from fragile natural reefs.

Most reef-forming corals belong to the stony or hard group of corals. There are many different types of hard corals, some branch-like, others rounded, their distinctive shapes determined by the budding pattern of the various polyp species. Corals are often named for their appearance and some common hard corals include **elkhorn**, with its thick stocky branches, and staghorn, which has smaller branches. Other branching colonies include flower, finger, pencil and ivory corals. Pillar and ribbon corals grow upright in clusters, and **brain corals** grow in rounded shapes. Soft corals also help build the reefs, their feathery forms including sea fans and gorgonians in a variety of vivid colors. **Sea anemones**, unlike the corals, do not have a skeleton and often look like flowers when their feeding end is open and their tentacles are fully extended. Brilliantly colored sponges, another aquatic animal, attach themselves to coral reefs, often in colonies. They vary in shape and size, and show little movement.

The shimmering tropical fishes found along coral reefs come in an assortment of shapes, sizes, colors and markings, which often change as the juvenile fish matures. **Angelfishes** are among the most beautiful of the small fishes that inhabit shallow reefs, their flattened disc-like shapes allowing them to slip through nooks and crannies. Their elaborate markings are often blue and yellow, or black with yellow stripes. They feed on sponges and the ectoparasites of other fishes. **Butterflyfishes** are similar to angelfishes with yellow

Golden Tube Sponge at Cane Bay Reef, St. Croix.

A reef shark looks for food along a barrier reef.

their dominant color. They travel in pairs, feeding on coral polyps, sea anemones, tubeworms and algae.

Blue tangs are another disc-like fish that live on the algae that grows on or among the coral. The juveniles are a lemon-yellow color, pre-adults are often part yellow and part blue, and adults are a blue to purplish gray. The size of reef fishes can vary, the butterflyfishes growing to about 6 inches, the angelfishes ranging from one to two feet in length, and the tiny cherubfish, which prefers deepwater reefs, reaching only 2 3/4" in size. **Parrotfishes** begin life as drably colored females, then turn into males with gaudy green and blue scales. They have molar-like teeth, which they use to grind algae off the corals, producing sand in the process.

Other members of the coral reef community include the **spiny lobster,** which hides in crevices by day and feeds at night, as does the **moray eel** – a snake-like fish that is harmless unless provoked. The tiny **sea horse** (ranging in length from 2 to 8 inches) is usually found swimming upright among the seagrasses, using its tail to hold onto a seaweed when resting. Seahorses, which utter musical sounds during the mating embrace, belong to the same family as the **pipefishes**, with which they share a unique breeding habit. The female's eggs are forced into a pouch on the male's underside, where they are fertilized and nourished until expelled as miniature versions of the adult.

Coral reefs attract a variety of feeding creatures, including **sharks,** which are heavy fishes with skeletons made of cartilage. A shark must keep moving in order to breathe, by taking water in through its mouth and passing it over its gills, which form a line of slits down both sides of the fish. There are over 250 species of sharks, ranging in size from 2 feet to 50 feet. Abundant in warm waters, not all sharks are predatory and few are interested in humans. Those considered harmless are the **nurse shark**, which grows to 12 feet in length, and the **Caribbean reef shark**, which grows to about 8 feet on a diet of reef fish, octopus, crabs and lobster. To detect their prey, sharks have electromagnetic senses on their snouts, which is why professional shark feeders wearing stainless-steel suits and gloves can hypnotize a reef shark with a gentle stroke of the hand. Not so placid are the **hammerhead** and **tiger sharks**, which are predatory and dangerous to humans.

Rays are flat-bodied fishes related to the shark. Shaped like kites with winglike pectoral fins that propel them through the water, rays also have long whiplike tails. There are three basic groups of ray: mantas, eagles and stingrays. Mantas are the largest, up to 22 feet in width and 3,000 pounds in weight. Mantas and eagles are active rays, whereas stingrays are bottom dwellers, lying like rugs on the sea floor as they dredge up shellfish and other small animals. The stingray's eyes and spiracles (breathing orifices) are on top of its head, its mouth and gill slits on the underside. Southern stingrays are common along Caribbean reefs, the females growing up to six feet in width. They have rows of spines along their tails which contain a poison that can inflict pain and be fatal to humans. Stingrays defend themselves against sharks by lashing with their tails but they rarely attack humans unless provoked or stepped on. They have no teeth, but their jaws are strong for grinding and sucking, which is why snorkellers at Stingray City on Grand Cayman will sometimes receive a hickey from a nuzzling stingray looking for food.

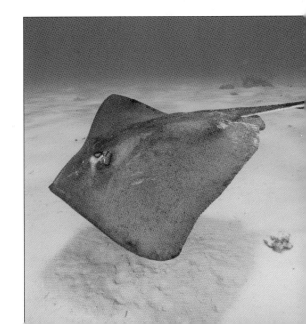

Southern stingrays are common in the Caribbean, living on the ocean floor near shores and in bays.

The loggerhead turtle, with its oversize head, grows to 450 pounds and nearly four feet in length.

Turtles are the world's oldest surviving reptile, in existence since the time of the earliest dinosaurs some 200 million years ago. Equipped with toeless, oar-like legs, these ancient mariners can swim at speeds approaching 20 miles per hour, and some will travel thousands of ocean miles along warm-water currents to reach their nesting sites. Once a source of food for sailors, the endangered **green turtle** is now protected by law, as are the hawksbill, leatherback and **loggerhead**, the latter named for its large head (up to 10 inches wide) and powerful jaws used to crush clams and crabs. The green turtle, named for the greenish color of its body fat, is a plant eater and can be seen grazing on seagrasses or sleeping under reef ledges. The **hawksbill turtle,** named for its narrow, pointed beak with which it pries sponges from coral reefs, was hunted nearly to extinction for its beautiful tortoiseshell, used in making jewelry. The **leatherback** has a rubbery dark shell and is the largest of all turtles, reaching lengths of eight feet and weighing up to 1,100 pounds.

The female nests on beaches where the warm sand incubates her eggs. She drags herself onto shore in the night, selects a site and digs a hole in which 100 or more eggs are laid. After covering them, she returns to the sea, having spent one to three hours on shore under cover of darkness. The two-inch-long hatchlings emerge two months later, again in the cool of the night, and crawl into the water. For years, the catching of females while they laid their eggs was a major factor in the marine turtle's decline, for as few as one in a thousand hatchlings survive to adulthood and it can take up to 20 years or more for some turtles to reach sexual maturity. Sea turtles spend their time feeding, sleeping under reef ledges and roaming the open ocean.

Caribbean waters host a range of marine mammals, including **Humpback whales** (average length – 45 feet) which migrate to warm tropical waters each winter to breed and calve. Other species sighted in the Caribbean include the small, toothed whales of the family Delphinidae, such as the **Killer Whale** (average length 25 feet) and the

Dolphins are highly intelligent, athletic and sociable, often seen travelling in large groups in the bow waves of ships.

Common Dolphin (average length 8 feet), the latter often travelling in huge herds of more than a thousand and often seen riding the bow waves of vessels.

Wave riding is also a favorite pastime of the acrobatic **Bottlenosed Dolphin**, which averages 9 feet in length and weighs about 350 pounds. These playful creatures swim in large schools and can reach speeds up to 30 mph. They can dive 70 feet and are capable of remaining underwater for 15 minutes. They sleep at night just below the water's surface, rising for air every three or four minutes. Their days are spent within a socially organized hierarchy. If one of the group is injured or sick, the others will try to rescue it and hold it above the water for air. When a calf is born, after a gestation of 12 months, a female assistant bites the umbilical cord in two and pushes the newborn to the surface to breathe. Mothers nurse their young for two years and practice group babysitting, with one female watching over several calves while their mothers hunt for food. With a beak holding 200 teeth, the bottlenose feeds on small fish, crustaceans and squid. When pursued by a shark or killer whale, the dolphins will try to outswim their predator or, as a group, they will try battering it to death.

The average lifespan of a bottlenose is 25 years, and its brain is large and convoluted, capable of complex functions. These fascinating mammals communicate with an extensive array of sounds, using the air sacs and valves in their blowholes, allowing them to converse with one another and convey instructions. Each dolphin is identified by its signature whistle, and a calf quickly learns to recognize its mother's whistle. Clicking and rapid creaking sounds are used for echolocation (projecting a sound beam and listening to the echo) with which the dolphin locates prey and avoids predators.

The bottlenose frequents inshore waters and is friendly to humans, often approaching close enough to be touched, and tales of dolphins rescuing people from drowning date back to Greek mythology.

However, man's fascination with these social creatures is now causing concern among animal-rights activists, who object to the recent proliferation of 'dolphin parks' in countries where there is little or no government regulation over the dolphins' capture and care. Visitors to these parks can swim and interact with the captive dolphins, but Richard O'Barry, the dolphin trainer for the 1960s television show *Flipper*, has compared one of these operations to an animal cage. Conflicting studies are cited by both sides as proof or disproof of the dolphins' distress. Meanwhile, the U.S. National Marine Fisheries Service has developed rules to limit the ratio of swimmers to dolphins, restrict the time each dolphin spends with people and provide a refuge to which the dolphin can retreat when tired of interacting with humans.

In contrast to the gregarious bottlenosed dolphin is the reclusive **manatee**. Also called a sirenian or sea cow, this large marine mammal descends from the same primitive group of land mammals as the elephant. The manatee spends its entire life in the water, surfacing to breathe at least every 15 or 20 minutes through nostrils on the upper surface of its snout, which close tightly like valves when the animal submerges. Shy and completely harmless, manatees live in warm, shallow and sheltered waters, where they consume up to 100 pounds of vegetation daily. The manatee can grow to 12 feet in length and weigh over 500 pounds, its thick, heavy body covered with hairless grey-brown skin. A sluggish, nocturnal bottom feeder, it propels itself with two weak flippers and a beaver-like tail. The female gives birth to one calf every two to five years and uses her flippers to hold the nursing calf to her chest. Both parents care for their young, one holding it while the other dives for food. An endangered species, the Florida manatee has no natural predators but is vulnerable to injury from boat propellers, and is found in the coastal waters of Central America, the West Indies and Florida, where it's protected by law.

A pair of manatees surfaces in the coastal waters of Florida.

PART II

The Voyage and The Ports

UNITED STATES

Houston

New Orleans
Mobile

Galveston

Florida

Port Canave

Tampa

Fort Lauderdale
(Port Everglades)

Mia

Key West

GULF of MEXICO

Havana

CUB

Progreso

Cancun

COZUMEL

Yucatan

CAYMAN IS.

Costa Maya
(Majahual)

MEXICO

Belize City

Western Caribbean Cr

BELIZE

Puerto Cortes

ROATAN IS.

GUATEMALA

HONDURAS

PACIFIC OCEAN

NICARAGUA

San Jose

Limon

COSTA RICA

Colon

PANAMA

Panama Canal

0   100   200   300   400   500
Statute Miles

A cruise is many things – a vacation, an adventure and, above all else, a voyage. Once the mooring lines are let go and the ship eases away from the dock, there's a remarkable sense of freedom as the bonds of land are broken and you head out to sea. Whether your ship takes you east, west or south, you may find yourself lingering at the ship's rail, relishing the sights and sounds of cruising – the fresh sea

HOME PORTS

Nautical Mile = 6,076 feet,
Statute Mile = 5,280 feet
Multiply Nautical Miles by 1.15
to get Statute Miles
The Caribbean Sea is approximately
2,000 by 1,200 statute miles
Average ship speed = 19 knots
(One nautical mile per hour = 1 knot)

air, the dolphins riding in the bow wave, the morning arrivals at tropical islands, the sun-filled days spent exploring new places, the evenings under the stars and the restful nights at sea as your ship carries you to the next port of call. There is a fragrance in the Caribbean, especially around the southern islands, which many months later you may recall when reliving your days on the Caribbean Sea.

A sunrise at Port Everglades

St. Augustine

Daytona Beach

Orlando

Port Canaveral

Florida's Turnpike

Atlantic Ocean

St. Petersburg **Tampa**

Sarasota

Venice

Gulf of Mexico

Lake Okeechobee

Charlotte Harbor

Fort Meyers

Naples

Palm Beach

Fort Lauderdale
(Port Everglades)

Miami

Florida

Cape Romano

Everglades National Park

0   30   60

Miles

Homestead

Key Largo

Florida Home Ports

Florida Bay

N

Key West

Straits of Florida

South Florida National Parks

Lake Okeechobee

Big Cypress National Preserve

Everglades National Park

Biscayne National Park

Dry Tortugas National Park

National Marine Sanctuary

©OCEAN CRUISE GUIDES

Entrance to Port Everglades

CHAPTER ONE

FLORIDA

lorida is America's answer to the Caribbean. Warmed by subtropical waters, cooled by trade winds, this southern state of swaying palms and coral cays has much in common with the history, culture and natural habitat of the West Indies. An international tourist destination, Florida is also a gateway to the Caribbean, and its cruise ports are among the busiest in the world.

Florida counts its visitors, and cruise passengers, in the millions. Every conceivable 'fun in the sun' attraction is here – palm-shaded swimming pools, championship golf courses, tennis camps, shopping malls, sporting events and theme parks galore. Yet it is water more than anything that defines Florida. The sea is readily accessible from any point in the state and some of the best beaches lie on barrier cays that line much of the splendid coastline. And the water doesn't stop at the seashore. Rivers and canals meander past cypress stands and waterfront homes, linking many of the lakes, lagoons and wetlands that make Florida an angler's paradise.

Lake Okeechobee is the largest of these lakes and is a chief source of water (along with Big Cypress Swamp) for the Everglades – a marshy, tropical savanna extending southward to Florida Bay. Covering more than 4,000 square miles, the Everglades is a unique wilderness region of slow-flowing water. Sawgrass and hammocks (island-like masses of vegetation) grow here in the solidly packed black muck, which has

Miami, a former trading post, is today the world's busiest cruise port with over three million passengers departing throughout the year.

formed over millions of years from vegetation decaying in the nearly stagnant water. Everglades National Park includes Florida Bay and its many islets and islands, and contains a great variety of flora and fauna, including palms, pines and mangrove forests, as well as such endangered species as the crocodile, alligator, egret and bald eagle.

Bird life abounds in Florida, where critical wetlands are now protected as wildlife refuges. A shoreline of seemingly endless beaches and holiday resorts has become dotted with parks, preserves and recreation areas. These conservation measures follow a century of unbridled development in which men with a passion for building – be it hotels, railroads, planned communities or theme parks – were attracted to Florida's broad, untouched landscapes.

The first 'developer' to arrive on Florida's shores was Spanish explorer **Ponce de Leon**. Seeking the fabled Fountain of Youth, he landed near the site of St. Augustine in 1513 during the Easter season (Pascua Florida) and mistook the long peninsula for an island, which he claimed for Spain. Turning south, he explored the coast to Key West, then headed up the west side to Cape Romano before retracing his route to Miami Bay and returning to his settlement in Puerto Rico, where gold and slave labor had made him a wealthy man. The next year the Spanish king commissioned Ponce de Leon to colonize the 'isle of Florida' but it wasn't until 1521 that he returned with 200 men, farm implements and domestic animals, his two vessels landing in the vicinity of Charlotte Harbor.

The development-minded conquistador's plans were, however, thwarted by the Native Americans already living in the area. Called Caloosas, they built their dwellings on high rectangular mounds surrounded by waterways and boat basins. These terraced mounds were interconnected with ramps and shell-covered causeways and canals, some of which led to burial mounds and other midden mounds where waste was discarded. Temples, storehouses and leaders' homes were built on the tallest mounds. These people, their urban culture over 2,000 years old, did not take kindly to the sight of strangers attempting to subdivide their land, and they attacked the Spanish party, fatally wounding Ponce de Leon with a poisoned arrow. The Spaniards retreated, sailing immediately for Cuba, where their leader died.

Spain abandoned any further plans to colonize Florida until the French began encroaching upon the area. St. Augustine was founded in 1565 to protect Spain's shipping route through the Straits of Florida. England, intent on expanding her American colonial holdings, was the next European country to threaten Spain's hold on Florida. At the end of the Seven Years War, England acquired Florida in the Treaty of Paris (1763), then returned it to Spain in 1783 at the conclusion of the American Revolution. But Spain's hold on Florida remained tenuous, and in 1819 Florida was reluctantly ceded to the United States, with official U.S. occupation taking place in 1821. Andrew Jackson was appointed military governor, and the next year Florida became a territory, with settlers from other states soon establishing cotton and tobacco plantations around the new capital of Tallahassee. The resident Native Americans – the Seminoles – resisted being displaced and a small band fled to the Everglades, where their descendants live today on reservations near Lake Okeechobee.

Florida, a slave-holding state, was admitted to the state of the Union in 1845, but seceded from the Union in 1861 to join the Confederacy. After the war, Florida's new constitution provided for black suffrage and the state was readmitted to the Union in 1868. A decade later, New York financier **Henry Flagler** paid a visit to Florida's east coast. He envisioned the state as the perfect winter playground and proceeded to build a business empire of railroads, steamships and palatial hotels, while anonymously donating to the construction of schools, churches and hospitals. Another industrial tycoon, Henry Plant, built railroads and hotels on Florida's west coast. Sections of the Everglades were drained, starting in 1906, and land booms caused real estate prices to soar one year and plummet the next.

Following World War II, sustained growth came in the form of manufacturing, especially in aeronautics after the opening of the John F. Kennedy Space Center at Cape Canaveral. Florida's population, now over 14 million, continues to grow with thousands of retired persons moving here. Nations of the Caribbean, most notably Cuba, are also a source of immigrants. In 1980, when Fidel Castro briefly opened the port of Mariel, more than 100,000 Cuban refugees were boat-lifted to Florida.

Rebuilt in 1926, the original Breakers in Palm Beach was built by Henry Flagler in the late 1800s.

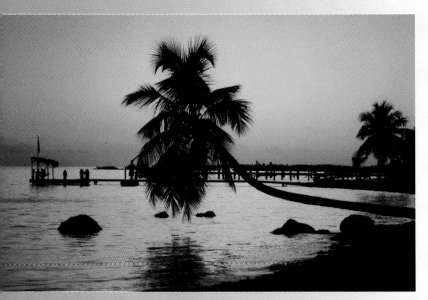

Florida's semi-tropical climate and miles of ocean coastline draw visitors by the millions. Shown here, a Key Largo sunset.

Florida's resources are diverse. A leading grower of citrus fruits, as well as vegetables, sugarcane and tobacco, the state also supports cattle and dairy farming, and the sea is a source of crab, lobster and shrimp. The state's timber is yellow pine, from which lumber and wood products are produced, and its mineral resources include phosphate rock, gravel and sand.

Florida is not without problems, however. Most pressing, many would say, is the degradation of the natural environment, with south Florida containing one of the most threatened wildlife habitats in the country. In the 1920s a ring dike was built around **Lake Okeechobee** to prevent water from blowing off the lake during hurricanes. This diking, along with land development in **Big Cypress Swamp**, disrupted the natural flow of water into the Everglades, and damaged plant and animal life. In the 1980s Florida instigated a massive conservation project which called for the reflooding of drained swampland and restoring to their natural state those areas previously cleared for agriculture and development. Sugar and vegetable farms have reduced the amount of phosphorus fertilizer discharged from their fields, and cleaner water is now running off their land into the imperiled Everglades ecosystem.

Tourism, which has contributed to Florida's environmental problems, may prove to be beneficial in the long run as areas of natural and cultural significance are preserved for the enjoyment of visitors, residents and, most importantly, for posterity.

Miami

Named for an American Indian tribe, Miami was a trading post when Henry Flagler, having built grand hotels at St. Augustine and Palm Beach, set his sights on this southern port. He made Miami a railroad terminus in 1896, the year it was incorporated, then proceeded to dredge the harbor to accommodate his fleet of steamships. Set on a low ridge overlooking Biscayne Bay, Miami is now the transportation and business hub of south Florida. It is also one of the busiest cruise ports in the world, with ships based here year-round for sailings to the Bahamas and the Caribbean.

Greater Miami encompasses the City of Miami, Miami Beach, Coral Gables, Hialeah and many smaller communities. About half of the City of Miami's population is Hispanic, many of Cuban descent, with hundreds of thousands of Cuban refugees moving here from the late 1950s to early 70s, settling in the city's Little Havana section. Calle Ocho (Southwest Eighth Street) is the main thoroughfare and scene of an annual Hispanic festival that's held in March and stretches the length of 23 lively blocks of music and dancing.

Miami Beach, located on a barrier island in Biscayne Bay, was a mangrove swamp until connected to the mainland by a wooden bridge in 1913. Opulent hotels and huge estates were soon built here, while the South Beach area was sub-divided into smaller lots and developed as a middle-class resort of modest hotels and apartments. Many of these buildings went up during the Depression, when visitors came to Miami Beach to temporarily escape their worries. The area suffered a decline following World War II. Then, in 1979, South Beach's square mile area of Art Deco structures, built between the two world

Miami Beach's revitalized Art Deco District is one of the trendiest hotel and restaurant strips in America.

wars, was declared a national historic district – the first containing registered buildings less than 50 years old. Their style, sometimes referred to as Tropical Deco, consists of smooth lines and white exteriors trimmed with hot colors. During South Beach's revitalization in the late 1980s and early 90s, many of the run-down hotels were refurbished and repainted in pastel colors. Today the area is one of the trendiest in America, where a steady stream of pedestrian and car traffic along Ocean Drive includes movie stars and fashion models dining at the stylish eateries. The Art Deco Welcome Center at 1001 Ocean Drive is a good place to start a tour of South Beach. Points of interest include the Cardozo Hotel at 1300 Ocean Drive, which was featured in the 1959 film *A Hole in the Head*, starring Frank Sinatra.

Coral Gables, situated four miles south of downtown Miami, was founded in 1925 at the height of the Florida land boom, which sparked an explosion of growth in the Miami area. A planned city designed by George Merrick, its Mediterranean architecture includes such highlights as the Venetian Pool – a huge municipal pool set in a coral quarry with caves, waterfalls and arched bridges. Merrick's boyhood home, a gabled plantation house on Coral Way, is open to the public. His dream city of canals, plazas and tree-shaded streets is also home to the University of Miami, where the Lowe Art Museum houses a permanent collection of Renaissance and baroque art, as well as Spanish and American paintings and artwork by North American Indians. The Orange Bowl Classic & Festival has been a major annual event in Miami since 1933 when the University of Miami played the Manhattan University.

The bustling Bayside Marketplace is located across the water from Miami's cruise port.

Coconut Grove, on the waterfront east of Coral Gables, was settled in the late 19th century by New England intellectuals and Bahamian seamen. The conical home of founding father Ralph Munroe, a New York yacht designer, is called the Barnacle and is open to the public at 3485 Main Highway. Also in Coconut Grove is the **Vizcaya Museum and Gardens** (3251 S. Miami Avenue), a restored Italian Renaissance-style villa completed in 1916 as a winter residence for industrialist John Deering. The 34-room mansion, set in grounds of formal gardens and amid fountains overlooking Biscayne Bay, has been designated a National Historic Landmark. It contains Renaissance and baroque antiques and artwork, and has been visited by such dignitaries as Pope John Paul II and Queen Elizabeth, and President Clinton who hosted the 1994 Summit of the Americas at Vizcaya.

A toll causeway links the mainland with Virginia Key, location of the Miami Seaquarium, and Key Biscayne, where the late Richard Nixon had a presidential retreat. Both islands contain parks, with a golf course and tennis stadium located on Key Biscayne.

GETTING AROUND

The **Port of Miami's** cruise port is a two-island complex in Biscayne Bay adjacent to downtown Miami. The port, consisting of a dozen passenger terminals, is located eight miles from Miami International Airport. It's a short taxi ride from the cruise terminals to **Bayside Marketplace**, a bustling waterfront development of shops, restaurants and open-air entertainment. Tour boats depart daily from Bayside on 90-minute narrated tours of the port, affording passengers a view of the Miami skyline, waterfront mansions and other sights. Trolley tours of Miami and Miami Beach also depart regularly from Bayside, as do water taxis, which ply the waters of Biscayne Bay, stopping at various waterfront attractions. The elevated Metromover links downtown Miami's major hotels and shopping areas.

Shopping, Dining & Staying – The selection of hotels in Greater Miami is extensive and includes a plethora of luxury properties. Yesteryear's elegance can be enjoyed at the Biltmore Hotel, built in 1926 as the centerpiece of Coral Gables. In a lovely setting of waterways, tennis courts and golf links, this is a classic grand hotel with a vaulted lobby and an opulent swimming pool/bar area. Nearby in Coconut Grove, overlooking Biscayne Bay, is the Wyndham Grand Bay Hotel – a modern boutique hotel offering golf, tennis and deepsea fishing. In downtown Miami, the Hotel Inter-Continental Miami contains a stunning lobby that features a massive marble sculpture by Henry Moore. Across the bay, in Miami Beach, the Casa Grande is highly touted, as are several small, stylish establishments in the Art Deco District of South Beach, including Merv Griffin's Blue Moon Hotel. A few blocks up Collins Avenue, in North Beach, the restored art deco hotels are considerably less expensive.

The **Bayside Marketplace** is a popular spot for cruise passengers with a good selection of waterfront restaurants and shops. Other areas that offer this combination are bohemian-flavored Coconut Grove, with its interesting shops, open-air bistros and sidewalk cafes along CocoWalk on Grand Avenue, and Coral Gables where its Miracle Mile – the main shopping thoroughfare on Coral Way between Southwest 42nd Avenue and Douglas Road – is lined with some of Miami's best restaurants. For a taste of Latin America and Miami's famous Cuban coffee, try one of the eateries on Calle Ocho in Little Havana.

For seafood lovers seeking a refined ambiance, The Fish Market (on Biscayne Boulevard at 16th Street) is recommended. In Miami Beach, the family-run Joe's Stone Crab Restaurant at 227 Biscayne Street has been a local favorite since opening in 1913. The South Pointe Seafood House in Miami Beach is a good spot to watch the cruise ships come and go, and for a sunset view of the Miami skyline, try The Rusty Pelican on Key Biscayne.

Golf – The Doral Resort near the Miami International Airport, has four 18-hole courses including one of the most challenging courses in the Miami area. The Links at Key Biscayne, a top-ranked municipal course, is built around lagoons and contains four waterside holes with views of the Miami skyline. The city-owned Biltmore Golf Course in Coral Gables opened in 1925 and was recently refurbished, and the Golf Club of Miami offers three different courses.

SOUTH OF MIAMI

Homestead, south of Miami, is the gateway to Everglades National Park, Biscayne National Park and the Florida Keys. The center of Florida's fruit and nursery production, one of its major attractions is Coral Castle, built from massive blocks of coral by a Latvian immigrant who labored alone from 1920 to 1940.

Biscayne National Park, nine miles east of Homestead on SW 328 Street, is an undeveloped underwater park containing miles of coral reefs. Its shallow waters are very clear and warm – a natural habitat for sponges, crabs, manatees and more than 500 different kinds of fish. The park is primarily accessible by boat, with tour boats operating out of park headquarters at Convoy Point.

EVERGLADES NATIONAL PARK

The Everglades, a slow-moving river about 50 miles wide and only a few inches deep, contains mangrove forests, sawgrass marshes, pinelands and hammocks. The tropical and sub-tropical foliage also includes six species of palm, and the park is a sanctuary for manatees, crocodiles, sea turtles and nearly 300 kinds of land and wading birds. Mosquitoes proliferate from May to November, and insect repellent is recommended year-round.

Parachute Key Visitor Center is located at the park's southeast entrance and another, the **Royal Palm Visitor Center**, is just inside the park. A road leads through the southern half of the Everglades to the **Flamingo Ranger Station and Visitor Center** on Florida Bay. In addition to canoe trails, boardwalks and nature trails in the Flamingo area, tours can be taken of Florida Bay and the backcountry for possible sightings of manatees, alligators and many varieties of birds, as well as the opportunity to disembark at a hammock to see Indian open-air dwellings. The Flamingo area has restaurants, accommodations, charter fishing boats and canoe rentals.

The 99-mile **Wilderness Waterway** winds between Flamingo and Everglades City, situated on the northwest side of the park, where airboat tours can be taken to the Ten Thousand Islands – a mangrove wilderness of islets, oyster bars and shell beaches.

The Keys

A chain of small coral islands extending 110 miles from the southern tip of Florida, the Keys are both exotic and all-American. Their tropical vegetation, steady trade winds and coral reefs are quintessentially Caribbean, while Key West's clapboard houses and white picket fences are reminiscent of a New England coastal town. The Keys' reef-riddled waters supported a thriving salvage industry in the mid-19th century before modern lighthouses and steam vessels brought an end to the steady stream of ships that were snared in the reefs off Key West.

Key Largo, the largest of the islands at the 'top' of the Keys, is famous both as the setting for the 1940s film classic *Key Largo*, starring Humphrey Bogart and Lauren Bacall, and as the location of John Pennekamp Coral Reef State Park – America's first underwater park, established in 1960. Over time, adjoining sanctuaries were established

Scenes from the '40s film Key Largo, starring Bogart and Bacall, were shot inside the Caribbean Club at Key Largo.

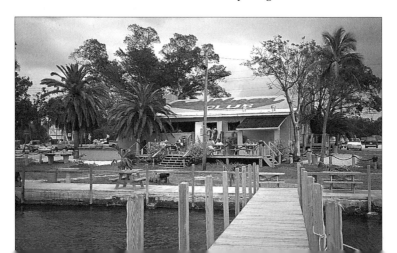

to protect the threatened reefs from boats grounding on them or hitting them with their props and anchors. Finally, in 1997, Florida's cabinet approved federal plans to establish Florida Keys National Marine Sanctuary, which encompasses the entire length of the Keys.

Key West

The southernmost point of the continental United States, and only 90 miles from Cuba, Key West is the largest center in the Keys, with about 25,000 residents. It was once a base of operation against pirates, who preyed on Spanish treasure ships as they sailed from Cuba to Spain via the Straits of Florida. When Florida was ceded by Spain to the United States in 1819, Key West became a haven for exiled Cubans, including revolutionary leaders trying to rid their country of Spanish rule. The sinking of the battleship Maine in Havana harbor in 1898 led the U.S. to declare war on Spain, and some of the 266 men who died in that incident are buried in the Key West Cemetery.

Key West has long been an enclave for writers and artists drawn to the tiny island's exotic locale. In 1912 the Keys became linked with the mainland with completion of Henry Flagler's railroad. The rail line was abandoned after sustaining hurricane damage in 1935, and was replaced a few years later with the 123-mile Overseas Highway that includes 42 bridges. Despite this tangible and well-travelled connection to the rest of Florida, the Keys have retained an island ambiance and sense of seclusion.

As a port of call, Key West holds many attractions. The cruise ship dock is located close to downtown with its tree-lined streets of shops, restaurants and colonial homes, a number of which are listed on the National Register of Historic Places and have been inhabited by some of the world's finest creative talents.

Of Key West's famous former residents, the one whose presence is most pervasive is **Ernest Hemingway**. For years Key West celebrated this Nobel Laureate with an annual Hemingway Days Festival, which included a writers' workshop, short-story contest, Caribbean street fair and a concert on the grounds of his former home. However, in 1997 Hemingway's sons denounced the festivities as tacky and threatened to sue if they weren't given control of the festival and a cut of the proceeds, prompting the festival's cancellation, but Sloppy Joe's bar still stages its annual Ernest Hemingway look-alike contest.

Other illustrious names associated with Key West are John James Audubon, Winslow Homer, Robert Frost and Tennessee Williams, all of whom spent time here, as did Harry Truman, whose presidential retreat is located in Key West.

Haitian-born and French-educated **John James Audubon**, for whom one of the oldest and best-known U.S. environmental organizations is named, visited Key West in 1832 to study and sketch the native birds. Born in 1785 in Haiti, the son of a French naval officer and Creole woman, Audubon was educated in France before moving to the family estate near Philadelphia in 1803, where he spent time observing birds. He began painting and taught for a while before finding a publisher for his bird drawings.

Another famous artist to spend time in Key West was Winslow Homer, a 19th-century painter best known for his watercolor depictions of the sea. Robert Frost, one of the 20th-century's most popular poets, and Tennessee Williams, one of America's foremost playwrights, also sought their muse in Key West.

GETTING AROUND

The cruise ship docks are near **1** **Mallory Square**, a bustling waterfront that attracts artists, entertainers and sunset watchers. Most major sights are within walking distance of the cruise pier but another option is to board either the **Conch Tour Train** at Mallory Square, or the **Old Town Trolley** at one of numerous stops, for a 90-minute narrated tour of Key West. Bicycles and mopeds can also be rented within the town.

Beaches & Watersports – Local scuba diving, snorkeling and sailing excursions are available. Departing just north of

Mallory Square are glass-bottom boat rides to the nearby coral reef. The beach at Fort Zachary Taylor is popular for swimming and snorkeling along its artificial reef.

Shopping – Clinton Square Market on Front Street contains a number of shops selling handcrafted jewelry and Caribbean clothing. Key West Hand Print Fashions, located in the Historic Curry Warehouse at 201 Simonton Street, is a good place to buy silk-screened fashions featuring original artwork.

LOCAL ATTRACTIONS

The **2** **Key West Aquarium,** beside Mallory Square, presents sea life of the Atlantic Ocean and Gulf of Mexico.

The **3** **Mel Fisher Maritime Heritage Society**, at 200 Greene Street, features artifacts and treasures retrieved from two Spanish galleons that sank off Key West in 1622. Beginning in the 1970s, Mel Fisher Enterprises, the legendary treasure hunters, recovered hundreds of millions of dollars in booty from these gold-laden ships.

The **4** **Audubon House & Tropical Gardens** at 205 Whitehead Street is housed in a restored 19th-century building. The museum commemorates John James Audubon's 1832 visit to Key West and contains a collection of his original engravings.

5 **Harry S. Truman Little White House** contains original furnishings and artifacts, which recreate the Truman era of the 1940s when the mansion was a presidential retreat.

At 322 Duval Street (near Eaton Street) stands Key West's oldest home, built in 1829 for a wrecker and sea captain. It now houses the **6** **Wreckers' Museum** with exhibits including marine artifacts and ship models. Other historic homes of note are the **Curry Mansion** (on Caroline near Duval) and the **Donkey Milk House Museum**, at 613

Key West's cruise docks are located beside Mallory Square, within walking distance of the town's main attractions.

Although Ernest Hemingway doesn't live here anymore, dozens of cats, relatives of the strays he adopted, still call this home.

Eaton Street, a restored 19th-century mansion listed on the National Register of Historic Places. Named for the back alleyway along which donkeys used to pull milk delivery carts, the award-winning mansion features hand-decorated ceilings, Spanish tile floors and verandas off every room.

7 Ernest Hemingway Home & Museum at 907 Whitehead Street is a Registered National Historic Landmark. The home was built in 1851 in the Spanish colonial style and contains furnishings and other items that Hemingway and his second wife, Pauline, collected in their travels to Spain, Africa and Cuba. Hemingway wrote some of his greatest works while living here in the 1930s and 40s, and his study in the loft of the pool house remains intact with his desk and typewriter on display. The home exudes Hemingway's forceful presence, and dozens of cats, descendants of those owned by the famous author, still wander the lushly landscaped grounds. Sloppy Joe's, Hemingway's favorite watering hole, was moved in 1937 from Greene Street to the corner of Duval and Greene. Its owner, Joe Russell, was Hemingway's boat pilot, fishing companion and a model for the character Freddy in *To Have and Have Not*, which was set in Key West and Cuba.

Recently restored and featuring a gift shop, the **8** Lighthouse Museum at 938 Whitehead Street includes the keeper's clapboard house and the lighthouse itself, built in 1847, with a magnificent view of Key West at the top of its 98 steps.

9 Fort Zachary Taylor State Historic Site was part of Florida's coastal defence system. Built from 1845-66, the fort became a base for the Union blockade of Confederate shipping during the Civil War, with captured ships brought to its harbor. Artifacts, models and one of the largest collections of Civil War armaments are on display.

Fort Lauderdale

The 'Venice of America', Fort Lauderdale is interwoven with more than 270 miles of natural and artificial waterways, including a navigable canal that connects with Lake Okeechobee. In neighborhoods crisscrossed with canals, both cars and yachts can be seen parked outside the palm-shaded homes.

Situated on the New River, this retirement and resort city of some 150,000 residents was settled around a fort built by Major William Lauderdale in 1837-38, during the Seminole War. Fort Lauderdale was incorporated in 1911 and the city grew rapidly during the Florida land boom of the 1920s. Its suburbs continue to expand, and today close to 4.5 million people live in the metro area. Fort Lauderdale has one of the most popular beaches in the country, one of the largest marinas in North America, and a cruise port that is fast becoming one of the busiest in the world.

Fort Lauderdale's seaport was originally a small lake used by recreational boaters. Locally known as Bay Mabel Harbor, it came to the attention of a developer and businessman named Joseph Young, who moved to the area in the early 1920s, purchased 1,440 acres adjacent to the lake and created the Hollywood Harbor Development Company. On February 28, 1927, expectant spectators gathered to watch an explosion that would remove the lake's rock barrier to the ocean. At the appointed time, President Calvin Coolidge pressed a detonator in the White House, but nothing happened. Nonetheless, the harbor was officially opened that day and the rock barrier was removed a short while later. In 1930, the new seaport was named **Port Everglades** – chosen from submissions to a naming contest.

Scenic Port Everglades is Florida's second busiest cruise port.

The port is located opposite the **John U. Lloyd Beach State Recreation Area**, situated on 251 acres of barrier island separating the Intracoastal Waterway from the Atlantic Ocean. The park is named in memory of a local attorney whose efforts helped bring about its creation. The park is entered at its south end via Dania Beach Boulevard, and its broad flat beach – popular for swimming and sunning – is also one of Broward County's most important sea turtle nesting beaches. A jetty at the north end is excellent for fishing and watching the comings and goings of cruise ships and small sailing craft.

The park also contains an open-air Environmental Education Facility. This timber structure and adjoining waterfront boardwalk were built by Port Everglades in 1991 as part of a wildlife protection/awareness project, which includes a comprehensive Manatee Protection Program. The Florida manatee is a protected species and in winter months these sluggish sea mammals frequent the Port, where they are attracted to the heated effluent from the Florida Power & Light plant. When calving mothers were found to be utilizing the FPL discharge canal, a section of it became designated a 'Manatee Nursery' and access to it was restricted. Manatees and other marine life also frequent the mangrove-lined tidal waterway that runs down the middle of the John Lloyd park.

GETTING AROUND

Located south of downtown, Port Everglades is an artificial deepsea port with a short, straight entrance channel. Its passenger terminals are modern and efficient, with long-term parking available in nearby self-parking garages. Less than two miles from Fort Lauderdale/Hollywood International Airport (and 30 minutes from Miami International Airport via I-95), Port Everglades is serviced by a fleet of taxis and by several car rental companies that provide shuttle service between the port and their rental lots.

Port Everglades viewed from John U. Lloyd Recreation Area.

Water taxis and tour boats are a popular way to explore Fort Lauderdale's scenic waterways. Water Taxi picks up at most waterfront hotels and restaurants north of the Brooks Memorial Causeway. Call 467-6677 for a pick-up; the one-way fare between two points is $7.50, the round-trip fare is $14 and an all-day pass is $16.

Shopping, Dining & Staying – Las Olas Boulevard, the 'Rodeo Drive' of Fort Lauderdale, is lined with boutiques, galleries and several fine restaurants, including Mark's Las Olas and the Grill Room at the Riverside Hotel, a heritage property built in 1936. In Lauderdale-By-The-Sea, the Sea Watch serves superb seafood, and American cuisine can be enjoyed at Burt & Jack's, co-owned by movie star Burt Reynolds and situated on a scenic lookout near the passenger terminals of Port Everglades. The huge Sawgrass Mills Mall on Sunrise Boulevard contains more than a mile of shops and bills itself as the 'World's Largest Outlet Mall'.

For a taste of 'Old Florida', the family-owned Riverside Hotel on Las Olas Boulevard is distinctly decorated with tropical murals and finely appointed rooms, with a pool area providing views of passing river traffic. The beachfront Lago Mar Resort Hotel & Club offers an elegant atmosphere with its bougainvillea-bordered swimming lagoon and luxurious lobby. Four restaurants, two swimming pools, tennis courts and miniature golf are among its extensive facilities. The Marina Marriott Hotel is conveniently located across the street from Port Everglades. North of downtown, in Lauderdale-by-the-Sea, the wide array of comfortable motels includes A Little Inn By The Sea, with its bright and airy rooms overlooking a beach-side swimming pool.

Beaches – Fort Lauderdale's famous stretch of beach used to attract crowds of college students on spring break. They go elsewhere now, and the beach has been given a multi-million-dollar facelift. A wave-themed beachfront promenade consists of wide walkways, crested gateways and neon lamp posts.

There are so many beaches in Florida, it is easy to find long stretches of sand all but deserted except for the resident gulls.

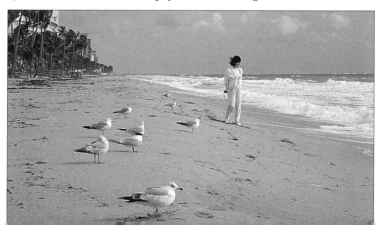

The oceanfront boulevard proceeds north to Lauderdale-by-the-Sea, an inviting stretch of sand, restaurants and motels. Beyond is Pompano Beach, Hillsboro Beach and Deerfield Beach, and south of Fort Lauderdale are the beaches of John U. Lloyd State Recreation Area, Dania and Hollywood. There are 23 miles of beach in the Fort Lauderdale area, the shoreline punctuated by fishing piers.

Golf – There are over 50 golf courses in the Fort Lauderdale area. The Emerald Hills Golf Club in Hollywood, about two miles south of the airport, is one of many open to the public.

LOCAL ATTRACTIONS

Las Olas Boulevard is an upscale shopping street of boutiques and restaurants. The Greater Fort Lauderdale Convention & Visitors Bureau is located at 200 E. Las Olas Boulevard

At the western end of Las Olas is **Riverwalk**, a lovely promenade on the north bank of the New River. Attractions in the Riverwalk area – also known as the Arts and Science District – include Esplanade Park, which features outdoor exhibits on astronomy and navigation; the Museum of Art; a complex housing the Museum of Discovery and Science and Blockbuster IMAX Theater; the Broward Center for the Performing Arts; and the Fort Lauderdale Historical Society Museum.

The eastern half of Las Olas runs through an exclusive residential area of canal-lined streets called **The Isles**. Nearby is the Bahia Mar Marina and the International Swimming Hall of Fame.

Across the road from Fort Lauderdale Beach is the **Hugh Taylor Birch State Recreation Area** with nature trails, picnic facilities and a museum. Directly south, on the other side of Sunrise Boulevard, is **Bonnet Hous**e, the 35-acre estate of the late Frederic Bartlett and his wife Evelyn, who built their 1920s dream home on land given to him by his first father-in-law Hugh Taylor Birch. Now a wildlife preserve, the tranquil grounds feature a swan pond, and the house contains the Bartletts' own paintings and an extensive seashell collection.

NORTH OF FORT LAUDERDALE

The coastal drive north of Fort Lauderdale to Palm Beach follows a scenic highway, bordered by the Atlantic Ocean to the east and the

Pleasant pathways can be enjoyed at Fort Lauderdale's Riverwalk.

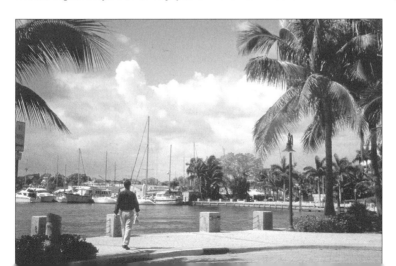

Intracoastal Waterway to the west. Spanish River Park, in Boca Raton, provides access to an ocean beach and contains a lagoon, nature trails and picnic sites.

Palm Beach is where you'll see some of Florida's most palatial estates along Ocean Boulevard, including the Kennedy compound (President Kennedy's Winter White House) at 1095 North Ocean Boulevard, which the family sold in 1995. For a taste of Old Florida, visit The Breakers (on County Road) – a luxury grand hotel originally built by tycoon Henry Flagler in the late 1800s. Rebuilt in 1926, the resort's Italian Renaissance architecture includes vaulted ceilings, frescoes and Florentine fountains outside the main entrance. Nearby, on Cocoanut Row, is Whitehall – a mansion built by Flagler in 1901 and now a museum containing original furnishings and railroad exhibits.

Port Canaveral

Cape Canaveral is better known as a spaceport than a seaport, but Port Canaveral is increasingly busy as a staging area for cruise ships. Only 50 miles east of **Orlando**, Port Canaveral is ideally situated for passengers looking to combine a Caribbean cruise with a visit to Walt Disney World. Those fascinated with space travel can begin or end their cruise with a visit to **Kennedy Space Center** and the Cape Canaveral Air Force Station.

Since 1947, the low sandy promontory of Cape Canaveral has been the principal U.S. launching site for long-range missiles, earth satellites, manned space flights and space shuttle missions. John Glenn, the

Port Canaveral's excellent harbor and nearby beaches.

first American to orbit the earth in 1963, and Neil Armstrong, the first man on the moon in 1969, were launched from this cape. In 1982, operational flights of the space shuttles began here. Missile launches can be watched from **Jetty Park** right in Port Canaveral. Other popular viewing spots include **Cocoa Beach** and the **Merritt Island National Wildlife Refuge**, location of Spaceport USA, which features multimedia displays on the U.S. space program, including a moon rock and an actual spacecraft. In its **IMAX** theatre you can watch footage of astronauts in space on a 5-1/2-storey screen. Bus tours of the Kennedy Space Center and Cape Canaveral Air Force Station begin at Spaceport USA. Nearby is the U.S. Astronaut Hall of Fame. The Wildlife Refuge is home to bald eagles and turtles, which nest here, along with alligators, which live in lagoons bordering the shuttle's landing strip and occasionally have to be shooed away by workers at landing times.

The Canaveral National Seashore, north of the Kennedy Space Center, contains 25 miles of unspoiled barrier beaches and grassy dunes, with swimming beaches at either end. The community of Cocoa Beach, south of Port Canaveral, features a downtown section called Olde Cocoa Village, in which restaurants and specialty shops are housed in heritage buildings along cobblestone lanes.

Tampa

Located on Tampa Bay, an inlet of the Gulf of Mexico, Tampa is the third largest city in Florida and one of the largest ports in the U.S. Incorporated in 1855, Tampa has long been a shipping and manufacturing hub on the Gulf Coast. First visited by Panfilo de Narvaez in 1528, the sole survivor of this Spanish expedition was rescued in 1539 by Hernando De Soto. He also negotiated a peace treaty with the Native

Unique Sunshine Skyway Bridge.

Americans, on the present site of the University of Tampa, but they remained hostile and for two centuries Europeans avoided the area.

The first white settlement began in 1823 and Fort Brooke was built the next year. A farming and fishing town grew around the fort, which was taken by Union troops during the Civil War. The late 1800s brought a surge in development with the construction of railroads, the discovery of phosphate, an expanding fishing industry and the introduction of cigar making in **Ybor City**, the center of Tampa's Hispanic population. During the Spanish-American War, Tampa became a military base with Theodore Roosevelt training his Rough Riders there.

A commercial center, Tampa also has a thriving arts and culture scene, which includes the Florida Symphony Orchestra and the Tampa Ballet. It's also a sports-oriented city, and several major league baseball teams have spring training camps in area.

Tampa shares the shores of Tampa Bay with neighboring **St. Petersburg** and **Clearwater**. St. Petersburg is a popular resort and retirement community, its places of interest including a municipal pier, the Salvador Dali Museum and a Museum of Fine Arts, all located on the Bay waterfront. Clearwater's white sand beaches have supported a thriving tourist industry dating back to 1896, when railroad baron Henry Plant built a luxury resort called The Belleview on a bluff overlooking the water. The Bay Area's beaches are concentrated on the barrier islands of Clearwater and St. Petersburg, a popular one being Indian Rocks Beach on Sand Key.

GETTING AROUND

Tampa International Airport, one of the top-rated airports in the U.S., is located 12 miles from downtown and the Garrison Seaport Center where the cruise ships dock. The Tampa-Ybor Trolley offers daily service around downtown Tampa, Ybor City and Garrison Seaport Center. A Visitor Information Center is located downtown at the corner of Ashley and Madison streets.

Shopping, Dining & Staying – Old Hyde Park Village in the historic Hyde Park area of Tampa contains more than 60 shops, as well as restaurants and movie theatres. Ybor Square is another historic marketplace, consisting of three large brick buildings converted into shops and ethnic restaurants. For unusal gifts, the Tampa Museum of Art in downtown Tampa and the Salvador Dali Museum in downtown St. Petersburg are worth visiting.

Some of the Bay Area's best hotels are situated on the shores of Tampa Bay, such as the Hyatt Regency Westshore and the Stouffer Renaissance Vinoy Resort, where the pink and palatial Vinoy Park Hotel was built in 1925 and is listed on the National Register of Historic Places. Nearby on the waterfront is the more modest Grayl's Lantern Lane, built in the Spanish style in 1922. Clearwater's best known heritage hotel is the Victorian-style Belleview Mido Resort Hotel, also listed in the National Registry of Historic Places. The largest occupied wooden structure in the world, this gracious hotel with four restaurants is surrounded by beautiful grounds containing swimming pools, red clay tennis courts and an 18-hole golf course.

Golf – There are over 90 courses in the Tampa Bay area, many of which are open to the public. Babe Zaharias Golf Course, Rogers Park Golf Course and USF Golf Course are all located north of downtown Tampa; the Rocky Point Golf Course is just west of the Tampa International Airport.

LOCAL ATTRACTIONS

The **❶ Florida Aquarium** is located right beside the passenger terminals at Garrison Seaport Center. It features sea creatures in near-natural habitats, as well as a fascinating exhibit in which visitors follow the path of a water drop from its underground source to the open sea, viewing aquatic animals and plants native to Florida along the way.

The **2** **Tampa Bay Performing Arts Center** and Tampa Museum of Art are located downtown overlooking the Hillsborough River. East on Franklin Street is the Spanish-Mediterranean-style **3** **Tampa Theatre**, a restored 1926 movie palace.

Across the Hillsborough River, on the University of Tampa campus, is the **4** **Henry B. Plant Museum**, housed in a wing of an opulent building originally built as the Tampa Bay Hotel by Henry Plant in 1891. It's a striking example of Moorish-Revival architecture and is a city landmark with its domed spires.

Northeast of the downtown core is historic **5** **Ybor City**. Settled by Cubans, Spaniards and other Europeans, this designated national landmark district features Mediterranean-style buildings housing art galleries, cafes and antique stores. Popular attractions here include the Tampa Rico Cigar Company (a retail store with cigar-rolling demonstrations) and tours of the Ybor City Brewing Company, located in a 100-year-old cigar factory.

Animals in their natural habitats can be seen at **6** **Lowry Park Zoological Garden,** which also operates a manatee research and rehabilitation center. The **7** **Busch Gardens** theme park is famous for its large African zoo, tropical garden and rides, such as the inverted roller coaster. Another area attraction is the **Florida Botanical Gardens**, 250 acres of themed gardens forming the centerpiece of Pinewood Cultural Park.

The Florida Aquarium is located beside Tampa's cruise terminal at Garrison Seaport Center.

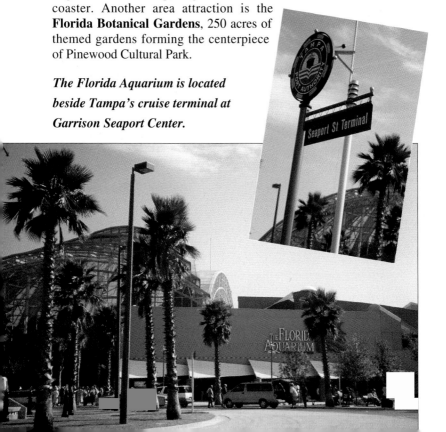

Gulf Coast

A drive south of Tampa takes in historic **Bradenton** and nearby **Anna Maria Island,** with its public pier and numerous white sand beaches. Next is **Sarasota**, a cultural center of Florida, its bay protected by a string of keys connected by bridges. One of Sarasota's noted attractions is the Ringling Museum of Art, located on the circus baron's winter estate built in the Italian Renaissance style with fountains, courtyards and gardens. The art museum's huge galleries are lined with priceless paintings, including one of America's largest Baroque art collections.

Venice, to the south of Sarasota, is another upscale community of palm-lined streets, waterfront restaurants and the highly touted Ritz-Carlton resort on Vanderbilt Beach Road, where the Grill Room serves superb contintental cuisine. Near Naples, off Route 846, is the Corkscrew Swamp Sanctuary, maintained by the National Audubon Society, where an easy-to-hike boardwalk winds through marshland which is habitat for great egrets, blue herons and alligators.

Fort Myers, about 50 miles south of Venice, was once a resort get-away for the wealthy, and the winter estates of Thomas Edison and Henry Ford now museums. Nearby **Sanibel Island**, a barrier island joined by a causeway to Fort Myers, is famous for the hundreds of species of sea shells that wash ashore, and ardent collectors assume the 'Sanibel stoop' while scouring the sandy beaches. Each summer hundreds of loggerhead turtles drag their heavy bodies onto shore to dig a nest and lay eggs, their welfare overseen by a group called Turtle Time, based in Fort Myers, which moniters the beach to ensure the hatchlings are undisturbed as they thrash their way out of the nests and make a nighttime dash to the sea.

The coastal drive south of Tampa to Fort Myers takes in numerous beaches and interesting towns.

CHAPTER TWO

GULF OF MEXICO PORTS

New Orleans

Louisiana's largest city, New Orleans – the 'Crescent City' – lies within a great bend of the Mississippi. It is one of America's oldest cities and its unique Creole culture, combining French, Spanish and African influences, is a source of fascination to all who visit New Orleans.

Founded in 1718 by the Sieur de Bienville on subtropical lowlands now protected by levees from flooding, New Orleans soon became the capital of the French colony of Louisiana. Transferred to Spain in 1762, it was a strategic port in the struggle for control of the Mississippi and was briefly returned to France before transferring to the United States with the Louisiana Purchase of 1803. The French-speaking Cajuns of Acadia arrived in 1763, and the westward movement of the 1800s brought growth and prosperity to New Orleans. As the queen city of the Mississippi, this thriving port earned a lasting reputation for elegance and extravagant living.

The Civil War marked the end of the golden era of river steamboats, sumptuous balls and wicked ways, but the city's exotic flavor lives on in its music, cuisine and literature. Jazz was born here among the city's black musicians in the late 19th century, and a park is named for native son Louis Armstrong. New Orleans is a city with soul, and its gusto for life reaches a feverish pitch during the annual Mardi Gras festivities.

A city that knows how to throw a party, New Orleans is also a busy commercial port and major U.S. point of entry, lying as it does at the junction of the Intracoastal Waterway with the Mississippi River. Imports here include coffee, sugar and bananas, which are unloaded at wharves that are themselves a local tourist attraction – as are most things in this sultry city.

LOUISIANA LITERATURE

New Orleans, a steamy mix of hedonism and Southern gentility, has stimulated the creativity of many a writer, including William Faulkner and Tennessee Williams. Mark Twain arrived in New Orleans in 1857, on his way to South America to make his

It takes eight hours of river cruising for ships to reach New Orleans' Julia Street Cruise Terminal, near the city's famous French Quarter.

fortune, and ended up working as a Mississippi River pilot, a vocation from which he took his pseudonym 'Mark Twain' – the river call for a depth of two fathoms – or twelve feet.

William Faulkner worked on his first novel, *A Soldiers' Pay*, while living in the city's French Quarter at 624 Pirate's Alley (then called Orleans Alley) which runs parallel with the west side of St. Louis Cathedral. The three-storey building, its narrow facade decorated with wrought iron and ferns, is now a bookstore called Faulkner House. Tennessee Williams also spent time in the French Quarter, living at 722 Toulouse Street in 1938. His Pulitzer-prize-winning play, *A Streetcar Named Desire*, was set on a tenement street of New Orleans. Streetcars no longer run along Desire Street, now the site of a housing project.

The playwright Lillian Hellman was born in New Orleans and lived in the stately Garden District, which is where Anne Rice – author of a series of bestselling vampire books – now resides in a Victorian mansion. This district of elegant old homes also contains a cemetery of graves and crypts built above ground, and F. Scott Fitzgerald rented an apartment overlooking this graveyard while reviewing the galleys of his first novel, *This Side of Paradise*.

GETTING AROUND

New Orleans International Airport is approximately 16 miles from the city core and location of the cruise ship terminal. The historic **French Quarter** is a short cab ride away from the cruise terminal, and in between are a number of waterfront attractions. In the other direction lies the Garden District, one of New Orleans oldest residential areas of grand homes and shady oaks. Local tour operators offer an eclectic choice of tours of these historic districts, including walking tours, cemetery tours and carriage rides.

Gray Line, its ticket office located beside the Jackson (Jax) Brewery, offers a variety of tours. For general sightseeing and shopping, its purple, green and gold trolley picks up passengers at 10 locations throughout the city and makes hourly stops at various attractions, allowing pass holders to hop on and off at their convenience.

The Regional Transit Authority (RTA) operates two streetcars – the red Riverfront Streetcar and the century-old St. Charles Streetcar. A one-day pass allows passengers to ride both cars as often as they like. The St. Charles streetcar, with its reversible wooden seats, rides the oldest working trolley line in the world through the business district. It can be boarded at the corner of St. Charles and Canal Streets. The Riverfront streetcar runs between the Convention Center and the French Market, past the Riverwalk Marketplace, World Trade Center and Aquarium of the Americas.

Horse-drawn buggies can be hired at Jackson Square or throughout the French Quarter for a half-hour tour ($10 per person or $50 for a private carriage). Paddle wheel steamboats, which dock on the waterfront between the cruise pier and Jackson Square, offer local river tours. A ferry runs between the foot of Canal Street and Algiers, on the other side of the river.

(Top) The Riverfront Streetcar runs between the cruise pier and the French Quarter. (Bottom) St. Louis Cathedral.

Shopping & Dining – Canal Street has long been famous as a shopping street, as has the French Quarter, with its fashion boutiques, museum shops and antique dealers selling everything from rare furniture to objets d'art. Canal Place features designer fashions, and the Jackson Brewery, which opened in 1984, is a shopping/dining/entertainment complex located beside Jackson Square in a renovated turn-of-the-century brewery. The French Market is an open-air produce and handicraft fair overlooking the river, and the Riverwalk Marketplace is a retail center located adjacent to the riverboat piers, just downstream of the cruise terminal.

Dining in New Orleans is done in the Continental style, its Creole and Cajun cuisine served with leisurely elegance in world-famous restaurants. The sophisticated sauces of Creole cooking are what distinguish it from the more robust Cajun dishes, but the two traditions – citified Creole and country Cajun – are often blended together and referred to as Louisiana cooking. Well-known and popular dining establishments in the French Quarter include Galatoire's, a French bistro on Bourbon Street, which serves classic French and Creole cuisine, and internationally renowned Antoine's on St. Louis Street. For Cajun cooking, K-Paul's Louisiana Kitchen on Chartres Street serves up blackened redfish and crawfish etoufee in a casual setting.

LOCAL ATTRACTIONS

The **French Quarter** (Vieux Carre) is the heart of New Orleans. It is a vibrant neighborhood of restaurants, hotels, jazz clubs, shops, museums and art galleries housed in 19th-century townhouses. The French Quarter burned twice in the late 1700s, and was last rebuilt by the Spanish, their Mediterranean influence reflected in ornamental cast-iron balconies and fountain courtyards. Most famous of the French Quarter's narrow streets and cobblestone alleyways is Bourbon Street, an entertainment strip packed with revelers during Mardi Gras. A **1 Visitor Center** is located at 529 St. Ann Street, opposite Jackson Square, a popular starting point for a tour of the French Quarter. **2 Jackson Square** (formerly the Place d'Armes) is the centerpiece of the French Quarter. Public meetings, celebrations and the welcoming of heroes have long been held in this square, its focal point a bronze equestrian statue of Andrew Jackson. In 1856 the Baroness de Pontalba transformed this dusty square into a garden park flanked by a pair of red brick apartment buildings which she had built. Fronting the square is the magnificent **3 St. Louis Cathedral**, completed in 1794, its Spanish style modified in 1851. On one side is the Cabildo, built by the Spanish in 1795, which now houses part of the Louisiana State Museum. Its French mansard roof was added in the mid-1800s. The Presbytere, on the other side of the Cathedral, is also part of the Louisiana State Museum, as is the 1850 House, which is an authentic re-creation of an antebellum townhouse.

Numerous other attractions are found in the vicinity of Jackson Square. These include the **4 Voodoo Museum** at 724 Dumaine Street, the **5 Preservation Hall** at 726 St. Peter Street, where traditional jazz bands perform each evening and the **6 Beauregard-Keyes House** at 1113 Chartres Street, which was built in 1826 and resided in by Confederate General P.G.T. Beauregard in the 1860s, then later restored by author Frances Parkinson Keyes. Also on Chartres is the Old Ursuline Convent, built in 1752.

Museum exhibits on jazz and Mardi Gras are housed in the **7 Old U.S. Mint** at the foot of Esplanade. This restored 19th-century building, an architectural blend of Classical Revival and Victorian, is backed by a courtyard in which stands the 'Streetcar Named Desire'. Beyond the French Quarter, major attractions include the **8 New Orleans Museum** of Art at #1 Lelong Avenue in City Park, and the **9 Confederate Museum**, at 929 Camp Street, which is the oldest museum in Louisiana and contains Civil War memorabilia.

Mobile

Situated at the mouth of the Mobile River and a relative newcomer as a base port for Caribbean cruises, this southern Alabama city and important seaport has a long and eventful history. Founded in 1710 by the Sieur de Bienville as the capital of French Louisiana, Mobile was eventually held by the British, then taken by the Spanish before being seized for the Americans by General James Wilkinson in 1813. Two forts stand at the entrance to Mobile Bay, and the city's rich past is reflected in its many beautiful antebellum homes, azalea-filled gardens and colorful Mardi Gras, an annual event dating to the early 1700s.

Galveston

Situated on an island at the entrance to Galveston Bay, this city of some 60,000 is connected by causeways to the Texas mainland and the city of Houston. Although Houston has a larger port, accessed from Galveston Bay by a ship channel, Galveston remains a key port of entry and industrial shipping center, as well as a growing base port for cruise ships servicing the Western Caribbean.

The Spanish were the first Europeans to discover Galveston Island, when Cabeza de Vaca was likely shipwrecked here in 1528. Settlement began in the 1830s but the natural port was plagued by hurricanes, including one that ruined the city and killed thousands of people in 1900. A 10-mile-long seawall was built against future hurricanes, and the city's beach and sportfishing resorts now thrive alongside its traditional shipbuilding yards and commerical fishing fleets.

Stately old homes grace many of Galveston's streets, their gardens brightened with the blooms of bougainvillea, pink oleander and other subtropical flowers. Of local interest is the Texas Heroes monument, and halfway between Galveston and Houston (about 50 miles away) is the Johnson Space Center and NASA headquarters.

(Above) Horse-drawn carriages take visitors along the historic streets of Galveston, its waterfront lined with beaches (opposite page).

Houston

Named for Sam Houston, the 19th-century frontier hero and statesman of Texas, the city of Houston is the fourth largest city in America, with a population exceeding 1.6 million. It began in 1836 as a muddy town on Buffalo Bayou and became a major deepwater port in 1914, after a ship channel was dug on Buffalo Bayou and Galveston Bay, linking Houston to the Gulf of Mexico. Phenomenal growth followed, with the city's suburbs spreading outward across the wide prairie, its expanding wealth based on oil, chemical production, shipbuilding and the aerospace industry. The city fell on hard times in the 1980s, when oil prices collapsed, but has since diversified its economy, manufacturing a great variety of products and attracting new industries, such as banking. The Texas Medical Center is the world's largest hospital complex and is a leading medical research facility.

The cruise ships dock at Barbours Cut, a 15-mile-long complex of port facilities situated at the head of Galveston Bay. The Houston International Airport is a 50-minute drive north of the port, while the William P. Hobby Airport is about half the distance to the south.

Visitor attractions in Houston include Hermann Park (with a zoo and planetarium), the Sam Houston Coliseum and Music Hall, the Jesse H. Jones Hall for the Performing Arts (home of the symphony orchestra) and the National Space Hall of Fame. Other places of interest include the Galleria (a massive mall filled with luxury stores), Old Market Square, Sam Houston Historical Park with its restored homes and the Astrodome and adjacent 'Astroworld' amusement center.

Progreso

Yucatan Peninsula

Cancun

Isla Contoy

Isla Mujeres

Merida

Chichen Itza

Playa del Carmen

Xcaret

Mayan Ruins

Coba

Xel-Ha

Cozumel Channel

Cozumel

Uxmal

Tulum

Coba

Tulum

Wall

0   100m

The Great Palace

Beach

Stela 2

Temple of the Diving God (Setting Sun)

Parking

El Castillo (used as watchtower)

Entrance

Building 20 Temple of the Frescoes

Temple of the First Series

Wall

Wall

Watchtower

Chacchoben

Majahual (Costa Maya)

Chetumal

Cayo Lobos

Belize

Punta Molas

Isla de la Pasion

Punta Norte

San Gervasio

Playa Bonita

North Hotel Zone

Playa San Juan

Town Pier

San Miguel

South Hotel Zone

Punta Langosta Cruise Pier

New Cruise Terminal

Punta Morena

Paradise Reef

Yucab Reef

Laguna de Chankanaab

Playa San Francisco

El Cedral

Punta Chiqueras

Playasol

Palancar Reef

0   2   4

Miles

Columbia Reef

Punta Sur

Cozumel

©OCEAN CRUISE GUIDES

N

CHAPTER THREE

COZUMEL, YUCATAN,
BELIZE & ROATAN ISLAND

The coral-fringed island of Cozumel was a sleepy hideaway when Jacques Cousteau paid it a visit in the early 1960s and introduced the world to one of the Caribbean's top dive sites. The documentary Cousteau filmed here captured the brilliance of Cozumel's extensive coral reefs which thrive in crystal clear waters teeming with tropical fish and other marine life. The clarity of the water is unsurpassed anywhere in the Caribbean, and the underwater caves and spectacular sponges are considered some of the best in the world. Understandably, about one third of Cozumel's visitors are divers, but the island is also popular for its beautiful beaches and fascinating Mayan ruins which have attracted such notable visitors as Jacqueline Kennedy who came to Cozumel in 1968 while touring the area's archaeological sites.

The ancient **Maya**, from which Cozumel's inhabitants descend, named the island 'Land of Swallows' and dedicated it to Ixchel, the moon goddess of fertility. Remnants of temples and religious artifacts have been found throughout the island which lies 12 miles off the Yucatan Peninsula. The Yucatan, low and flat like Cozumel, is a limestone tableland covered with thin topsoil which supports subsistence crops as well as tobacco and corn. It is also one of the world's most important henequen-growing regions, the leaves of these tropical plants containing a strong fiber used for making binder twine. The uncultivated areas are covered with a dense growth of scrub, cactus, sapete wood and mangrove thickets. No rivers run through this area and the light rainfall is absorbed by the porous limestone where it collects in underground rivers and wells (cenotes), and in surface pools called *aguadas*.

Scattered throughout the low hills are thousands of pre-Columbian archaeological sites, for the Yucatan was once the seat of the great Mayan civilization that flourished for three millennium, beginning in about 1500 B.C. **El Mundo Maya** (The Maya World) extended from the Yucatan peninsula, which encompasses modern Belize and northern Guatemala, into parts of El Salvador and Honduras. An advanced society with an understanding of astronomy and engineering, the Maya built their pyramidal structures oriented to the spring and fall equinoxes, and one of the world's earliest suspension bridges was built by the Maya in the 7th century in Yaxchilan, near Mexico's border with Guatemala. The Maya formed a hierarchical society based on patrilineal descent, in which kinship played a major role, but there was no widespread political organiza-

COZUMEL
& the YUCATAN

(Above and right) San Miguel's charming museum features a replica Mayan home. (Below) Tulum was an ancient trading center of the Maya-Toltec.

(Top) Chichen Itza is an important Maya-Toltec site on the Yucatan peninsula. (Middle, right) San Miguel's main shopping street is lined with lively restaurants. (Middle left) A Mayan family sells crafts outside walls of Tulum. (Below) A cruise ship off Cozumel.

tion of the Maya – each city state had its own internal structure of dynastic status and power. Their civic centers followed a pattern in which pyramidal structures and temples were built around a central plaza. Kilns were used to reduce the region's limestone into lime, which was mixed with white earth and water to create the mortar used in constructing the walls, corbelled arches and roof combs of these massive stone temples – often decorated with elaborate carvings and ceramic paintings.

A common feature of the civic centers was a ball court with stone hoops. Opposing teams played with a heavy rubber ball that players kept in the air by bouncing it off any part of the body except the hands and feet. It's believed these games were sometimes used as a peaceful means to settle disputes between leaders, with the loser giving up his land and followers to be assimilated with the winning team's people. Another theory is the losing team offered a human sacrifice – often the team captain.

Mayan civilization reached its height during the Classic period (300 to 900 AD), followed by a rapid decline during which the population plummeted. In the Yucatan, however, settlement persisted due to the arrival of the Toltec from Central Mexico. Also an advanced civilization, Toltec society was based on a warrior aristocracy. These master builders dominated the Yucatan's Maya from the 11th to the 13th century, at which time the nomadic Chichimec brought about the fall of the Toltec empire, soon to be followed by the rise of the Aztec. Toltec art depicts male nobility in feathered headdresses inspired by the brilliant plumage of the quetzal. A chief god of the Toltec and Aztec was Quetzalcoatl, who was identified with the wind and air, and was symbolized by a feathered serpent.

The first Europeans to arrive at the Yucatan were most likely a pair of survivors from a 1511 Spanish shipwreck. One man joined the Maya, the other was rescued by Hernan Cortes in 1519 and became his interpreter. Spanish battles with the Maya began in 1527, with Cozumel used as a staging base, and continued until 1546 when a Mayan revolt was crushed. However, resistance to Spanish (and later Mexican) rule continued into the early 20th century.

The rural Maya lived in small dwellings made of perishable materials, in contrast to the massive civic centers built of stone.

During the Spanish colonial period, administrative centers were established by Spaniards who imposed their own religious and political organization on the Mayan population. Assimilation, however, was far from complete. The indigenous elite were incorporated into the new colonial system but the rural peasants were left alone. The Spanish were disinterested in the Yucatan, due to its lack of mineral wealth and export crops. Its offshore islands of Cozumel and Isla Mujeres also were of little value to the Spaniards, but they did attract pirates such as Henry Morgan and Jean Lafitte who hid in coves to lie in wait for passing ships laden with gold and other treasures.

Chacmool statues represent reclining idols.

In the late 18th century, a growing world demand for cordage and fibers prompted the establishment of huge henequen plantations throughout the northern Yucatan. The local Maya's village lands were expropriated and, as the plantations grew in size, former land owners were pressed into labor. Tensions reached a boiling point in the mid-1800s and sparked a rebellion in which the Maya tried to drive all Europeans off the Yucatan peninsula. They were unsuccessful, but the Spanish were never able to completely suppress the indigenous population, and isolated pockets located outside the plantation zone remained autonomous throughout the 19th century.

Mexico gained independence from Spain in 1821, but widespread political turmoil continued. The social order inherited from Spanish colonialists consisted of two groups: Spanish-speaking whites and ladinos who resided in the major towns and maintained control of the region's commercial interests, and the much larger group of Mayan-speaking farmers who lived in rural villages. Following the Mexican Revolution of 1910-17, a land redistribution program guaranteed the rural Maya would no longer have their village lands expropriated.

In the early 1970s, flush with oil revenue, the Mexican government decided to build a world-class resort and once again the Yucatan became the focus of outside interests. The location for a master-plan resort – carefully chosen for its white sand beaches, Caribbean climate, clear waters and access to Mayan ruins – was Isla Cancun, lying off the northeast coast of the Yucutan Peninsula. Modern civilization is very much in evidence at Cancun where hotel towers line the powdery beaches, their design elements including pyramidal forms, stucco walls and other architectural features first used by those accomplished master builders – the Maya.

Cozumel

Cozumel is a flat island, its highest point only 35 feet above sea level, and is covered with scrub jungle. The majority of islanders live in the town of San Miguel, located on the island's sheltered west coast overlooking Cozumel Channel. While no longer the quiet seaside town that greeted visitors back in the 1950s, San Miguel has retained much of its early charm. Safe and compact, the port is laid out in a grid pattern with streets running parallel and perpendicular to the waterfront. The locals, of Mayan descent, are generally shorter than the average Mexican and most speak Spanish as well as some English.

GETTING AROUND

A new cruise ship pier is situated about three miles south of San Miguel and is a $5 taxi ride into town, while another pier (Punta Langosta) is within easy walking distance of the town plaza and main shopping strip along Avenue Rafael E. Melgar. Ships that anchor off San Miguel transport their passengers by tender to the town pier, right in the heart of downtown opposite the plaza. A cab ride from San Miguel to Chankanaab Lagoon is about $8, to San Francisco Beach – $12, and to Playasol – $15. A passenger ferry runs between Cozumel and Playa del Carmen on the mainland, which is a disembarkation port for cruise passengers taking organized shore excursions to the Yucatan's Mayan sites.

Shopping – Cozumel offers excellent shopping. The local flea market is located off 5th Avenue between Calles 2 and 4, while the town's upscale boutiques and restaurants are located on the waterfront's Avenue Rafael E. Melgar. Mexican handicrafts are among the finest in the world and include ceramics, tiles, pottery, cop-

Cozumel's Punta Langosta cruise pier is within easy walking distance of San Miguel's shops and attractions.

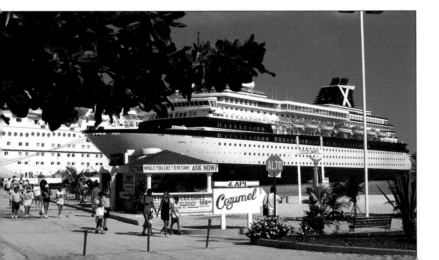

perware, glassware and whimsical hand-painted wooden animals. Quality leather goods include wallets, belts, sandals and cowboy boots, while hand-woven products range from baskets, rugs and hammocks to embroidered blouses, fine beaded tapestries and colorful woolen shawls called *serapes*. Gold and silver filigree (intricate ornamental work) is another Mexican specialty, creating exquisite earrings, necklaces and bracelets. All Mexican-made products are duty-exempt and good buys are available in products made of silver, onyx and leather. Small discounts are often given for cash purchases and most stores accept U.S. dollars. Passengers visiting the mainland will also have an opportunity to buy local Mayan crafts at outdoor markets.

Beaches – An excellent beach, Playa San Juan, lies a few miles north of San Miguel where the North Hotel Zone is situated, and many more are located south of town, in the vicinity of the South Hotel Zone. South of Chankanaab Lagoon are San Francisco Beach and Playasol Beach, two of the island's most beautiful and busiest beaches.

Dive & Snorkel Sites – A strong current flows through Cozumel Channel, so drift diving is how the offshore reefs are explored. The continual current carries food to the reefs, which is why the sponge growth is so spectacular. One of the Caribbean's most famous dive sites is three-mile Palancar Reef at the southern tip of the island, with seven different dive sites ranging from 35 to over 80 feet. Other good dive sites include: Columbia Reef; Punta Sur with caverns and steep drop-offs; Santa Rosa Reef with its huge coral mounds; San Francisco Reef's valleys and vertical wall; and Yucab Reef, an extensive and shallow dive site encompassing a wide variety of coral formations and fish species.

Playasol, south of San Miguel, is one of Cozumel's best beaches.

Cozumel's reefs were protected by presidential decree in 1980, so construction of a new cruise pier at Paradise Reef in the late 1990s was greeted with protests from several environmental groups, as well as local residents and dive operators. Not far from Paradise Beach is Paradise Wall which begins at a depth of 50 feet and contains an abundance of marine life including giant sponges.

The best **snorkel sites** are the shallow reefs at Playa San Francisco and at Chankanaab Bay, site of Chankanaab National Park ($7 admission) which contains a natural underwater preserve connected to the sea by underground channels ('chankanaab' means 'small lake' or 'little sea' in Mayan). This beautiful lagoon is filled with bright corals and surrounded by a botanical garden, where visitors can stand and watch the colorful fish. The lagoon itself is off-limits to snorkeling and swimming to protect the marine life from harmful suntan lotions, but there is good snorkeling among the reefs of Chankanaab Bay.

LOCAL ATTRACTIONS

1 Main Square, located opposite San Miguel's town pier, is pleasant to stroll with its shaded areas, large gazebo, clock tower and a monument to motherhood.

2 Museum de le Isla de Cozumel, located on the waterfront between Calle 4 Norte and Calle 6 Norte, is a welcome retreat from the busy street and bustling boutiques. For a small admission charge, you can enjoy exhibits ranging from Cozumel's natural habitat to its Mayan and colonial history. A highlight is the replica Mayan house, set in a courtyard, with a garden outside and authentic tools and furnishings inside. A Mayan host demonstrates the various stone tools, identifies foodstuffs on display and generally brings to life the workings of a typical village home. An open-air restaurant on the museum's second floor provides a lovely view out to sea.

DOWNTOWN SAN MIGUEL
©OCEAN CRUISE GUIDES

▣ **Cozumel Archaeological Park** contains full-size replicas of Mayan and Toltec stone carvings set in a jungle setting. A guided walking tour is included in the admission fee.

Although there are numerous archaeological sites on Cozumel, none reach the scale and architectural significance of those found on the Yucatan peninsula. The most important island site is the Mayan temple of Ixchel located at **San Gervasio**, about 10 miles from San Miguel.

Yucatan Peninsula

The lure of Mayan ruins and dazzling white beaches has prompted the construction of several cruise ship ports on the Yucatan Peninsula. Progreso, a tiny fishing village on the north coast, is now home to a cruise pier providing access to Merida (22 miles) and the Mayan sites of Uxmal (49 miles) and Chichen Itza (72 miles). Another new cruise port, called Costa Maya, has been built at Majahual which is situated 107 miles south of Cozumel and provides access to several southern Maya sites.

MERIDA

Once called the White City for its clean streets of gleaming white build-ings where rooftop windmills are used to pump water from under-ground wells and streams, this Spanish colonial town was founded in 1542 by Francisco de Montejo, who conquered the Yucatan peninsula after his father withdrew due to fierce resistance. Built on the site of a ruined Mayan city, Merida became the cultural center of the Yucatan peninsula, its Cathedral of San Ildelfonso completed in 1599. Today, as the Yucatan state capital with a population exceeding 1/2 million, Merida's colonial heritage endures in its public buildings and the ele-gant old mansions of Paseo Montejo.

UXMAL (PRONOUNCED OOSHMAL)

Situated in the Puuc hills, this important center of education flourished between 600 and 900 and is considered one of the finest examples of the Maya's Late Classic architecture. The site's impressive structures include the unique Pyramid of the Magician; the Governor's Palace, its facade decorated with some 20,0000 carved stone elements; and the Nunnery Quadrangle, the equivalent of a modern university.

CHICHEN ITZA

This well-restored and popular Mayan site was founded around two large cenotes (deep, natural wells) in circa 514 by the Itza – the last strong, independent Mayan tribe. A political and religious center, the site was occupied at various times until 1194 when it was abandoned for the last time. The buildings span two periods of Mayan civilization. The Classic style is reflected in massive structures and heavy, decora-tive sculpture; the Post-Classic period, with a strong Toltec influence, produced plainer buildings, columns and sculpture based on the

Mexican feathered serpent motif. The site's highlights include the Castillo temple, a ball court and, unusual among Mayan buildings, a round tower called the Caracol (snail shell) which was built in the Post-Classic period, probably as an astronomical observatory. Offerings, including human sacrifices, were thrown into Chichen Itza's sacred well which was a mecca for pilgrimages by other Mayan tribes of Central America and Mexico.

CANCUN

Originally a Mayan settlement, its name meaning 'vessel at the end of the rainbow', Cancun consisted of a few hundred inhabitants before an international holiday resort was built on its offshore island in the early 1970s. Long and narrow, the island is lined with powdery white beaches and connected to the mainland by a bridge at each end. Its hotel zone contains first-class hotels and recreation facilities that draw over two million visitors annually, mostly from the U.S. The L-shaped island forms a lagoon where water sports can be enjoyed, and the outer beaches are sheltered by coral reefs. Isla Mujeres is a short ferry or water taxi ride from Cancun, and this tiny island (5 miles long and 1 mile wide) of secluded beaches and lagoons contains the National Marine Park El Garrafon at its southern tip. A snorkeling and diving paradise, the Park's popularity has, in recent years, threatened the very reefs and other marine life that attracted visitors, so a plan has been put in place to protect the Park's underwater habitat while continuing to welcome day-trippers to the island.

◭ COBA

Dozens of stone roads and causeways once led to Coba – a commercial hub of the Maya, which flourished from 400 to 1100. The largest settlement found to date, much of this site is still overgrown but those structures that have been excavated include the 80-foot-high 'Iglesia' temple-pyramid, the 'Crossword' pyramid, and the 'Nohochmul' pyramid which is the tallest on the Yucatan peninsula with 120 steps climbing to the top of its 138-foot-high face.

(Opposite page) The famous beach resort of Cancun.
(Above) Beautiful beaches lie at the base of Tulum.

Calica is a cruise terminal located about six miles south of Playa del Carmen. Two natural parks are in the vicinity, the nearest being **Xcaret** ('little inlet'), which is an eco-archeological park built around the ruins of a Mayan ceremonial center. Visitors can don life vests and ride the gentle currents along an underground river, through caves illuminated by shafts of sunlight. The grounds include a botanical gardens, butterfly pavilion, turtle farm, swimming lagoons and restaurants.

Further south (about 15 miles) along the coast is **Xel-Ha**, touted as the world's largest natural aquarium. The park's limestone shoreline has been sculpted by the sea and freshwater springs, forming turquoise lagoons filled with tropical fish that can viewed from wooden platforms above the rocky shore. Snorkelers can swim in the lagoons and along the Xel-Ha river. A footpath also leads to the river and into the jungle where two cenotes and the Cave of Miracles, a massive underground cavern, can be viewed.

TULUM

The only known walled city of the Maya, this ancient trading center is a stunning sight perched on the edge of a bluff overlooking the sea. Its stone buildings are surrounded on three sides by a stone wall that dates from 1200 AD and is said to be 16 feet thick in places. Tulum, 'City of the New Dawn', was the only Mayan city still occupied when the Spanish arrived in the early 1500s. The protected cove at the base of this site is ideal for swimming and snorkeling off its white sand beach.

COSTA MAYA

This new cruise port at Majahual provides access to **Chetumal**, the capital of the state of Quintana Roo, where one of the Yucatan's best museums on Mayan culture is located. The city itself is mostly modern, rebuilt after its destruction by a hurricane in 1955. Other excursions take in the ruins at Oxtankah and Chacchoben, both Mayan centers dating to the 4th century.

Banco Chinchorro, a huge coral reef the size of Cozumel Island, lies offshore and provides diving and snorkeling opportunities.

Belize City

The tiny country of Belize, squeezed between Guatemala and the Caribbean Sea, was part of the Mayan civilization before the arrival of Europeans. The Spanish paid the region little notice, but British buccaneers preying on Spain's treasure ships began hiding out in the white-sand cays that dot the coast. When British settlers from Jamaica started colonizing the area, several battles ensued between Spain and England until a decisive defeat of the Spanish at St. George's Cay in 1798 settled the matter. Known as British Honduras until gaining independence in 1981, Belize had been claimed by Guatemala since 1821 as part of its inheritance form Spain. Finally, in 1991, Guatemala officially recognized Belize's sovereignty.

Belize City, devastated by three hurricanes in the last century, was the country's capital until 1970 and it remains the commercial center and major port for Belize, the only Central American country with English its official language, although Spanish is widely spoken. The Belize Dollar is worth 50¢ US, and American currency is accepted almost everywhere. The city is situated at the mouth of the Belize River and has retained the air of a British colonial port with its canals, wooden houses and fishing boats. Offshore the cays (low islands) are sheltered by the longest unbroken reef in the Western Hemisphere. **Dive and snorkel** excursions can be taken to several of these cays where the nearby reef's underwater attractions include Hol Chan (Mayan for 'little channel') and Shark Ray Alley where southern stingrays and nurse sharks congregate.

In addition to dive trips and fishing charters, shore excursions can be taken from Belize City to the nearby Mayan ruins, such as the sprawling site of **Altun Ha**. There, amid hundreds of mounds, archaeologists discovered the Green Tomb, so named for its stash of jade treasures that included a carved head representing the Mayan sun god, now one of Belize's national symbols. Nearby **Lamani**, still occupied when Spanish conquistadors sailed up the New River, is an immense site of some 700 structures standing on high ground that is now home to howler monkeys. An excursion to Lamani still requires a boat trip up the river, past mangroves, crocodiles basking on the banks, and a variety of birds and tropical flowers.

In between these two Mayan sites is the **Crooked Tree Wildlife Sanctuary**, its guided tours touted as one of Belize's best nature experiences. Established by the Belize Audubon Society in 1984, the sanctuary is habitat to a wealth of bird life and encompasses the fishing and farming village of Crooked Tree, a lagoon upon which boat trips can be taken, a system of trails, observation towers and an elevated boardwalk. South of Belize City is the 98,000 acre **Cockscomb Basin Wildlife Sanctuary**, well known for the world's first jaguar reserve.

Roatan Island, Honduras

The sultry Bay Islands, lying off the Caribbean coast of Honduras, were once a 17th century hideout for the Welsh pirate Henry Morgan who established his base at Port Royal on Roatan Island, the largest of the three main islands making up this archipelago. Two centuries later, shortly after Britain relinquished the Bay Islands to Honduras, the American fillibuster William Walker sought refuge here amongst the English-speaking islanders until forced to surrender to the Royal Navy.

Today, Roatan Island is a popular tourist resort of powdery white beaches and clear turquoise water protected by a reef that surrounds the island. Seaside towns hug the coastline of this long, narrow island, home to about 15,000 seafaring inhabitants who are as likely to hop into a boat as a car to get somewhere on the island. **Taxis**, however, are plentiful and visiting cruise passengers – who are tendered ashore at **Coxen Hole** – should agree on a fare before setting out (riding *colectivo* is the cheapest way to go, which means the driver can pick up more fares along the way). The best beaches are at the island's western end, about five miles from Coxen Hole. **West Bay Beach** is considered the island's most beautiful, with **good snorkeling and diving** along the protected reef, especially in the Blue Channel. **Half Moon Bay** is also good for snorkeling, and semi-submersible glass-bottomed boat tours operate out of both bays.

Grand Cayman Island

N

Conch Point

Cayman
Turtle Farm
Hell

West
Bay

Governor's Harbour

Governor's Residence
Westin Casuarina
Beach Club Colony

Seven Mile Beach

West Bay Road

The Links
at SafeHaven

Taxi Stand

Hyatt Britannia
Golf Course

Rum Point

Little Sound

Stingray City

North Sound

Crewe Rd.

South Church St.

Walker's Rd.

George Town

North-Side Rd.

North
Side

Old Man Bay

Mastic
Trail

Queen Elizabeth
Botanic Park

Bodden
Town

Savannah

Pedro St. James
Castle

South Sound

Bodden Bay

Frank Sound Rd.

Frank Sound

Blow Holes

East End

Caribbean Sea

0   1   2
Miles

©OCEAN CRUISE GUIDES

Chapter Four

GRAND CAYMAN

Grand Cayman, an international center for offshore banking, is one of the best-rated dive locations in the world. A person needn't even get wet to enjoy some of the island's remarkable aquatic sights, for a variety of vessels and observatories allow visitors to see the reefs, wrecks and marine life for which the Cayman Islands are famous.

Grand Cayman is the largest of a three-island group which includes Little Cayman and Cayman Brac – a Gaelic word for cliff. The name Cayman is derived from a Carib word for crocodile, although the Caymans were first called Las Tortugas by Columbus when he observed, in 1503, the hundreds of turtles living on these uninhabited islands. The Spanish paid these flat coral outcrops little attention as the soil was poor and there were no precious metals to mine, but English, Dutch and French ships pulled in regularly to take on fresh water and salted turtle meat. Today, the green sea turtle is an endangered species and in 1978 the United States banned the import of all turtle products, even those raised at the Cayman Turtle Farm, which releases young turtles into local waters.

Sea turtles are not the only species protected in the Cayman Islands. In 1978 a marine conservation law was passed, and four preservation zones were established in 1986. The Replenishment Zones provide year-round protection of conch and lobster breeding grounds, as well as every other kind of marine life. Line fishing

Stingray City is a highlight for visitors to Grand Cayman.

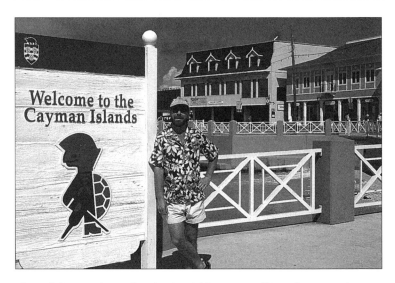

Grand Cayman's tender pier is within easy walking distance of George Town's attractions and harbor based sightseeing boats.

from shore or beyond the drop-off are the only forms of harvesting allowed. Permanent moorings have been installed to protect the reefs which were becoming damaged by the anchors of dive boats. These progressive conservation measures have extended onto land with the establishment of animal sanctuaries and the opening of a botanical park by Queen Elizabeth. Grand Cayman's indigenous animal species include iguanas and parrots. Bird watching is popular here, with more than a hundred species of birds observed, including those on spring and fall migrations.

The Cayman Islands, a British Crown Colony since 1670, were a dependency of Jamaica when transferred from Spain to Great Britain under the terms of the Treaty of Madrid. Shortly thereafter the Cayman Islands were settled by a motley collection of British army deserters, shipwrecked sailors, retired pirates and African slaves who gained freedom when ships carrying them foundered on Cayman reefs.

Slavery was abolished by Britain in 1833, a year after a representative government was established on the Cayman Islands. When Jamaica opted for independence from Britain in 1962, a debate ensued among Cayman residents who eventually voted to remain a British Crown Colony. About 30,000 people live on the three islands, the majority on Grand Cayman. Of mixed origin and free of racial tensions, they descend from the English, Irish, Scottish and Africans who first settled the islands. With few natural resources on these mangrove-covered islands, the Cayman men traditionally made their living from the sea – turtle fishing, ship building and serving in the merchant marine. As recently as the 1950s, those working on foreign-owned ships were sustaining the local economy with the money they sent back home.

Grand Cayman remained an isolated backwater until 1954, when an airfield was built. But it wasn't until the island's troublesome mosquitoes were brought under control in the 1970s that tourists began arriving in droves. The climate is ideal, the beaches are beautiful and the marine life prolific due to the varied underwater terrain which ranges from shallow coral reefs to submarine canyons. Meanwhile, Cayman's political stability and attractive tax laws make it an ideal environment for offshore banking interests. Some 70 financial institutions, six of which are clearing banks, operate on Grand Cayman where local services include offshore incorporation, company management and private banking. This thriving financial industry, which includes major accounting firms, is subject to strict government controls – which apply to both its banks and its customers. But professionalism and integrity do not provide good material for a Hollywood script, so Caymanians were more than happy to cooperate with Paramount Pictures when its film crew arrived at Grand Cayman to shoot scenes for *The Firm*, a movie of intrigue and corruption based on John Grisham's book and starring Gene Hackman, Tom Cruise and Jeanne Tripplehorn.

The movie's underwater scenes were shot at Soto's Reef and Rhapsody – two dive sites close to George Town. A sheltered cove on North Sound is where the fictitious 'Abanks Dive Lodge' was built, an attraction that will be left intact. The pool bar at the Grand Hyatt Hotel was another film location, as were Seven Mile Beach and a bank in George Town.

GETTING AROUND

The cruise ships anchor off George Town and tender their passengers ashore. A visitor information booth and telephones are located at the north tender pier. The town's sights and stores are all within easy walking distance of the waterfront, and shuttle vans transport visitors between George Town and Seven Mile Beach for a fee of $4 per person. A regular taxi ride between Georgetown and Seven Mile Beach is $12. The Holiday Taxi Stand is located at the

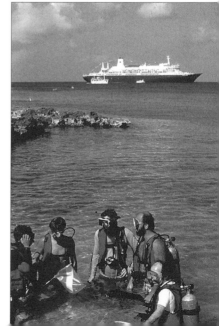

A cruise ship anchors off George Town where shore excursions include snorkeling and scuba diving.

(Above) Seven Mile Beach

Westin Casuarina Resort. Ship-organized excursions cover most of the island's attractions, concentrating on the western end of the island where Stingray City and Seven Mile Beach are located. Passengers interested in touring the island independently can hire a taxi (about $40 US to East End) or rent a car (approximately $40 a day plus $7.50 for a temporary driving permit) as well as mopeds, motorbikes and bicycles. Driving is on the left.

Shopping – A free port, Grand Cayman carries an assortment of duty-free goods. George Town, where the majority of shops are located (many of which are closed on Sundays), is very clean and orderly with no roadside pedlars. Local items to look for include numismatic jewelry, crafted from old coins retrieved from sunken vessels and featured in exquisite gold-and-diamond settings. Unique to the Cayman Islands are sculptures and jewelry made of an earth-toned, hard dolomite stone called caymanite that was discovered at East End. Another island specialty

(Below) The Cayman Islands National Museum is housed in Grand Cayman's oldest surviving building, a former courthouse.

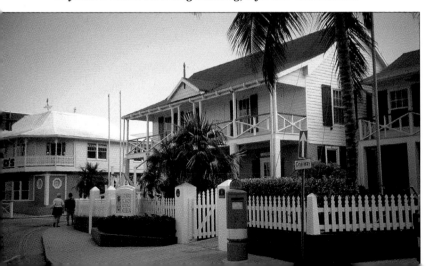

is Tortuga Rum Cake, baked according to a century-old family recipe and coated with an aromatic syrup made with specially blended, five-year-old Tortuga Gold rum stored in oak barrels.

The Cayman Island dollar equals about $1.25 US, but American currency is accepted throughout the islands. American and Canadian visitors should be aware it is against customs regulations to import turtle products into their countries.

Local Sights – Overlooking the pier area is the **1 Cayman Islands National Museum**, housed in the former courthouse and containing displays on the islands' natural and cultural history, including artifacts of pirate lore. Cardinal, one of the main shopping streets, leads to the post office and the adjacent **2 Elizabethan Square**. A few blocks north on Edward is the Public Library. Across the street is a small park containing a massive fig tree. At the intersection of Edward and Fort Streets is **3 Clock Tower**, a monument to Britain's King George V. Fort Street leads down to the waterfront where the remains of Fort George can be seen, built in the 17th century to protect the island from pirate attacks. Nearby, on Harbour Drive, is the restored 19th-century **4 Elmslie Memorial Church**.

Best Beaches – The natural choice for cruise passengers is Seven Mile Beach, one of the finest in the Caribbean, which starts just north of George Town and stretches for about five miles along the island's western shore. Lined with hotels, this beautiful white-sand beach is ideal for swimming, snorkeling and other water sports. The cruise lines often arrange with one of the hotels for their passengers to utilize its beach-front facilities for a small fee. Sailboards and other equipment can be rented at a sports center beside the public beach which is usually uncrowded. **Government House**, the Governor's official residence, is near the public beach area.

©OCEAN CRUISE GUIDES

A diver swims with the tropical fish in George Town's harbor.

Dive & Snorkel Sites – Grand Cayman is the top of a submerged mountain and its offshore coral reefs form the famous 'Cayman Wall'. An estimated 60 miles of drop-offs encircle Grand Cayman where the underwater visibility extends to depths of 150 feet. There are more than a hundred dive sites surrounding the island, and they include numerous shipwrecks as well as coral gardens, grottos, caves and canyons which are habitat for rays, turtles, tropical fish and huge, colorful sponges. Whether snorkeling, shore diving or deep diving, Cayman Island offers crystal clear water, an abundance of marine life and a variety of underwater terrain.

This fascinating marine world can also be viewed from vessels that operate out of George Town, including a glass-bottom boat, a semi-submersible and a submarine. There are reefs and wrecks to explore right in Hog Sty Bay, such as Cheeseburger Reef and the wreck of the *Cali*. Other easily accessible dive sites include Eden Rock and Devil's Grotto, just south of George Town, as well as those along Seven Mile Beach. Dive boats take certified divers to the island's incredible drop-offs, such as the West Wall which lies about nine miles offshore. Atlantis Submarine operates out of George Town and offers non-divers the opportunity to view the famous Cayman Wall. Several dive and snorkel shops are located within walking distance of the tender pier, and the cruise lines also offer snorkel and dive excursions.

Golf – There are two golf courses on Grand Cayman, both a few miles north of George Town along West Bay Road. Closest to town is the Hyatt Britannia Golf Course, designed by Jack Nicklaus and offering three courses in one: a nine-hole championship course, an 18-hole course and one played with a special Cayman ball. The Links at SafeHaven is an 18-hole championship course and is reminiscent of those in Scotland.

ISLAND ATTRACTIONS

Stingray City, located in the protected waters of North Sound, has been described in National Geographic as "one of the most rewarding experiences in the undersea world." Visitors are taken by boat to this shallow sandbar where for decades fishermen used to clean fish, their discarded entrails attracting stingrays who would arrive at the sound of a ship's motor. In 1987 some divers began frequenting this spot, bringing squid for the normally shy stingrays who gradually got used to the divers' presence. Now 30 to 50 stingrays show up daily to be hand fed, stroked and held by humans. Visitors can watch from an observatory or snorkel with the stingrays.

Cayman Turtle Farm is situated in a tidal creek of North Sound. Originally established in 1968 to raise and market turtle products, the farm now concentrates on research and breeding. Green sea turtles and hawksbill turtles are bred, hatched, raised and tagged before being released into Cayman waters. Tours of the facility are self-guided. While many visitors like to stop at nearby **Hell** so they can send a postcard, the real attraction is the weathered outcrop of iron shore which, although said to look like the charred remains of a hell fire, is actually made of black limestone about 1.5 million years old.

East of George Town the attractions include **Pedro St. James Castle**, an 18th-century great house beautifully situated on landscaped grounds atop a bluff. **Bodden Town,** with its legendary Pirate Cave, is where pirates are said to have hidden their loot in a series of tunnels. Nearby is the Meagre Bay Bird Sanctuary and further east is the **Botanic Park**, officially opened by Queen Elizabeth in 1994. The park's 60 acres of grounds include a floral garden and an interpretive trail that winds through woodlands, wetlands, swamps and thickets. Adjacent to the park is the **Mastic Trail**, a restored 200-year-old footpath that winds for two miles through primary woodlands and mangrove swamps. The island's eastern shores contain **The Blow Holes**, saltwater geysers spouting from the coral rock as waves crash onto shore. **East End** is the oldest town on the island, founded in the late 17th century.

Cayman Turtle Farm

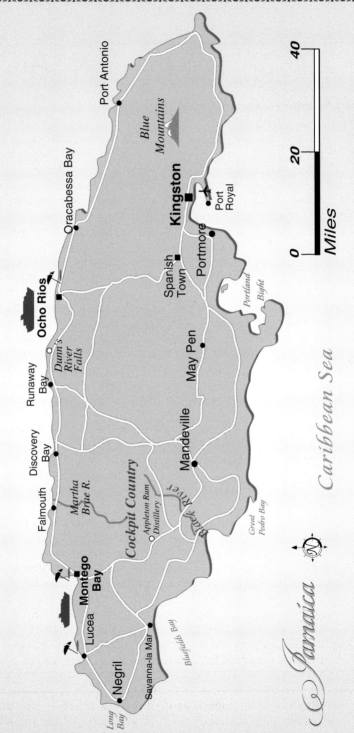

Jamaica

Caribbean Sea

©OCEAN CRUISE GUIDES

Miles

0   20   40

Port Antonio

Oracabessa Bay

Blue Mountains

Kingston

Port Royal

Portmore

Spanish Town

Portland Bight

Ocho Rios

Dunn's River Falls

Runaway Bay

May Pen

Discovery Bay

Mandeville

Falmouth

Martha Brae R.

Cockpit Country

Appleton Rum Distillery

Black River

Great Pedro Bay

Montego Bay

Lucea

Bluefields Bay

Savanna-la-Mar

Negril

Long Bay

N

Chapter Five

JAMAICA

Jamaica, third largest island of the West Indies after Cuba and Hispaniola, is one of the most beautiful in the Caribbean. A lush and mountainous island where rivers rush to the sea and white beaches line sparkling bays, Jamaica has long attracted a diversity of peoples to its shores, from famous buccaneers to famous artists. The country's official motto is 'Out of Many, One People' – acknowledging the range of races and nationalities that have colonized this island nation. Its history is turbulent and social problems still exist, but a 'No problem mon' attitude sums up the buoyant spirit of Jamaicans.

A limestone plateau more than 3,000 feet above sea level, Jamaica has a mountainous backbone that rises at its eastern end to the Blue Mountains and the island's tallest peak at 7,402 feet. Narrow coastal plains lie on either side of the mountain chain where fertile slopes and broad river valleys support the country's export crops of sugarcane, bananas, ginger, citrus fruits, cocoa, pimento, tobacco and its famous Blue Mountain Coffee. Most of these crops are grown on large plantations while small farms grow subsistence crops such as yams, breadfruit and cassava.

Rainfall, abundant in the mountainous regions, diminishes westward across a rugged plateau of streams and subterranean rivers. The heart of this plateau, called the Cockpits, is used for livestock grazing. During Jamaica's colonial days, escaped or freed slaves – called maroons – fled to Cockpit country where they lived in villages and organized frequent uprisings against the European landowners.

Arawaks, an agricultural people, were the first to inhabit the island about a thousand years ago and they called it Xaymaca – 'land of woods and streams'. The Spanish began colonizing Jamaica in 1509 under licence from Christopher Columbus's son, and the Arawaks soon died out under Spanish occupation. Captured by the British in 1655 and formally ceded to England in 1670, the island was a haven for buccaneers before becoming a major sugar producer in the 18th century.

Half of Jamaica's population is still rural, with much of the work force employed in agriculture. However, the continuing trend is one of migration to the cities. Of the country's 2.6 million residents, about 600,000 live in the capital of Kingston. Situated on a deep, landlocked harbor, Kingston was established in 1692 after an earthquake destroyed Port Royal at the tip of the peninsula that forms the harbor. This British outpost and pirate haven suddenly sank 33 feet into the sea, taking

JAMAICA

*(Above) Jamaica's scenic north coast. (Below) River rafting
on the Martha Brae. (Opposite page, top) The waterfront at
Ocho Rios . (Middle) A resort at Turtle Beach.
(Bottom) The tiered falls at Dunn's River.*

2,000 inhabitants with it. When a subsequent tsunami swept ashore, a British naval frigate was carried across the sunken townsite and desposited inland.

Plans are now underway to recreate 17th-century Port Royal, which wasn't properly excavated until 1965, although some of its treasure was salvaged at once. The most famous name associated with Port Royal is Sir Henry Morgan, a Welsh privateer whose daring exploits included the sacking of Portobelo in 1668 and the capture of Panama in 1671. He was eventually arrested on charges of piracy and sent to England where, with war against Spain threatening once more, he was knighted and returned to Jamaica as deputy-governor.

The entire north coast, from Negril at its western end to Port Antonio at its eastern end, is dotted with beach-lined bays and palm-shaded resorts, including some of the most exclusive in the Caribbean. It also contains Jamaica's two main cruise ports – Ocho Rios and Montego Bay.

Many a famous person has spent time living or vacationing in Jamaica, beginning with Christopher Columbus who first stepped ashore in 1494 at Rio Bueno. On his fourth voyage to the West Indies in 1503, Columbus beached his damaged ships on the island's north shore and spent a year on Jamaican soil awaiting rescue. In more recent times, the swashbuckling movie star Errol Flynn pulled into Port Antonio in his private yacht to escape a storm and ended up building a home there on Navy Island.

For a relatively small country, Jamaica has had a far-reaching impact on the rest of the world with its music, dance and art. Jamaicans are international in outlook and many of its citizens have migrated to other countries, most notably Britain. Over 90% of Jamaicans are of West African descent with Asians and Europeans adding to the cultural tapestry of this dynamic island nation. Yet, the country's rich social fabric has at times appeared to be unraveling, with political tribalism resulting in election violence.

The People's National Party (PNP) was founded in 1938 by Norman Manley. His cousin, Sir Alexander Bustamante, founded the Jamaica Labour Party (JLP). These two parties, their roots in rival trade unions, have dominated Jamaican politics since 1944 when universal adult suffrage was introduced. Jamaica gained its independence from Britain in 1962 but remains a member of the British Commonwealth. The country's economy is one of the more prosperous in the West Indies, despite a recession that persisted throughout the 1970s and 80s. After embracing socialism in the 1970s, Jamaica now has a free market economy based on tourism, agricultural products and the export of bauxite, from which alumina is extracted.

Hurricane Gilbert caused widespread devastation when it swept the length of the island in 1988 and the country's tourism industry was crippled. The island has since regained its prominence as a popular

Caribbean destination but many tourists stay at all-inclusive resorts. The government is trying to counter this insular attitude with a Meet the People program in which the tourist board will arrange for a visitor to spend time with a Jamaican host who shares a common interest.

Cruise passengers who might be apprehensive about venturing ashore can simply book a shore excursion. Those who prefer to strike out on their own will find the Jamaican people, despite their reputation for aggressively selling their wares (including narcotics), are an outgoing and friendly people who will respond to a polite but firm 'No thank you' with a 'No problem mon' wave of the hand. Most Jamaicans have a good sense of humor and this is usually the best way to fend off persistent advances.

REGGAE & RASTAFARIANISM

Rastafarianism is a religious-cultural movement that began in Jamaica in the 1930s when Haile Selassie (also named Ras Tafari) became Emperor of Ethiopia, as predicted by Jamaican hero Marcus Garvey. Selassie was hailed as the movement's messiah, Ethiopia was the promised land, and Garvey was considered a major prophet and early leader in creating black awareness and unity.

Reggae,which originated in the 1960s among the poor blacks of Kingston, is the protest music of the Rastafarian faith. Its sound is characterized by an off-beat rhythm that draws on American soul and traditonal African and Jamaican folk music. Reggae's most famous performer is the late Bob Marley, a Jamaican singer, songwriter and guitarist to whom a museum is dedicated in Kingston.

Born in 1945 and deserted by his white Jamaican father, Marley was raised by his mother in Nine Miles village on Jamaica's north coast. As a youth, he and his mother moved to the poor shanty area of Kingston where he worked in the welding trade while seeking success as a musician. Fame finally came to Marley in the 1970s when his new group began playing reggae and their songs soared in the charts. When Marley died of cancer at the age of 36, he had achieved international stardom and received his country's highest public honor, the Order of Merit. The worldwide popularity of reggae is attributed in large part to Marley, whose songs supported his belief in nonviolence and the Rastafarian religion.

Bob Marley, the 'King of Reggae Music' died at age 36.

Rastas, who object to shaving and cutting hair, wear their hair in long braids called dreadlocks – a symbolic connection with the Ethiopian lion. They are vegetarians who prefer natural foods and many of them smoke ganga, locally grown marijuana. Not everyone wearing dreadlocks is a Rasta and most 'real' Rastas are congenial, generally preferring the country to urban areas.

Ocho Rios

The original Spanish name for Ocho Rios was Las Chorreras – The Waterfalls – an appropriate name for a port situated at the base of lush mountains where rivers and streams spill into the sea. A former fishing village, Ocho Rios has been developed as a tourist destination with high-rise hotels and condominiums lining the beaches to the east of Ocho Rios Bay. The local population numbers about 11,000 and residents speak an English-based patois. Ocho Rios Bay contains two piers – the Reynolds Pier and the new cruise ship pier which is joined by a jetty to shore where telephones, tourist information and a handful of shops are located.

GETTING AROUND

 The cruise lines offer organized excursions to the major attractions, or you can hire a taxi. A visitor information booth is located in the terminal building and the taxi fares to various destinations are posted nearby. A dispatcher is also stationed there and, upon telling him where you want to go, he will hail you a driver whose car will carry the red Public Passenger Vehicle (PPV) license plates. If you want to visit a number of destinations, negotiate the fare with your driver before getting in. The fare is per taxi, so travelling in groups of four is the most economical. Some sample taxi tour rates for one to four persons: Dunn's River Falls – $20; Prospect Plantation – $30.

Shopping – Jamaica offers good buys in duty-free goods and great bargains in locally produced clothing, wood

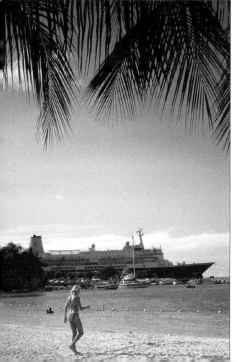

(Left) Turtle Beach. (Opposite page) A jetty leads ashore from the cruise pier at Ocho Rios.

carvings, coffee and rum. Beautiful, hand-carved walking sticks can be bought for $15 and tee shirts screened with unique Jamaican designs sell for as little as $5. More expensive are the beautiful batik cottons and silks. The exchange rate is approximately 45 Jamaican dollars for 1 US dollar, but there's no need to exchange money because American currency and credit cards are widely accepted.

Within walking distance of the cruise ship pier are the **1 Taj Mahal Centre** and **2 Soni's Plaza**, or you can take a shopping shuttle which costs $2 per person. In between are the **3 Old Market Craft Shoppes** and **4 Craft Park**, where local artisans sell their wares. Excellent arts and crafts can also be bought at the Dunn's River Falls marketplace, and paintings by acclaimed Jamaican artists are on display at the **9 Harmony Hall Gallery**, five miles east of the cruise port.

Best Beaches – Beautiful white sand beaches line the shoreline east of Ocho Rios Bay. Most of these are backed by hotels and have controlled access to protect tourists from pedlars. The admission fee is usually $1.00 per person. Closest to the pier is Turtle Beach, and an excellent beach lies on the other side of The Point at Mallards Bay.

Dive & Snorkel Sites – excursions are available out of Ocho Rios to nearby shallow coral gardens, some of which have been damaged in recent years by hurricanes. Serious divers recommend going deeper to see an abundance of coral and sponge life. Wall diving is popular at Runaway Bay.

Sandal's Golf & Country Club, overlooking Mallards Bay, is considered one of the most scenic in Jamaica, situated 700 feet up into the mountains. This 18-hole par-71 course was designed by P.K. Sanders and totals 6,500 yards.

LOCAL ATTRACTIONS

A botanical garden and bird sanctuary, **5 Shaw Park Gardens**' hillside location provides panoramic views in a tropical setting. The Coyaba River flows through **6 Coyaba Garden** where riverside paths and boardwalks lead past waterfalls and pools filled with koi carp and turtles. The museum contains pre-Columbian artifacts and the gallery displays creative works by Jamaicans.

AREA HIGHLIGHTS

7 Fern Gully, a former riverbed that went dry following an earthquake, is a three-mile stretch of road that winds into the Blue Mountains and leads, eventually, to Kingston on the other side of the island. The many species of fern that grow in this gully form a lush canopy for vehicles passing beneath it.

One of Jamaica's most popular attractions, **8 Dunn's River Falls** consist of clear mountain water flowing seaward across a tiered limestone bed. Visitors are charged $5 US to enter the park area, which includes a guided climb up this stunning set of falls. Guides lead visitors, in single file, along a known route. Operators of the park are fairly insistent you remain part of a guided climb to prevent personal injury. For an additional $5, a guide will hold your camera and other belongings as you scramble up the falls. A pair of running shoes or aqua socks (which can be rented) are recommended for the climb over slippery stones and rushing, knee-deep water. Dunn's Falls are about 1.5 miles by road from Ocho Rios and can also be reached by boat, a popular excursion being one of the party cruises that depart the cruise pier for a relaxing yacht ride to the mouth of Dunn's River and back, with time allowed for climbing the falls. Mountain biking excursions are also popular and involve an uphill drive followed by a downhill bike ride from Murphy Hill to Dunn's River Falls. Dolphin Cove, located beside Dunn's River Falls, is a new attraction where visitors can feed, pet and swim with dolphins.

Anyone interested in Jamaican folk art will enjoy a visit to **9 Harmony Hall**, a restored Victorian great house. Set on a small plantation estate four miles east of Ocho Rios, it contains an art gallery, craft and book shops, boutique and restaurant.

10 Prospect Plantation is a working plantation estate where guides take visitors on tractor-drawn jitneys past various flora and agricultural crops including bananas, sugarcane and coffee, as well as the White River Gorge and Sir Harold's Viewpoint, where Cuba, about 100 miles due north, can be seen on a clear day. Horseback tours are also available on each of three varied trails that traverse the 900 acres of grounds, which also contain a miniature golf course and a gift shop selling local crafts and souvenirs.

About 10 miles east of Prospect Plantation, **11** **Brimmer Hall Plantation** is another working plantation providing tours by tractor-drawn jitney. The beautiful grounds contain an 18th-century great house open for viewing, as well as a swimming pool, bar and shops.

Firefly, Noel Coward's "earthly paradise" set atop a plateau with a dramatic view of the surf pounding into Saccabus Bay, was the famous playwright's home for the last 25 years of his life and the place where he wrote some of his most celebrated works. Screen stars and British royalty would come to visit, but when Coward died in 1973 he asked that no fuss be made, and the site of his grave was where he often sat with friends sipping a pre-dinner cocktail while looking out to sea. Coward's home and contents were bequeathed to Jamaica in 1975 and restored as a museum run on behalf of the National Heritage Trust by Island Outpost, which is owned by Chris Blackwell, the multi-million-aire founder of Island Records. However, Firefly failed to attract enough visitors and in early 2000 plans were made to auction many of Coward's belongings and rent the property out for private receptions.

At **Oracabessa** ('Golden Head' in Spanish), the road winds past Goldeneye, an estate overlooking a private cove. This was the former winter retreat of the late Ian Fleming, who wrote his James Bond novels at this idyllic location. Noel Coward referred to Fleming's rather plain U-shaped house as the "Goldeneye, nose and throat clinic" while describing the cove's crescent beach of dazzling white sand as "unbelievable." Chris Blackwell's Island Outpost now owns the property and has converted it into a boutique-style luxury resort.

Other Excursions – Helicopter flightseeing trips can be taken from the heli-pad at Reynolds Pier. A 20-minute flight takes in the lush and varied coastal sights of the Ocho Rios area, including aerial views of Dunn's River Falls, sumptuous seaside villas and beaches lapped by an azure sea.

River rafting on the **Martha Brae**, which lies between Montego Bay and Ocho Rios, is a popular attraction. On bamboo rafts carrying two people, the raft man uses a pole to guide the raft gently downstream past bamboo groves and chirping birds. The drive from Ocho Rios to Martha Brae takes 1-1/2 hours along the winding coastal highway, and the river ride is just over an hour in length. An organized shore excursion lasts about five hours, often with a stop at Columbus Park, near Discovery Bay, where Columbus first landed at Jamaica. Other notable places along this stretch of coastline include Nine Miles village, the birthplace and gravesite of **Bob Marley**, and the 18th-century Georgian town of Falmouth near the mouth of the Martha Brae, about 20 miles east of Montego Bay.

Greenwood Great House, located 16 miles east of Montego Bay, was built by relatives of poet Elizabeth Barrett Browning, and the stately mansion is furnished with antiques and contains a rare-book library. A tour of Greenwood gives visitors an inside look at the privileged lives once enjoyed by plantation owners.

Rose Hall, a British mansion built in 1770, lies about 10 miles east of Montego Bay and is Jamaica's most famous great house thanks to a legendary mistress by the name of Annie Palmer. She lived here around 1820 and is said to have murdered three husbands and numerous slave lovers whom she controlled through witchcraft. According to one version of the legend, she was finally murdered by a lover who felt he was destined to be next on Annie's hit list.

Montego Bay

Jamaica's second-largest city, Montego Bay is one of the Caribbean's most popular resorts, beautifully situated on a beach-lined bay surrounded by green hills. A commercial center and shipping port, it's a growing city of over 70,000 residents, many of whom live in shanty towns on the outskirts. On the lower slopes of the Miranda Hills are luxury hotels set in manicured grounds.

GETTING AROUND

 The cruise ships dock at Freeport, about three miles from downtown. An information booth and telephones are situated on the dock. Nearby is the Montego Freeport duty-free shopping area. The taxi fare into town is about $12 for up to four people, and only JUTA (Jamaica Union of Travellers Association) taxis and mini-vans should be rented.

Best Beaches – Doctor's Cave Beach, located just north of the town center, is Montego Bay's most celebrated beach. At the turn of the century it was a fashionable health resort and many distinguished visitors came to bathe here. Today it's Montego Bay's most popular beach, with an entry charge that includes change facilities. Other good stretches of sand are found at Walter Fletcher Beach, south of Doctor's Cave, and at Cornwall Beach, which lies directly north of Doctor's Cave with a Jamaican Tourist Board office situated at its south end. Coral sea gardens can be viewed by glass-bottom boat in the clear, sheltered waters of Doctor's Cave, and snorkel and dive excursions can be arranged through local operators or your ship's shore excursion office. A championship golf course (7,130 yards, par 72) is located at the **Half Moon Golf Course**, near the sea on the eastern outskirts of Montego Bay.

Local Sights & Shopping – The city's business district includes a few historic landmarks, most of them situated on or near **1 Sam Sharpe Square** – named for a Jamaican hero who was hanged in 1831 for leading a slave revolt. On the southwest side of the square stands the Court House, an early-19th century colonial building. The Cage, a small building of the same period on the square's northeast corner, was used for detaining runaway slaves. Nearby, on Church Street, are a number of restored Georgian buildings including St. James's Parish Church which was rebuilt after suffering major damage in a 1957 earthquake. South of Church Street, near the water, is the colorful **2 Crafts Market**. A few blocks to the north, along the waterfront, stand the remains of Fort Montego which was built by the British in 1752. From here Gloucester Avenue, the main shopping thoroughfare, wends north past the hotel strip.

Area Attractions – **3 Rockland Bird Sanctuary**, nine miles south of Montego Bay, is popular with visitors, as is the **4 Appleton Estate Express**, a train that departs daily from Montego Bay and heads into Cockpit Country, location of the famous Appleton Rum Distillery and the Ipswich Caves with their limestone stalagmites and stalactites.

East of Montego Bay are Rose Hall, Greenwood Great House and the Martha Brae River (see pages 173 and 174).

Famous beaches lure visitors to Montego Bay.

New Providence Island

Atlantic Ocean

Cabbage Beach
Salt Cay
(Blue Lagoon Island)
Atholl Island
Paradise Island
Sea Gardens
Montagu Bay
Yamacraw Beach

Silver Cay
Bay St.
Shirley St.
NASSAU
Fort
Charlotte
Discovery Is.
Cable Beach
Ardastra Gardens
Eastern Rd.
Bernard Rd.
Prince Charles Dr.
Fox Hill Rd.
East St.
South Beach
South Beach Rd.
Cowpen Rd.
Bacardi
Rum Distillery
Carmichael Rd.
Gladstone Rd.

Delaporte Point
Lake Cunningham
John F. Kennedy Dr.
West Bay St.
Lake Killarney

Love Beach
Western Rd.
NASSAU INT'L AIRPORT
(Windsor Field)
Coal Harbor Rd.
Carmichael Rd.
Adelaide Rd.

Lyford Cay
Goulding Cay
South West Bay
Coral Harbour

0   2.5   5
Miles

©OCEANCRUISEGUIDES

CHAPTER SIX

BAHAMAS

An archipelago of some 700 islands and islets, the Bahamas start about 50 miles off southeast Florida and extend 600 miles in a southeasterly direction toward Haiti. Small and snakelike in shape, these limestone islands lie low on the horizon and are surrounded by clear turquoise seas filled with coral gardens and sunken wrecks. A diver's delight, they were treacherous waterways in the days of piracy when buccaneers, intent on pillage, would lure passing ships into these shallow reef-strewn waters. Spanish galleons laden with gold and silver had to pass through the Straits of Florida and around the top end of the Bahamas on their way back to Spain, so they became easy prey for pirates like the notorious Blackbeard who would escape Spanish convoys by retreating to the port of Nassau on New Providence Island.

Two centuries earlier these far-flung islands were home to a much different breed of seafaring people – a tribe of Arawaks called Lucayans who lived here in fishing villages. Travelling by canoe, the Lucayans had migrated from South America to these remote and riverless islands to avoid the aggressive Carib tribes. Their solitude was shattered in 1492 by the arrival of an unexpected visitor.

The Bahamian island of Guanahani was where Christopher Columbus first stepped ashore in the New World after crossing the Atlantic into the unknown. Relieved to have reached what he assumed were the islands of Asia, Columbus called the island San Salvador and claimed it for Spain. The Spanish, whose goal was to find gold and other treasures, were not interested in colonizing these islands situated in what Columbus called a *baja mar* (shallow sea). They did, however, enslave the Lucayans to work in the gold mines on Hispaniola, and the first inhabitants of the Bahamas were soon exterminated.

The islands remained deserted until the mid-17th century when a group of English Puritans arrived from Bermuda. They settled at Preacher's Cave on Eleuthera and tried to scratch out an existence, but conditions were harsh. The Bahamas rise from a vast submarine plateau, their brackish lakes connected with the ocean by underground passages, and rainfall or desalinization are the main sources of fresh water. The settlers on Eleuthera slowly cultivated the thin soil for growing cotton, tobacco and vegetables. Meanwhile, another settlement was established on New Providence Island. Originally called Charles Towne, it was renamed in 1695 for England's King William III, a member of Europe's Orange-Nassau dynasty. The settlement

***Fort Fincastle has overlooked
Nassau Harbour since 1793.***

quickly grew and Fort Nassau was built in 1697 to ward off Spanish invasions.

A period of lawlessness prevailed in the Bahamas, which had become a rendezvous for pirates. The British did little to discourage the plundering of Spanish ships until the Bahamas were made a crown colony and Captain Woodes Rogers was dispatched to Nassau in 1718 to restore order. The town was so squalid he chose to live on board his ship while overseeing the cleaning of streets and wells. Local forts were improved and manned with regular garrisons. Woodes Rogers also restructured the island government and issued a proclamation guaranteeing freedom for slaves from Bermuda and the American colonies, with which the islanders had close trading ties. Runaway slaves fleeing the American colonies would stow away on board Bahama-bound merchant ships, and when the American Revolutionary War broke out in 1776, hundreds of loyalists also fled to the Bahamas.

American revolutionists captured and held Nassau for three days – long enough to raid the port for arms and ammunition. Then, in 1781, Spain captured Nassau and took possession of the whole colony which was returned to Great Britain in the Treaty of Paris (1783). The British built two more forts (Charlotte and Fincastle) to protect Nassau from any future invasions but the islands were largely ignored. Many of the loyalists, their plantation farms failing, returned to England.

During the American Civil War, the islanders profited from blockade running into Southern ports. The islands also became a base for rum-running during the prohibition era that followed World War I. However, the islands remained in relative isolation, their inhabitants developing a unique culture of Goombay music, Junkanoo dance and straw crafts. Yet the influence of British colonialism remained strong with English nobility maintaining beautiful homes and gardens on New Providence Island. Wealthy Americans also began vacationing in the Bahamas in the 1860s, arriving by steamship from New York.

Nassau is one of the Caribbean's busiest cruise ports.

In 1900 the Florida railroad baron Henry Flagler built the huge Colonial Hotel in Nassau and offered steamship service from Miami. The hotel, destroyed by fire in 1929 but quickly replaced, was favored by European royalty and high society, but it wasn't until after World War II that tourism flourished, as did social activism. Black Bahamians began to challenge the ruling white party and in 1967 the Progressive Liberal Party, led by Bahamian-born and London-educated Lynden Oscar Pindling, won control of the government with a close but surprising victory. His party, campaigning for independence, won an overwhelming majority in 1972 and began negotiations with Britain. The following year, Britain's Prince Charles presented the new Constitution of the Bahamas to Prime Minister Pindling and a former crown colony of Britain became the Commonwealth of the Bahamas.

Pindling, in power for 25 years, was defeated in 1992 amid accusations of mismanagement. Offshore banking has grown in the major centers of Nassau and Freeport on Grand Bahama Island, but tourism remains the number one industry.

About a quarter million people live on the islands. Nassau, on New Providence Island, is the capital and principal city. Other main islands, called 'out islands' or 'family islands', include Grand Bahama, Great and Little Abaco, Andros, Eleuthera, Cat Island, San Salvador, and Great and Little Inagua. The Turks and Caicos Islands, lying southeast of the Bahamas, are geographically part of the archipelago but have been separately administered by Great Britain since 1848.

The Bahamas are blessed with beautiful beaches, crystal clear waters, coral gardens, exotic birds and an ideal climate. Their proximity to Florida and the enticement of casinos also add to their appeal. Still, many of the islets and cays remain uninhabited and undeveloped, just as they were when Christopher Columbus first laid eyes on the New World.

By horse-drawn buggy is a popular way to tour the streets of Nassau.

Naussau

Nassau, one of the busiest cruise ports in the world, is a vibrant city with a population of about 150,000. Its pink buildings and white gloved bobbies are part of the British colonial charm of this bustling port.

GETTING AROUND

Nassau is fairly compact and the major historical sights can be seen on foot, although there is some uphill walking. Another option is to see the local sights by horse-drawn buggy. These can be hired in Rawson Square and the usual fare is $10 for a half-hour ride, but settle on a price before climbing in.

Jitney buses to Cable Beach leave from the British Colonial Hilton every 10 or 15 minutes and the fare is 75¢ per person. A one-hour island tour costs $30 to $40. The water taxi to Paradise Island is $3 each way and takes about half an hour (plus a ten-minute walk if you're heading to the Atlantis Resort). A cab ride, which is much faster, costs $6 per person each way, plus a $2 bridge toll.

Rental cars and scooters are available in Nassau. Driving is on the left and helmets are mandatory for people on scooters.

Shopping – Nassau and Hong Kong have been touted as the two best places in the world to buy watches. Other duty-free items to look for in Nassau include jewelry, crystal, china, leather and liquor. Bay Street (from East Street to the British Colonial Hilton) is where the majority of shops are located, as is the famous Straw Market where handcrafted baskets and other items are sold. The Bahamian Dollar is on par with the U.S. dollar and the two currencies are used interchangeably. When paying with American money, ask for

Cable Beach, near Nassau, is a popular beach for cruise passengers.

your change in the same currency or you'll receive Bahamian currency. Travellers cheques and credit cards are widely accepted.

Beaches – Closest to the cruise pier and within easy walking distance is the beach in front of the British Colonial Hilton. West of downtown is popular Cable Beach, while a few miles farther along Bay Street is secluded Love Beach which offers ideal snorkeling just one mile off the shore. Among the excellent beaches on Paradise Island, lovely Cabbage Beach is bordered by the cooling shade of casuarina trees. The beautiful beaches of Blue Lagoon Island can be reached by 30-minute boat shuttles from Paradise Island.

Dive & Snorkle Sites – Excellent snorkeling and diving can be enjoyed in the waters off Nassau, and several dive operators are located on Paradise Island and in Nassau at the foot the Paradise Island bridge. Local snorkeling sites include the reefs at Silver Cay (see Crystal Cay Marine Park) and Athol Island's Sea Gardens (see page 185). Divers can explore numerous wrecks immediately north of Paradise Island. About 10 miles east of Nassau is the famous Lost Blue Hole – a massive oceanic hole which begins at 45 feet and contains coral heads, moray eels and other creatures.

The southwest coast also has great snorkeling and diving, and many a filmmaker has shot underwater footage here. The shallow reef areas at Goulding Cay contain magnificent elkhorn coral – featured in such movies as *20,000 Leagues Under the Sea* and *Splash*. A number of James Bond flicks have also been filmed in these waters, including *Thunderball*, *For Your Eyes Only* and *Never Say Never Again*. Sunken movie props include the *Vulcan Bomber* and *Tears of Allah* freighter, both of which are popular dive sites. Natural attractions include Tunnel Wall, Southwest Reef and Shark Wall, a drop-off along the edge of a deep-water abyss called Tongue of the Ocean.

Golf – There are plenty of golf courses to choose from in the Nassau area, a popular one for cruise passengers being the par-72 course at the Paradise Island Golf & Country Club.

LOCAL ATTRACTIONS

The **1 Tourist Office** is located right beside the cruise pier on the edge of **2 Rawson Square**, named for a former governor. Horse-drawn buggies wait here for hire.

Clustered around a statue of Queen Victoria in **3 Parliament Square** are the Houses of Parliament, built from 1805 to 1813. When facing Queen Victoria's statue, the House of Assembly is to the right, the Senate Building is straight ahead and the old Colonial Secretary's Office and Treasury is to the left. South of these buildings are the Supreme Court and Garden of Remembrance with a cenotaph.

The octagonal-shaped **4 Public Library**, once used as a prison and complete with dungeons, stands at the corner of Parliament and Shirley Streets.

(Top) Parliament Square
(Above) Christ Church Cathedral

5 **The Royal Victorian Gardens** offer a shady spot to rest before tackling the **6** **Queen's Staircase** where 66 steps, cut into a limestone gorge by slave laborers in the 18th century, lead up the hill to **7** **Fort Fincastle**. The fort was built in 1793 to ward off Spanish invasions. Nearby is a water tower where visitors can take the stairs or an elevator (for a small charge) to the top for a commanding view of the fort and harbor beyond.

8 **Government House** is one of Nassau's most photographed buildings with a statue of Columbus standing on the steps leading to its front entrance. The building isn't open to the public and sentry guards man the gates on either side of the grounds, but they will allow visitors to walk through. Edward, Duke of Windsor, resided here when he was governor of the Bahamas from 1940 to 1945. A former King of England who renounced his throne to marry American divorcee Wallis Warfield Simpson, the Duke was suspected of either inadvertently or intentionally leaking Allied secrets to the Nazis. To keep him a safe distance from the war raging in Europe, the British government sent him to the Bahamas in July, 1940.

9 **St. Andrew's Presbyterian Church**, begun in 1810, stands at the corner of Duke and Market streets, and **10** **Christ Church Cathedral** at the corner of George and King streets was built in 1837. Across the street is the **11** **Pirates of Nassau Interactive Museum** where exhibits include dioramas depicting pirates battling on the high seas.

Dominating the waterfront, the **British Colonial Hilton** stands on the former site of Fort Nassau and was built soon after the original Colonial Hotel was destroyed by fire in 1929. Since acquired as a Hilton property, this historic landmark has undergone a $68-million restoration and renovation.

(Above) The main entrance to Government House.
(Below) The Queens Staircase leads to Fort Fincastle.

(Left) Vendue House.
(Below left) A sentry at
side gate to
Government House.
(Opposite page) Atlantis
on Paradise Island.

12 **Vendue House**, which stands on the site of a former slave market, dates back to 1769 and was rebuilt in the early 1900s. It now houses the Pompey Museum of Slavery and Emancipation, opened in 1992 as part of the Columbus Quincentennial. The museum is named after a slave and Bahamian hero who lived on Exuma.

The **13** **Straw Market**, in the heart of Nassau's shopping district, is a traditional Bahamian market where shoppers bargain with the vendors for items which include jewelry, t-shirts, carvings and, of course, an array of straw woven products. Most of the more-than-500 vendors are women whose stalls and craft skills have been passed down through generations. In fall 2001, a fire swept through the Straw Market and a temporary market was opened on the block between the Pompey Museum on Bay Street and Woodes Rogers Walk.

ISLAND ATTRACTIONS

About a mile west of downtown Nassau stands **Fort Charlotte**. Built on a hilltop from 1787-94, this imposing fort features a moat and dungeons, and provides impressive views. Nearby are **Ardastra Gardens and Zoo**, a 5-1/2 acre nature park which is home to nearly 300 animals in a tropical garden setting. Amid the lush foliage there live peacocks, parrots, monkeys and some famous marching flamingos, featured here since the 1950s. They were initially trained by a Jamaican horticulturist, and subsequent trainers have simply introduced a few young flamingos at a time who follow the veteran members of the group and quickly learn the maneuvers.

The turquoise waters of the Bahamas are a major attraction, whether for swimming, snorkeling, diving or simply observing the colorful marine world that thrives just below the sea's surface. Glass-bottom boats, catamarans and other excursion vessels depart from the cruise pier on harbor tours and trips to nearby beaches and coral gardens.

Crystal Cay Marine Park, located on **Silver Cay** in Nassau Harbor, is connected by a bridge to the mainland or can be reached by a short ferry boat ride from the cruise pier. Its admission fee includes access to various tanks holding sharks, stingrays and turtles, in addition to an underwater observatory for viewing coral reefs and tropical fish. Also located here is a white sand beach, snorkel trail, equipment rental, change facilities, bars and a restaurant.

Beach-lined **Paradise Island** was once a playground for the wealthy, and the Astors, Rockefellers and Vanderbilts all built winter residences here in the 1920s. Called Hog Island, its name was changed to Paradise Island when Huntington Hartford bought the island and developed it into a holiday resort. A unique attraction is the Versailles Gardens and French Cloister, a ruined 14th-century Augustinian monastery transported from France. The island's modern resorts include the **Atlantis**, a huge Sun International Resort and Casino (formerly owned under a different name by Merv Griffin) which features a spectacular water park of pools, waterfalls, underground grottos and various lagoons, one containing sharks, barracudas and stingrays.

Thirty-minute boat shuttles are available from Paradise Island ($20 round trip) to **Blue Lagoon Island**, popular with day trippers and where Dolphin Encounters offer participants the chance to pet and hug an Atlantic bottle-nose dolphin in a controlled setting.

The waters surrounding **Athol Island**, lying east of Paradise Island, are referred to as the **Sea Gardens**, for they are filled with shipwrecks, coral colonies and schools of tropical fish. Seaworld Explorer's tours begin at Captain Nemo's Dock (just east of the cruise pier) with a 20-minute boat tour of Nassau Harbor en route to Athol Island, where passengers transfer to an observatory vessel in which they sit five feet beneath the water's surface for a submarine-like viewing experience.

Atlantis Submarine, based at the west end of New Providence Island, departs from West Bay near Lyford Cay for deep-water viewing of the area's renowned reefs and wrecks.

Freeport

The cruise port of Freeport/Lucaya, located on Grand Bahama Island, was developed as a tourist destination and world-class dive resort in the 1950s and '60s. The island, 75 miles long by 15 miles wide, is an exposed portion of the Little Bahama Bank, where a combination of shallow waters and deep chasms creates a diver's paradise of shallow, medium-depth and deep reefs as well as dramatic drop-offs.

Beaches, nature parks, golf courses, gambling casinos, duty-free shopping and every conceivable water sport await visitors to Freeport. Cars, mopeds and bicycles can be rented, and metered taxis are available at the cruise terminal which is about five miles from town. Local attractions include the **Garden of the Groves,** an 11-acre botanical garden containing the Grand Bahama Museum, and the **Rand Memorial Nature Center**, 100 acres of natural woodland containing trails and a bird sanctuary. **Lucaya National Park**, 25 miles west of Freeport, contains an underground system of limestone caverns, shady trails, pine forests, a mangrove creek and ocean beach.

 Shopping can be enjoyed at the International Bazaar & Strawmarket and at the Port Lucaya Marketplace & Marina. At the Perfume Factory, a restored 18th-century Bahamian mansion located next to the International Bazaar, shoppers can mix, bottle, label and name their own fragrance.

Beaches abound on Grand Bahama and they line the shores of Freeport and Lucaya. Those with hotels and facilities include Xanadu Beach (about five miles from the cruise pier) and Lucaya Beach, located across the street from the Port Lucaya Marketplace.

The Underwater Explorers Society (UNEXSO), a famous scuba diving school, is located at **Port Lucaya**. Their organized dives include a daily trip to Shark Junction, where a dozen or more Caribbean Reef Sharks often appear and feed on bait. Also popular is The Dolphin Experience at Sanctuary Bay, the world's largest dolphin sanctuary, where Atlantic Bottlenose dolphins swim with divers both in a sheltered lagoon and in open water along an offshore coral reef. For wild dolphin encounters, White Sand Ridge off the northwest point of the island is a good place to interact with a resident pod of Spotted Dolphins that frequent these waters. A number of local dive boats offer snorkel trips to this area.

 Golfers can choose from three PGA-rated courses – Princess Ruby Golf Course, Princess Emerald Golf Course and Lucaya Golf & Country Club.

Barbary Beach

Churchill Beach

Garden of the Groves

Taino Beach

Midshipman Rd.

GRAND BAHAMA ISLAND

Grand Bahama Highway

Lucaya Beach/
Port Lucaya Marketplace

Seahorse Rd.

Silver Cove

Queens Hwy

Beachway Dr.

FREEPORT

W. Sunrise Hwy.

Xanadu Beach

Borco

Cruise Ship
Harbor

Freeport

5

2.5

0

Miles

N

©OCEANCRUISEGUIDES

Puerto Rico

Atlantic Ocean

Aguadilla
Quebradillas
Arecibo
Dorado
Bacardi
Rum
Factory
Old
San Juan
Condado
Isla Verde
San Juan
Luquillo
Fajardo
Las Cabezas
Celiba
Mayaguez
Ponce
Humacao
El Yunque
Rain Forest
Isla de Culebra
Isla de Vieques
St. Thomas

El Morro

©OCEAN CRUISE GUIDES

Miles
0   10   20

Atlantic
Ocean

El Morro
**Old
San Juan**
C. Fortaleza
Cruise
Piers
Ave. Munoz Rivera
Ave. Fernandez
Ponce de Leon
Cano de San Antonio
Frontier Pier
Aeropuerto de
Isla Grande

Fort San
Geronimo
Laguna de
Condado
CONDADO
OCEAN
PARK
Ave. Ashford
Baldorioty de Castro Exp.
26
Ave. Ponce de Leon
Munoz Rivera Exp.
3 mi. to
In'l Airport

Miles
0   1   2

©OCEAN CRUISE GUIDES

CHAPTER SEVEN

SAN JUAN

S an Juan, a busy base port for Caribbean cruises, is also one of the best-preserved ports of colonial Spain. The walled city of Old San Juan, the oldest Spanish settlement under American sovereignty, is a World Heritage Site. Its cobblestone streets are paved with ballast from Spanish galleons and the impenetrable citadel of El Morro was once a symbol of Spanish domination in the Caribbean. In contrast to the historic feel of Old San Juan is the nearby Condado area, where modern high-rise hotels line the beaches and a sizzling night life can be enjoyed in the night clubs and casinos.

Puerto Ricans number over three and a half million and they refer to their Connecticut-sized island as the 'continent' of Puerto Rico due to its geographical diversity. Mountains here soar to over 4,000 feet and vegetation ranges from lush rainforests to low-lying mangrove swamps. Beautiful beaches line much of the coastline and, in the northwest, an extensive system of caves has been carved by one of the world's largest underground rivers.

Puerto Rico is a self-governing Commonwealth of the United States and its infrastructure includes a major airport, well-maintained roads, luxury resorts and championship golf courses. Industrialization came to Puerto Rico in the 1940s when Operation Bootstrap was introduced and its tax exemptions promoted American investment. Manufacturing, pharmaceuticals and the production of high-tech equipment are now major industries, along with agriculture and tourism.

Puerto Ricans enjoy the highest annual income in Latin America and are a well-educated work force. Few deny that the island's ties to America are beneficial and worth preserving, but an ongoing debate revolves around the 'statehood versus status quo' issue. The electorate is fairly evenly divided, with those supporting the status quo concerned about preserving their Spanish culture. Those supporting statehood accuse their opponents of 'wanting to have their cake and eat it too'. A small minority support independence, a movement that began in the last century when Puerto Rican statesman and journalist Luis Munoz Rivera led a growing demand for self government, which resulted in Spain granting its Caribbean colony some autonomy in February 1898. However, the Spanish-American war began a few months later and American troops soon occupied the island. By December, Spain had ceded Puerto Rico to the United States.

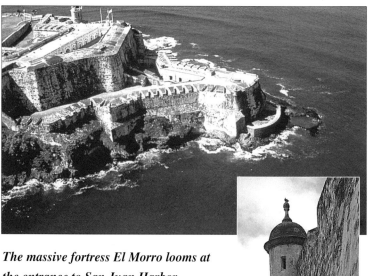

The massive fortress El Morro looms at the entrance to San Juan Harbor.

Puerto Rico remained under direct military rule until 1900 when Congress passed the Foraker Act, setting up a local administration with a U.S. Governor, an elected house of delegates and an upper chamber appointed by the U.S. President. Munoz Rivera, who had moved to New York where he published the Puerto Rico Herald before becoming the resident commissioner of Puerto Rico in Washington, was again a driving force for greater autonomy. In 1917 the Jones Act pronounced Puerto Rico a U.S. territory, granting its occupants U.S. citizenship and increased internal self-government.

While Puerto Ricans were making political gains, economic and social conditions were worsening. Much of their subsistence land was encroached upon by the establishment of large sugar plantations. The situation, aggravated by overpopulation, went from bad to worse when the sugar market fell in the 1930s. Recovery measures were taken under Franklin Roosevelt's presidency and the governorship of Rexford Tugwell. In 1948 Puerto Ricans elected their governor for the first time, and in 1952 the Commonwealth of Puerto Rico was proclaimed.

The smallest and easternmost of the Greater Antilles, Puerto Rico was originally inhabited by Taino Indians who called the island Borinquen. Christopher Columbus visited in 1493 and named the island San Juan Bautista (St. John the Baptist) but sailed on to Hispaniola to establish a settlement. Juan Ponce de Leon began the Spanish conquest of Borinquen, after finding gold there in 1508. He established a settlement on the shores of San Juan harbor, calling it Puerto Rico – rich port. The names were eventually switched, and rich is what Ponce de Leon became as governor of the island, with the lure of new conquests drawing him away from Puerto Rico from time to time.

In 1521, the Spanish colonists moved their settlement from a low-lying location across the bay to the present-day site of San Juan. Ponce de Leon was in Florida at the time, trying to establish a new colony, where he was felled by the poisoned arrow of a Native American. His party sailed immediately for Cuba where their leader died, his body returned to Puerto Rico for burial.

Meanwhile, hardship, disease and Spanish massacres had eliminated the Tainos and they were replaced with African slaves, first introduced in 1513. Once the island's placer gold deposits were depleted in the 1530s, the Spanish turned their attention to sugar plantations. Distractions came in the form of raids by Carib Indians and by British, French and Dutch pirates and roving corsairs, all of whom were attracted to this important outpost of the Spanish empire.

Twice a year two armed convoys were sent from Spain to collect precious gems, gold and silver. The Spanish ships entered the Caribbean Sea near Puerto Rico, one fleet heading to Veracruz to pick up Mexican gold and silver, the other heading to Cartagena to await treasures arriving from the Isthmus of Panama. The two fleets would then rendezvous at Havana for the return voyage to Spain. To protect her shipping interests, Spain established several military fortifications, the most strategic being San Juan harbor which Spain's King Philip II called 'the key to the West Indies'.

The famous **El Morro** fortress was built at the east side of the harbor entrance. It began as a round masonry tower which, over time and following various enemy assaults, was strengthened and expanded until it was a massive citadel. The main purpose of this fortification was to prevent Spain's European enemies from gaining possession of the port and using it as a base for attacks on Spanish settlements and trading ships.

Britain's Sir Francis Drake, justly feared by the Spanish and emboldened by his successful sackings of Santo Domingo, Cartagena and St. Augustine in Florida, was the first to test El Morro. In 1595 he forced the entrance to the harbor but was repulsed, with heavy losses suffered by the Spanish defenders. Three years later Britain's Earl of Cumberland successfully besieged El Morro, his brief occupation cut short by an outbreak of dysentery. The Dutch were next, in 1625, sacking and burning the town before being driven off by the Spanish.

In response to these attacks, Spain built several fortresses, making San Juan virtually impregnable. Massive walls of sandstone, some 50 feet high and 20 feet thick at the base, were raised around the town. A redoubt named San Cristobal was built about a mile east of El Morro to protect the town from a land-based attack. But it wasn't until the end of the Seven Years War (1756-1763), which left Spain and Britain the two powers in the Caribbean, that San Juan was transformed into the strong-hold we see today. Thomas O'Daly, an Irish-born military engineer, was hired by Spain's King Charles III to oversee the completion of the wall, expand San Cristobal into the largest fortress built by Spain in the Americas, and turn El Morro into an impenetrable citadel. Hundreds of workmen were employed in this massive undertaking which took 20 years to complete. San Juan remained impregnable for more than a cen-tury and was one of Spain's last remaining holdings in the Americas when a revolution in Cuba sparked the Spanish-American War. A United States naval flotilla, in search of the Spanish war fleet, bom-barded San Juan in May of 1898, and two months later American troops landed on the south coast of Puerto Rico. As soldiers advanced to the outskirts of San Juan, an armistice was signed. Spain's four-cen-tury rule of Puerto Rico had come to an end.

GETTING AROUND SAN JUAN

San Juan's main cruise port is located adjacent to the walled city; its secondary cruise pier (**Frontier Pier**) is two miles east of the main port. In between the airport and the cruise piers lie the hotel-lined beaches of Isla Verde, Ocean Beach and Condado, where the majority of passengers stay if spending extra time in San Juan before or after their cruise. Two **hotels** located right in Old San Juan are the El Convento (a former convent) and the new Wyndham Old San Juan Hotel on the harbor front. Tourist **taxis** are painted white and they offer fixed rates (per car) to and from tourist zones. The fare from the airport to Isla Verde is $8, to Condado is $12, and to the cruise piers in Old San Juan is $16. From Isla Verde to the cruise piers the fare is $16 and from Condado, $10. From Frontier Pier to Old San Juan is about $10.

Parking is limited in Old San Juan and its streets are best explored on foot or by using the free trolley service which originates at the Covadonga parking lot, a block up from the cruise ship piers. Five trol-ley buses, equipped with wheelchair ramps, operate daily and cover two routes: a central one to Plaza de Armas and a northern route to the grounds of El Morro. Passengers can hop off and on at any stop.

To see some of the city's outlying districts and area attractions, such as the El Yunque National Forest, tours can be booked through the cruise lines' shore excursion office or at the tour desks of the major hotels. Another option is to rent a car. Rental agencies are numerous in the San Juan metropolitan area, including Avis, Budget and Hertz.

Spanish and English are the official languages. Spanish is predomi-nant, but English is taught in school and is widely spoken. Long-dis-tance phone calls can be made at 'Phones & More' located inside Pier 6 and other phones are opposite Pier 4. A post office is located opposite Pier 1 where San Justo intersects with Comercio.

 Dining – San Juan has become a restaurant town, serving both traditional creole cuisine and the new Puerto Rican cuisine,

San Juan's inviting waterfront promenade leads from the main cruise port to the walled city.

which has taken traditional recipes featuring native Indian, Spanish and African foods, and enhanced them with new seasonings and presentation. A good place to sample some local fare is Amadeus, a popular bistro-style bar and restaurant across from the Plaza San Juan.

Shopping – San Juan has duty-free shopping at its airport and at several factory outlets in Old San Juan. The main shopping streets are Cristo, Fortaleza, San Francisco and Cristo, where a Pusser's Store and Polo/Ralph Lauren Factory Store are located. Numerous art galleries are situated in the shopping area and on San Jose Street. Traditional items include *cuatros* (handmade guitars), bobbin lace (*mundillo*) and small wood carvings of religious figures called *santos*. Other local crafts include straw work, ceramics, hammocks and carnival masks. The Institute of Puerto Rican Culture operates the Popular Arts and Crafts Center, located at the bottom of Cristo Street near the Capilla de Cristo, where a variety of island crafts are displayed and

(Below) The new Wyndham Old San Juan Hotel.
(Right) El Convento, a heritage hotel building.

San Juan

Fort
El Morro

Atlantic Ocean

San Juan
Cemetery

San Juan
Bay

CRUISE SHIP DOCKS

(Frontier Pier)
Two Miles

Pier 6
Pier 4
Pier 3
Pier 2
Pier 1

Cataño
Ferry
Terminal

Ave. Muñoz Rivera
Ave. Ponce De León
Covadongo
Comercio
Recinto Sur
Tetuan Sur
La Puntilla
Paseo La Princesa
O'Donnel
Capilla
Tanca
Sol
San Francisco
San Justo
Luna
Las Monjas
Sol
Norzagaray
Beneficencia
San Sebastian
Norzagaray
Cruz
Fortaleza
San Jose
Cristo
San Juan
El Morro
P.O.

(1) La Casita
(2) Aduana
(3) El Arsenal
(4) Paseo La Princesa
(5) La Princesa
(6) La Puerta de San Juan
(7) La Fortaleza
(8) Plazuela de la Rogativa
(9) Casa Blanca
(10) El Morro
(11) Ballaja Barracks
(12) Plaza del Quinto
Centenario
(13) San Juan Cemetery
(14) Plaza de San Jose
(15) San Juan Cathedral
(16) Capilla de Cristo
(17) Plaza de Armas
(18) Plaza de Colon
(Columbus Plaza)
(19) San Cristobal Fort
(20) Capitol Building

©OCEAN CRUISE GUIDES

offered for sale Monday through Saturday. On weekends, local crafts can be purchased at an outdoor market beside La Casita information center and along La Princesa promenade. This market is a popular venue for local musicians.

Rum is another Puerto Rican specialty, with free tours and samples provided at the Bacardi Rum Factory – reached by harbor ferry from the cruise ship pier. Gourmet coffee drinkers may want to purchase a pound or two of flavorful Puerto Rican coffee. If you're looking for fine cigars, there's a boutique catering to connoisseurs at El San Juan Hotel on Isla Verde. Shoppers looking for interesting books and souvenirs should check out the museum gift shops, such as the one at El Morro, where visitors can purchase replica gold and silver coins of the 16th century.

Beaches – Good beaches in the metropolitan area include Escambron Beach and Isla Verde Beach, both of which are balnearios (government-run beaches with facilities, lifeguards and security personnel). About 20 miles east of San Juan is highly popular and beautiful Luquillo Beach – rated one of the world's top ten by National Geographic. A favorite with children is Seven Seas in Fajardo at the northeast end of the island. More beautiful beaches lie west of San Juan at Dorado where a public beach is located near the hotel and golf resorts.

(Above) The cuatro is a traditional handmade guitar. (Below) Ocean Park Beach.

Golf – Puerto Rico boasts a dozen public golf courses, including four at the Hyatt Resorts west of San Juan. Designed by Robert Trent Jones Sr., the par-72 East course at Dorado Beach contains a par-5 thirteenth hole, rated by Jack Nicklaus as one of the top ten in the world.

VIEJO SAN JUAN

(Right) Pablo Casals Museum. (Below) Paseo La Princesa.

(Top) La Fortaleza viewed from the water. (Right) Aerial view of El Morro and Old San Juan. (Below) Spanish townhouses line a cobblestone street leading to the Church of San Jose.

(Above) The waterfront promenade leads to San Juan Gate.

(Opposite) Children play in Small Plaza of the Religious Procession.

LOCAL ATTRACTIONS:

The cruise ships dock right at the doorstep of Old San Juan, a seven-block area packed with historical and cultural sights which include Gothic churches, restored colonial buildings, townhouses with inner courtyards and wrought-iron balconies, museums, art galleries, boutiques, plazas, fountains and gardens. An **information center ℹ** is conveniently located beside Pier 1 inside **1 La Casita (The Little House)** and is an ideal starting point for a self-guided walking tour of these historic streets and fortifications. Refreshments can be enjoyed along the way at various restaurants and sidewalk cafes, or from street vendors who sell bottled water and soft drinks. Piraguas (fruit-flavored snow cones) and helados (coconut and pineapple ices) are popular with the locals. **2 Aduana**, the beautiful pink building overlooking the harbor, is a U.S. Customs House. Nearby **3 El Arsenal** was built in 1800 as a base for patrol boats and houses Divisions of the Institute of Puerto Rican Culture. Three art galleries are located within the grounds. An elegant promenade, **4 Paseo La Princesa**, runs parallel with the city wall and is where Spanish gentry of the 19th century once strolled. Restored for the Columbus Quincentennial, the esplanade is lined with palms and ornate street lamps, and features a large bronze fountain titled Raices (Roots), its human figures representing Puerto Rico's Indian, African and Spanish founders.

Paseo La Princesa leads past **5 La Princesa**, a former jail, which has also been restored to its former colonial grandeur and is now the headquarters for the Puerto Rico Tourism Company, the island's official tourism body. The promenade curves along the waterfront at the base of the city wall, called La Muralla, which is guarded at strategic points by garitas (sentry boxes). **6 La Puerta de San Juan (San Juan Gate)** is one of six heavy wooden doors once positioned along the wall and which, for centuries, were bolted shut at sundown to secure the fortified city from enemy attack.

Pass through this gate and make an immediate right on Recinto Oeste Street for a look at **7 La Fortaleza (The Fortress)** which overlooks San Juan Bay. Built as a fort in 1540, its location proved poor for military defence and its role reverted to that of governor's mansion – the oldest one in use in the Western Hemisphere. The grounds are open weekdays to organized tours that start every hour in a small plaza beside the building.

A turn to the left upon passing through the San Juan Gate will take you to the top of a hill where **8 Plazuela de la Rogativa (Small Plaza of the Religious Procession)** is a popular gathering place for local residents and the staging of children's puppet shows. A bronze sculpture here depicts an event of 1797 when Old San Juan was under attack by British ships. In desperation, the residents of San Juan, led by their bishop, marched through the streets one night carrying lit torches and praying for their safety. The British apparently mistook this parade of lights for Spanish reinforcements and retreated from the harbor. Opposite the Plazuela de la Rogativa is the Museo Felisa Rincon de Gautier (the former home of a popular mayor) and behind it the Museo del Nino (Children's Museum).

North of Plazuela de la Rogativa you will come to a fork in the road. On the left is Casa Rosada (Pink House) which was built in 1812 for the Spanish army. To the right an upper road leads past a plant-decked wall to a doorway from which steps lead into the lovely gardens of **9 Casa Blanca (White House)**. Built in 1521 as the city's original fortress, this is the oldest Spanish colonial building in Old San Juan and has been modified over the years. It was a gift from Spain's monarch to Ponce de Leon for his settling of Puerto Rico. Ponce de Leon died the year the original wooden house was built, but his family resided there until 1779, when it was sold to the Spanish government. Following the Spanish-American war in 1898, the Commander of the U.S. Army lived at Casa Blanca until 1967. It was declared a National Historic Monument in 1968. Recently restored and furnished with authentic 16th- and 17th-century pieces, the mansion now contains two museums – the Juan Ponce de Leon Museum and the Taino Indian Ethno-Historic

(Above) A cruise ship approaches San Juan Harbor. (Bottom)
Visitors approach El Morro from its landward side.

Museum. They are open Tuesday through Sunday, 9:00 a.m. to noon and 1:00 p.m. to 4:30 p.m.

Between Casa Blanca and the grounds of El Morro stand two impressive colonial buildings. Asilo de Beneficenica, its facade consisting of wrought-iron fencing and green shutters, contains the headquarters of the Institute of Puerto Rican Culture and several galleries which are open Wednesday through Sunday. The red-domed building beside it was built in the 1800s and now houses a school of fine arts.

One of the most popular attractions in Old San Juan is the dramatic fort of **10** **El Morro**, open daily from 9:00 a.m. to 5:00 p.m. Admission is free and a brochure map is available at the entrance. Administered by the National Park Service, El Morro's full name is Castillo de San Felipe del Morro or 'Castle St. Philip of the Headland'. The fort is reached by a long, straight path which leads across a broad grassy area called a glacis. This cleared land was smoothed and sloped by the Spanish so that attacking troops had no shelter from the fort's cannon fire. Beneath the ground are tunnels in which kegs of gunpowder were planted should enemy troops try to lay siege to the fort.

From this landward approach, the fort strikes a surprisingly low profile, so engineered to make it a small target for enemy troops approaching by land. This was achieved by a dry moat which was dug along its length so the main wall could be sunk into the ground, yet still present a formidable height for scaling. The ocean side of the fort, in contrast to the landward side, consists of six tiers of batteries that loom above the water, protecting the fort from sea attacks. The lowest gun platform, the Water Battery, is washed by ocean swells while the uppermost ramparts – the Ochoa and Austria Bastions – stand 145 feet high.

Inside the fort, its entrance guarded by a drawbridge, are storerooms, gun rooms, troop quarters, a chapel and prison. These all open onto a central courtyard beneath which are cisterns. Tunnels and stairways connect different parts of the fort, and a museum is located in one of the bombproof vaults.

The El Morro lighthouse, which took a direct hit during the Spanish-American War, stands on the fort's fifth level. First constructed in 1846, it has been replaced three times since then. A working lighthouse, it helps guide ships entering one of the Caribbean's busiest ports.

Returning to the city streets, the next historic site is **11 Ballaja Barracks** where Spanish troops and their families once lived. The Museum of the Americas is on its second floor. On the eastern side of the barracks is **12 Plaza del Quinto Centenario (Quincentennial Square)**, constructed for the 1992-93 celebration of the 500th Anniversary of the discovery of the New World. This multi-level square affords a sweeping vista of El Morro and, from its upper western level, a view of the **13 San Juan Cemetery**.

The steps of the square lead to **14 Plaza de San Jose** where a statue of Ponce de Leon stands outside San Jose

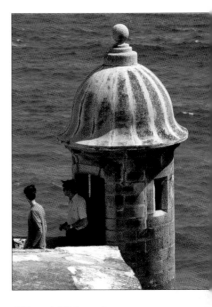

(Above) Visitors inspect one of Old San Juan's sentry boxes. (Below) Outdoor dining on Cristo Street, near Christ Chapel.

Church – the second oldest church in the Western Hemisphere, built in 1532, and the family church of Ponce de Leon's descendants. A beautiful example of Gothic architecture, the church was originally built as a chapel. Next to the church is the Convento de los Dominicos, containing the Institute of Puerto Rican Culture book and music store. Tucked in a corner townhouse of the plaza is the Museo de Pablo Casals, a small museum containing memorabilia of the famous cellist who spent his final years in San Juan. On the plaza's eastern side is Casa de las Contrafuertes (House of Buttresses), which contains the Museum of Latin American Prints and a Pharmacy Museum.

Cristo Street leads from Plaza de San Jose down the hill to **15 San Juan Cathedral**. Built in 1540 with early 19th-century modifications, the cathedral contains the marble tomb of Juan Ponce de Leon. Two blocks south of the Cathedral, at the foot of Cristo Street, you will see **16 Capilla de Cristo (Christ Chapel)** dedicated to the Christ of Miracles. It was built following a 1753 incident in which a youth was racing his horse down the hill at such a speed that rider and horse could not possibly stop before hurtling over the city wall. One legend is that both miraculously came to a halt just in time, another says the horse stopped but the boy flew over the wall, and a third version claims they both met their maker at this spot. Beside Capilla de Cristo is the small

Parque de las Palomas (Pigeon Park) with a fine view of the harbor. Lying opposite is Casa del Libro (House of Books), a small museum and library with a collection of rare, pre-16th century books.

(Top) Quincentennial Square.
(Left) San Juan Cathedral.

Plaza de Armas (Army Plaza) lies a block east of Cristo Street on San Francisco. Several government buildings surround the square, which was originally used for military drills, when built in the 16th century, and is now a social gathering place. City Hall, completed in 1789, stands on the plaza's north side and was designed to resemble its counterpart in Madrid; it contains a visitor information center. An administration building, at the west end of the plaza, and the provincial delegation building at its northwest corner, are fine examples of 19th-century neoclassical architecture. The century-old statues gracing the plaza represent the four seasons.

At the eastern end of Fortaleza Street, where it intersects with O'Donnel, you'll find **Plaza de Colon (Columbus Plaza)** and Teatro Tapia, a 19th-century theatre. A few blocks north is the entrance to **San Cristobal Fort**, open daily from 9:00 a.m. to 5:00 p.m. East of the historic quarter is the dome-roofed (20) Capitol Building.

Area Highlights

El Yunque National Forest – A 45-minute drive from San Juan, this 28,000-acre tropical forest is one of Puerto Rico's natural wonders. Set in the Luquillo Mountains and named for anvil-shaped El Yunque peak, the park contains 240 species of tropical trees, flowers and wildlife, including ferns, orchids, parrots and tiny tree frogs called coqui. Cool and often rainy, the park's verdant forest contains a dozen hiking trails and a lookout tower. Its highest peak is 3,532-foot-high El Toro. A popular restaurant at the entrance to the park is Las Vegas where both Puerto Rican and American cuisine is served.

Las Cabezas de San Juan Nature Reserve – This peninsula at the northeastern tip of the island is often referred to as El Faro, which is the name of the 1882 lighthouse located here. Beautifully restored, El Faro now houses a scientific research center with an observation deck added to the building's exterior. The reserve, situated on land acquired by the island's Conservation Trust, encompasses a dry forest, mangroves, lagoons, beaches, reefs and offshore cays. Guided tours, by reservation only, are conducted in safari buses and include informative walks along trails and boardwalks to observe the various species supported by this diverse habitat.

El Faro Lighthouse

CHAPTER EIGHT

U.S. VIRGIN ISLANDS

The natural allure of the Virgin Islands prompted Christopher Columbus to name them, in 1493, for the legend of Saint Ursula and her 11,000 virgin martyrs. But not even Columbus could have predicted their potential as a tourist mecca. As recently as 1917, when the United States bought these tropical treasures from Denmark for $25 million, it was not for possession of their beautiful beaches and fragrant flowers but to protect America's shipping interests. At the time, after decades of economic decline, the Danish West Indies were valued mainly for their strategic proximity to the recently opened Panama Canal.

A 100-island chain, the Virgin Islands are divided into the U.S. Virgin Islands and the British Virgin Islands. The U.S. Virgin Islands consist of three principal islands – St. Thomas, St. John and St. Croix – and dozens of smaller islands. They contain many sheltered harbors and lie directly in the path of easterly trade winds, which made them an ideal stop-over point for trading vessels in the days of sail.

The capital of the U.S. Virgin Islands, Charlotte Amalie (pronounced *ah-mahl-ya*), is located on the south coast of St. Thomas and overlooks one of the finest harbors in the Caribbean. The downtown's narrow streets and colonial buildings look much as they did in the mid-1800s when Charlotte Amalie was one of the most important trading centers of the West Indies, bustling with the comings and goings of naval ships, whalers, merchant traders and fishing boats. Import firms flourished here, their warehouses lining the waterfront, and wealthy merchants lived on the surrounding hillsides where they enjoyed the sea breezes and magnificent harbor views.

Haagensen House, a restored 1820s townhouse in Charlotte Amalie.

Their gleaming white houses, set among terraced gardens and coconut palms, were rectangular in shape with hipped roofs designed to collect rainwater along the gutters. Inside these homes were polished mahogany floors and comfortable furnishings which included rocking chairs and a large sideboard for holding carafes of chilled drinks. Block ice was imported from Boston and stored in wooden ice houses, the spaces of their triple-layered walls filled with sawdust as insulation from the hot sun. The bedrooms contained huge four-poster beds from which hung mosquito netting. As a fire-safety precaution, the kitchen was contained in a separate building, as were the servants' quarters. Mode of travel around the island, up steep winding roads, was by horseback. Life on St. Thomas, however, centered around the town. As the 19th-century Danish naturalist A. S. Orsted wrote, "If you know the town, you know the whole island."

The town began in 1672 when the Danish West India Company established the first permanent settlement here. Fort Christian was completed in 1680 and the port quickly became a leading slave-trading center of the West Indies. Denmark allowed the Brandenburg American Company to operate here for a while and the town's four busy taverns soon earned it the name 'Tap Hus' (Beer Hall). In 1691 the settlement was officially declared a town and named Charlotte Amalie, in honor of the Danish Queen who was consort to King Christian V.

In 1717 the neighboring island of St. John was claimed by Denmark and a fort built at Coral Harbor. Neither St. Thomas nor St. John were ideally suited for agriculture, however, so in 1733 Denmark purchased St. Croix from France. That same year a slave rebellion took place on St. John and the rebels held the island for six months before French soldiers from Martinique helped the Danes recapture it. St. Thomas, meanwhile, was declared a free port and it became a thriving trade center and exporter of contraband trade from the strictly regulated Spanish colonies. It also became a refuge for pirates who sold their cargo here and often hid in the hills overlooking the harbor. The legendary Blackbeard is said to have holed up in a watch tower with a spyglass and supply of rum.

The islands became a Danish royal colony in 1754 and remained

Fort Christian, St. Thomas

thus, apart from two British occupations – the first in 1801, when Denmark allied itself with Russia, and again from 1807 to 1815 when Denmark was allied with Napoleon. St. Croix was devoted to the cultivation and production of sugar, molasses and rum, its countryside covered with sugarcane fields and dotted with windmills. The island prospered and the port of Christiansted became Denmark's colonial capital. A town of well-planned streets and handsome buildings, it was protected by Fort Christiansvaern, built of yellow brick and dominating the harbor entrance.

In contrast to the orderly development of Christiansted was the haphazard growth of Charlotte Amalie. Between 1804 and 1832, six fires swept through the town's narrow streets. Building codes were eventually enforced that banned frame construction in the commercial area along the waterfront. These masonry warehouses were fitted with fire-

Fort Christiansvaern, St. Croix

proof roofs of tile or brick which were eventually replaced with corrugated metal due to hurricanes. Following emancipation in 1848, many freed slaves moved into town where existing residential lots were re-subdivided into smaller ones.

By the mid-1800s, the Danish West Indies had reached their zenith as colonial holdings. The price of sugar cane had dropped and, with steamships replacing sailing ships, St. Thomas was losing its importance as a stop-over point. Then a labor insurrection on St. Croix in 1878 prompted the remaining shipping companies in Charlotte Amalie to shut down. However, the protected harbors of St. Thomas and St. John were still of military value, prompting the purchase of the Danish West Indies by the United States in 1917 to prevent their being used as a German submarine base. The U.S. Navy handled initial administration of the islands, and residents were granted U.S. citizenship in 1927. Local government was established in 1954, with a governor and senate locally elected.

During World War II, the U.S. military constructed a submarine base, airfield, roads and housing on St. Thomas. Tourism began to

St. Thomas Harbor, viewed from atop Paradise Point.

flourish following the war, especially after the closing of Cuba to American tourists. A total of 26,650 visitors arrived at St. Thomas by ship or by airplane in 1950. Today that annual number is approaching two million. The U.S. Virgin Island, have established themselves as America's vacation paradise and Charlotte Amalie is once again the busiest free port in the Caribbean.

St. Thomas

Charlotte Amalie is serviced by two cruise ship terminals, the main one being the West Indian Company Dock which is located on the east side of the harbor, about a mile and a half by road from downtown. The other cruise terminal at Crown Bay is about two miles west of downtown. When ships anchor in the harbor, their passengers are tendered ashore to Kings Wharf on the downtown waterfront. The passenger ferry dock, with regular departures to St. John, is at the west end of the harbor, across from Hassel Island which is a national park. St. Thomas is fully geared for visitors with many of the island's 50,000 residents employed in tourism-related industries. English is the official language

Complimentary shopping shuttles run between the main cruise pier and nearby Havensight Mall.

and the U.S. dollar is the legal tender. Long-distance calls can be direct dialed to the U.S. mainland, and overseas service to Europe is excellent. A post office is located on Main Street, west of the Grand Hotel.

GETTING AROUND

St. Thomas is only 13 miles long and four miles wide, so the island's beautiful beaches are easily reached by taxi. A number of car rental firms operate on the island. Keep in mind that the roads are narrow and winding, and traffic keeps to the left. The port itself is usually busy with car traffic, and is best explored on foot. Open-air shuttle buses run regularly between the main cruise dock and downtown ($3 per person).

Officially licensed taxis carry a dome light and the letters TP on their license plates. Their rates have been set by the Taxi Commission and approved by the Virgin Islands' Legislature. Some sample fares per passenger: main cruise dock to downtown – $3.00; Crown Bay Dock to

(Above) U.S. Post Office on Main Street. (Below) Magens Bay Beach.

downtown – \$4.00; Charlotte Amalie to: Magens Bay – \$6.00, Morningstar Beach – \$5.50, Red Hook ferry terminal (for ferry to St. John) – \$8.00. **Paradise Point Gondola**, located across the street from Havensight Mall, whisks visitors up the mountainside for a sweeping view of the harbor. The complex contains a spacious sun deck, a restaurant/bar with umbrella tables, and a handful of gift shops.

Shopping – The Caribbean is famous for its duty-free shopping, and most famous of all is St. Thomas, where American visitors to the U.S. Virgin Islands can take advantage of a \$1,200-per-person duty-free allowance. The prices in St. Thomas are generally 20% to 50% less than stateside and there's no sales tax. Imported liquor, jewelry, china, crystal, designer leather goods, watches and other items are all offered at substantial savings. Dozens of duty-free stores are housed in restored warehouses of the town's historic section, the shopping area concentrated along Main Street, the waterfront and the narrow, palm-shaded alleyways and pedestrian malls that connect these two busy streets. Additional duty-free shops, including branches of downtown retailers, are located at Havensight Mall beside the main cruise dock. The gift shop at Fort Christian sells locally made crafts including hand-carved mahogany rocking chairs, made to order.

Dining – For a taste of authentic Caribbean fare in a casual setting, try The Jamaican Ackee Tree & Bar, popular with local business people at lunch time and conveniently located across the street from Havensight Mall. Downtown, the Back Street (one block up from Main Street) is a good place to momentarily escape the crowds with a lunch stop at a number of good restaurants, including Cuzzin's at the corner of Back Street and Raadets Gade.

Beaches – Magens Bay, on the north coast, has been rated by National Geographic as one of the ten most beautiful beaches in the world. Admission is \$3.00 and change facilities are available.

Other recommended beaches include Morningstar Beach and Limetree Beach southeast of Charlotte Amalie. On the northeast side of the island are Sapphire Beach and Coki Beach – good for snorkeling and adjacent to Coral World where change facilities are available.

Dive & Snorkel Sites – Off the island's south coast lie Cow and Calf Rocks, named for two humpback whales once seen at this dive site, which contains dramatic caves, archways and cliff overhangs from 25 feet. The Pinnacle (French Cap), about a mile offshore, consists of two stone pillars atop a seamount at 45 feet. Two miles out, at Buck Island, a World War I freighter is resting in 40 feet. Atlantis Submarine has a dive site at Buck Island, taxiing passengers by boat to the submarine which submerges to depths of 90 feet, providing views of the corals and fishes. On the north coast, the calm waters off Coki Beach are excellent for snorkeling and beach dives, with a dive shop right on the beach. Lying opposite is Thatch Cay, another popular diving area.

Golf – Mahogany Run on the north coast is an 18-hole Fazio-designed championship course. Its famous 'Devil's Triangle' consists of three dramatic holes overlooking the Atlantic.

DOWNTOWN CHARLOTTE AMALIE

The **1 Legislative Building**, a two-storey green building of Italian Renaissance design, is the seat of the U.S. Virgin Islands Senate. Built in 1874 as barracks for the Danish police, it was later used as housing for U.S. Marines Corps. It's open to visitors Monday through Friday.

2 Fort Christian, built of red brick and rubble, is the oldest standing structure on St. Thomas. It was begun about 1666, completed in 1680 and altered in 1874 when the watch tower was removed and its north facade, with a crenelated clock tower, was added. The fort was later used as a jail, and is now a museum and National Historic Landmark. **3 Emancipation Garden**, the site of many official ceremonies, commemorates the freeing of slaves in 1848 and contains a bust of Danish King Christian and a small replica Liberty Bell. A tourist information office *i* is located nearby at the corner of Tolbod Gade and Veterans Drive, opposite which is the open-air Vendors Market. The **4 Grand Hotel**, originally called the Commercial Hotel & Coffee House, is a Greek Revival structure which occupied an entire block when built in 1840. Formerly three storeys tall, the top floor was presumably damaged by a hurricane sometime after 1896. The former hotel now houses a jewelry studio featuring designs by local artisans.

The **5 Frederick Lutheran Church**, the official church of the Danish West Indies, was established in 1666 with worship services held in the homes of planters and soldiers, and then at Christensfort. The present building was built in 1793, gutted by fire in 1826 and damaged by a hurricane in 1870, after which the tower was added.

6 Government House, completed in 1865, is a three-storey

the U.S. Virgin Islands

(Above) Government House.
(Left) Havensight Mall.
(Below) A shopping street in downtown Charlotte Amalie.

(Above) Legislative Building. (Right) Frederick Lutheran Church (Below) Charlotte Amalie's harbor.

masonry building built in the neo-classical design. Its brick walls are painted white, as are the cast-iron verandahs that run the length of the first two storeys. Government offices are located here, including the Governor's Executive Offices. The Governor's official residence is the former Danish Consulate, an imposing two-storey mansion atop Denmark Hill. Two sets of stairs, the westerly one called **7 The 99 Steps**, lead up the hillside behind Government House, past **8 Haagensen House**, a restored 1820s townhouse which is now a museum. Standing atop Government Hill is **9 Skytsborg** (Blackbeard's Castle), a five-storey conical tower constructed of rubble masonry by the Danish in 1678, with later changes. Now part of a hotel, the stone watch tower is said to have been used by the infamous pirate Blackbeard. **10 Hotel 1829** (formerly Lavalette House) was built as a residence for a French sea captain and now houses one of Charlotte Amalie's finest restaurants. **11 St. Thomas Reformed Church**, constructed in 1846, is a good example of Greek Revival building. **12 Beracha Veshalom U'gemilut Hasidim**, built of cut stone and brick in 1833, is the second-oldest synagogue in the Western Hemisphere.

The **13 Camille Pissaro Building** is where the famous impressionist painter lived above the family store in the 1840s. Born in a small Jewish community of Charlotte Amalie in 1830, Pissaro left St. Thomas in 1855 to study art in Paris. He became a teacher and friend of Gauguin and Cezanne, and died near Paris at the age of 73. The Pissaro building now houses the Tropicana Perfume shop and upstairs, above an inner courtyard entered off Main Street, is an art gallery.

14 Market Square was, in 1946, officially named Rothschild Francis Square to honor the public service of this champion of civil rights and liberties. The square has long been a central meeting place where fresh produce, fish and spices are sold, with French farmers from the north side of the island bringing their fruits and vegetables to town by donkey. In the early 1900s, an open-air iron shed called the Bungalow was erected and the regular female vendors, called 'Market Women', each had their own spot under the shade of the bungalow – to the exclusion of any male vendors. The annual Carnival Food Fair is held here each April.

AREA ATTRACTIONS

West of Downtown – **Frenchtown**, founded as a fishing village by French Huguenots from St. Barts, lies west of Charlotte Amalie on the way to the Crown Bay cruise pier. Its restaurants and bars now create a lively night scene. The University of the Virgin Islands was founded in 1963 and the campus contains the Reichhold Center for the Arts where concerts and other events are held in its open-air amphitheatre.

East End – Coral World at Coki Point is a popular attraction with its underwater observatory, natural reef exhibit, aquarium and semi-submarine rides along a coral reef. Sharks, moray eels, stingrays and pink flamingos are some of the exotic creatures that can be seen here. Tillet Gardens, on the way to Coral World, is the site of an historic Danish cattle farm and a gallery featuring local arts and crafts.

North of Town – Drake's Seat, said to be used by Francis Drake as a lookout for Spanish ships while his fleet lay concealed in Magens Bay, offers breathtaking views of Magens Bay and the British Virgin Islands. **Estate St. Peter Great House & Botanical Gardens**, a former plantation estate, has been developed into a beautiful botanical garden with breathtaking ocean views from its mountainside location. The elegant, open-plan house is wrapped with white latticework and broad decks from which visitors can gaze at more than twenty offshore islands. Local art is on display and outside, on the lushly landscaped grounds, are more than 500 varieties of plants and trees.

A drive to **Mountain Top**, highest viewing point on the island, provides stunning views of St. John, the British Virgin Islands and Charlotte Amalie Harbor. Refreshments served here include the original banana daiquiri. The attractive complex includes Caribbean shops, an aviary and aquarium.

St. John

In contrast to bustling Charlotte Amalie, a shopper's paradise, is the peaceful island of St. John, a nature lover's paradise. Lush and mountainous, St. John is indented by numerous bays at the head of which lie some of the world's most beautiful beaches. The island is also a botanist's delight with its proliferation of tropical plants and flowers.

When A. S. Orsted, discoverer of plankton, travelled by barkentine to the Danish West Indies in 1845, he was so captivated by the plant life he found that he changed his field of study from zoology to botany. Born of an illustrious Danish family, Orsted was especially besotted with St. John where uncultivated slopes presented him with an array of indigenous plant species, including bamboo, guava berry, century plant and coconut palms. A century later, in the early '50s, Laurance Rockefeller paid St. John a visit. A member of the wealthy American family famous for its philanthropy, he too arrived by sailboat and he too was so impressed with the serene and natural beauty of the island that he purchased about two thirds of it, which he donated to the United States federal government for the establishment of the Virgin Islands National Park in 1956. The park has expanded since its inception and now covers about three-quarters of the island.

Residents of St. John, who number about 3,000, call their island 'Love City' and most visitors do fall in love with this protected paradise. Its highest point is Bordeaux Mountain at 1,277 feet, and the island's steep slopes provide dramatic vistas of distant islands and nearby cays where a deep blue sea fades to pale aquamarine at the head of beach-lined bays.

GETTING AROUND

Cruise ships stopping at St. Thomas usually offer shore excursions to nearby St. John. Independent travellers can take one of the passenger ferries that connect St. John with St. Thomas, and these depart regularly from both Charlotte Amalie and Red Hook on St. Thomas for Cruz Bay on St. John. The Red Hook/Cruz Bay ferry leaves every hour on the hour both ways, is a 20-minute ride and costs $3.00 one way. The Charlotte Amalie/Cruz Bay ferry ride takes 45 minutes, costs $7.00 one way, and leaves Charlotte Amalie at one- to two-hour intervals throughout the day.

Cruz Bay is the main town on the island and open-air safari buses await here to transport visitors around the island. A Visitors Center at Cruz Bay provides information on the Park – its beaches, trails and activities, including organized hikes and historic bus tours.

Beaches – Inviting beaches line St. John's northwest coast, including the sugary white sands and clear turquoise waters of Trunk Bay – considered one the most beautiful beaches in the world. Excellent for swimming, Trunk Bay also has an underwater snorkel trail. On shore are shaded picnic areas and a snack bar. Cinnamon Bay has open-air dining and a watersports center that rents snorkel gear and beach chairs. Sailing and windsurfing can also be enjoyed here, as well as National Park interpretive programs. Other lovely beaches include those at Hawksnest Bay and Caneel Bay, where a resort owned by Laurance Rockefeller is located.

Dive & Snorkel Sites – Cinnamon Bay has good snorkeling and a watersports center that rents snorkel gear. Trunk Bay has an underwater snorkeling trail with red, white and blue markers to guide snorkelers and identify the coral and marine life. Caneel Bay is recommended for the chance to view stingrays, green turtles, cushion sea stars, pipes-of-pan sponges and sargent majors. Popular dive sites are Steven's Cay, Carval Rock and Congo Cay.

Shopping – Cruz Bay is where most of the island shops are located, offering both duty-free goods and local arts and crafts. Mongoose Junction, across from the National Park Dock, is a pleasant shopping complex built of Caribbean stone. Its multi-level design of shaded terraces and tropical foliage contains fine shops, galleries and open-air restaurants.

Island Attractions – Points of interest on the island include the Annaberg Sugar Mill ruins, beautifully situated on the north side of the island overlooking Sir Francis Drake Passage. Also of note are the prehistoric petroglyphs at Reef Bay.

(Opposite, top) The ruins of Annaberg Sugar Mill.
(Opposite, bottom) Cruz Bay is the main port on St. John.
(Right) St. John's Trunk Bay is undoubtedly one of the world's most beautiful beaches, ideal for swimming and snorkeling.

St. Croix

Hams Bluff

Davis Bay

Cane Bay

Salt River Bay

Buck Island

Green Cay

Buck Island Channel

Grapetree Bay

Sprat Hall Beach

Rainbow Beach

CARAMBOLA GOLF COURSE

Botanical Gardens

Frederiksted

Centerline Rd.

Cruzan Rum

Whim Distillery

Plantation

Cormorant Beach

Mini-cruiseship pier

Protestant Cay

Buccaneer Beach

Christiansted

Great Pond Bay

Cruise Pier

Long Pt

Sandy Point

Caribbean Sea

Protestant Cay

0   2   4
Miles

©OCEANCRUISEGUIDES

St. Croix

St. Croix (pronounced Croy) was first settled by people who had migrated along the Lesser Antilles from South America. By the 4th century AD they had established a village at Salt River Bay on the island's north coast and eventually constructed the only ceremonial plaza/ball court discovered to date in the Lesser Antilles. When Columbus arrived at Salt River Bay in 1493, on his second voyage to the Caribbean, the boat party he sent ashore was met by a canoe filled with Carib warriors. A skirmish took place that resulted in the death of two Caribs and one Spaniard – the first fatal confrontation between Europeans and New World natives. Columbus called the island Santa Cruz (Holy Cross) but it was the English and Dutch who first colonized St. Croix, followed by the French who sold the island to Denmark in 1733. In the late 1700s and early 1800s, St. Croix was one of the wealthiest sugar islands in the West Indies and Christiansted's waterfront was busy with ox-drawn carts driven by slaves and laden with barrels of sugar and molasses to be loaded onto waiting ships.

In 1803, Peter von Scholten arrived as a young officer and rose through the ranks to become Governor-General of the Danish West Indies in 1827. Born of an aristocratic family (his father served as Commandant of St. Thomas in the early 1800s), von Scholten governed the colony with military efficiency. His companion Anna Heegaard was a woman of color, and in 1848 von Scholten issued a decree abolishing slavery. Denmark's king confirmed the emancipation decree but von Scholten paid dearly for his benevolence, for he was dismissed from office and stripped of his pension. Returning to Denmark, he died a few years later.

Before Peter von Scholten's arrival in the West Indies, a distinct class of Free Blacks had already begun to escape slavery on St. Croix. With money saved selling produce at the local market, they would buy their freedom; others earned it with faithful service. In a designated section of town, established in 1747 and called Neger Gotted (Free Gut), they built their own houses and worked as merchants, tradesmen and fishermen. In 1834 the Free Blacks gained full equality. As for Peter von Scholten, he is today honored throughout the U.S. Virgin Islands.

GETTING AROUND

St. Croix, about 20 miles long and seven miles wide, is the largest of the U.S. Virgin Islands and its topography is fairly flat. Most ships dock at Frederiksted at the west end of the island; a small cruise ship dock is located at Chistiansted. Centerline Road, a four-lane highway that runs the length of the island, connects the two ports with taxi vans running regular shuttles ($14 per person round trip). A three-hour island tour by taxi costs $20-25 per person. Several rental car companies are located in Frederiksted, and the roads on St. Croix are well maintained.

(Above) A Buck Island beach. (Below) The cruise pier at Frederiksted.

Shopping – The stores on St. Croix offer both duty-free goods and local crafts, but on a much smaller scale than St. Thomas. The largest selection of stores (and restaurants) is at Christiansted, where Queen Cross and Strand are the main shopping streets. In Frederiksted, most of the shops are located on Strand Street facing the harbor.

Beaches – Lovely beaches abound on St. Croix and those closest to Frederiksted are Rainbow Beach ($6 round trip taxi fare from Frederiksted), Sprat Hall Beach ($7 round trip) and Sandy Point where the beach closes each spring when sea turtles come ashore to lay their eggs. Popular beaches near Christiansted include Buccaneer Beach, Cormorant Beach, and Protestant Cay which is a $3 ferry ride from the Christiansted waterfront. Buck Island, famous for its coral reefs, also offers pristine beaches. Charter boats out of Christenstad provide access to this uninhabited islet once used as a goat pasture.

Dive & Snorkel Sites – St. Croix is a superb snorkel and dive destination, with its clear waters and extensive coral gardens. **Buck Island Reef National Monument**, a mile-long volcanic islet lying off St. Croix's northeast tip, is one of the most popular underwater sites in the Virgin Islands. First protected in 1948 and proclaimed a national monument in 1961, it encompasses 176 acres of land, 704 acres of water and a magnificent coral reef system. Numerous endangered species nest at Buck Island, including the brown pelican and the hawksbill, leatherback and green sea turtles. Much of this dry-forest island is surrounded by an elkhorn coral barrier reef that reaches 30 feet in height. The lagoon, formed by the barrier reef, contains clear calm water and large brain corals that nearly reach the surface. A snorkel trail with underwater interpretive signs lies off the east end of island. Good snorkeling can also be found at Green Cay and at Cane Bay. One of the island's most beautiful dive sites is the Old Frederiksted Pier where the marine life includes orange sea horses.

Golf – There are three golf courses on St. Croix. Closest to Frederiksted and one of the best in the Caribbean is the 18-hole course at Carambola Golf Club, designed by Robert Trent Jones. At the eastern end of the island is The Buccaneer Hotel's 18-hole course and a 9-hole course called The Reef.

Christiansted

Christiansted is one of the Caribbean's best-preserved colonial ports and is ideally suited to a self-guided walking tour. The town's historic buildings are located on or near the waterfront and are administered by the National Park Service. Their architectural designs reflect the West Indian neo-classical style that dominated the Danish islands during their golden age of colonial wealth. A Visitors Bureau **i** is located in the Scale House, built in 1856 to replace a wooden structure, in which imports were inspected and sugar was weighed prior to export.

The gift shop at the entrance to **1 Fort Christiansvaern** contains an official map and guide to the historic area. There is a small admission fee to enter the fort, which was completed in 1749, with later additions in 1835-41. Built of yellow brick brought to the island as ship's ballast, this carefully preserved fort once protected the town from pirates and slave uprisings. Under the governorship of Peter von Scholten from 1827 to 1848, Christiansvaern was well manned with a

Government House is a showcase of Danish colonial architecture.

(Above) Fort Christiansvaern is now a National Historic Site, and the former Scale House (right) is a Visitors Bureau.

garrison of 215 officers and men, and Free Blacks serving in the fire corps. In 1840 the **2** **Customs House** was constructed and the town's post office was located upstairs. The **3** **Danish West India & Guinea Company Warehouse** was built in 1749 to house offices and storerooms, its courtyard used for auctioning slaves.

On the waterfront near the fort is a dock used by the passenger ferry that runs between Christiansted and **Protestant Cay**, the location of a hotel and beach. The small island was formerly a burial ground for Protestants barred from the Catholic cemetery. The ferry ride costs $3 for adults and $1 for children.

A short walk from Christiansted's waterfront is the **4** **Steeple Building**, St. Croix's first Lutheran Church, completed in 1796. In 1831 the congregation moved to the **5** **Lutheran Church** on King Street which had been built in 1744 as the Dutch Reformed Church. The Church's steeple was added by the Lutherans.

6 **Government House** comprises two palatial townhouses that were built in the mid-1700s and connected in the 1830s. Usually open to the public, the second-floor reception hall has been restored to its 1840s appearance.

Frederiksted

Frederiksted's shaded streets and arcaded sidewalks contain a number of historic buildings, many of them rebuilt in the Victorian ginger-bread style following the 1878 labor riots during which much of the town was burned. **1** St. Patrick's Catholic Church, **2** Holy Trinity Lutheran Church and **3** St. Paul's Anglican Church were all begun in the 1840s. **4** Victoria House and the **5** Customs House were built in 1803. **6** Fort Frederick, overlooking the local beach, was begun in 1752. Now a museum, it has been restored to its 1820s appearance.

ISLAND ATTRACTIONS

Whim Plantation Museum, featured in most island tours, is located two miles east of Frederiksted on Centerline Road. This sugar planta-tion estate consists of an elegant, 18th-century great house built of stone and elegantly furnished with colonial antiques. Other buildings on the grounds include a cookhouse, sugar mill and gift shop that sells West Indian crafts and prints. Tours run every half hour, Monday through Saturday.

Other island attractions include the Cruzan Rum Distillery, with tours and a tasting bar; St. George Botanical Gardens, with self-guided tours of this 17-acre park; and the restored ruins of Estate Mount Washington Plantation. Oil refining has replaced sugar production on St. Croix, and just outside of Christiansted is the sprawling Hess Oil Refinery – one of the largest in the world.

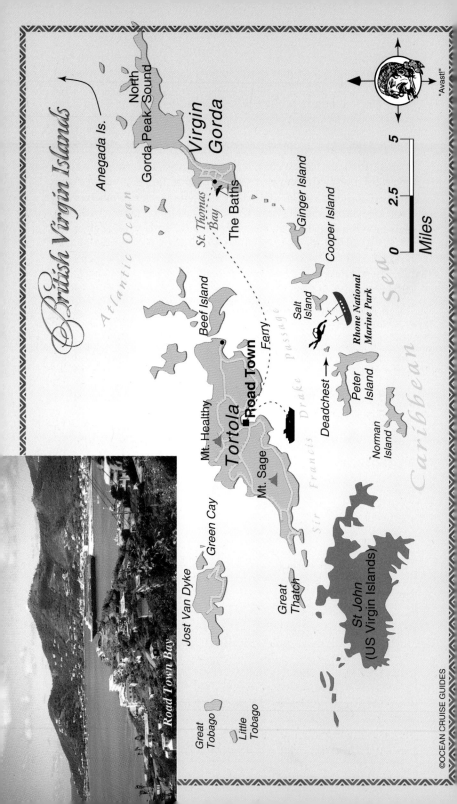

British Virgin Islands

Anegada Is.

Atlantic Ocean

North
Gorda Peak Sound

Virgin Gorda

St. Thomas Bay

The Baths

Ginger Island

Cooper Island

Beef Island

Road Town

Ferry

Tortola

Mt. Healthy

Mt. Sage

Salt Island

Rhone National
Marine Park

Drake Passage

Deadchest →

Peter Island

Norman Island

Sir Francis

Green Cay

Jost Van Dyke

Great Thatch

St John
(US Virgin Islands)

Caribbean Sea

Great Tobago

Little Tobago

Road Town Bay

0	2.5	5

Miles

"Avast!"

©OCEAN CRUISE GUIDES

CHAPTER NINE

BRITISH VIRGIN ISLANDS

Christopher Columbus named the Virgin Islands in 1493, but Francis Drake set the tone a century later when he sailed along the channel now bearing his name. Sir Francis Drake Channel runs through the middle of the British Virgin Islands, commonly called the B.V.I., which are a labyrinth of islands and channels rich in pirate lore and legend. The island of **Jost Van Dyke**, popular with yachtsmen who frequent famous Foxy's Tamarind Bar, was named for a Dutch pirate. **Norman Island** was possibly the inspired setting for Robert Louis Stevenson's Treasure Island, an adventure story published in 1883 about a search for Captain Kidd's buried treasure. And **Peter Island** is associated with the pirate Blackbeard who is said to have anchored in Deadman's Bay after a successful raid. While splitting the booty, an argument ensued and Blackbeard marooned 15 of his men on the nearby island of Dead Chest with a bottle of rum and their sea chests. The following lyric is attributed to this incident: Fifteen men on dead men's chest, Yo ho ho and a bottle of rum!

The B.V.I., with their steady breezes and pristine anchorages, have long been a mariner's mecca. They were ideal for buccaneers who hid in secluded coves while fleeing enemy ships, and today they attract island-hopping yachtsmen from around the world. Large charter fleets are moored at marinas on the main islands of **Tortola** and **Virgin Gorda,** and boat bunks account for nearly half the total tourist beds in the B.V.I. There are no high-rise hotels in this chain of 30-plus islands, just plenty of white beaches and blue bays dotted with sailboats.

Inhabited by Taino Indians when discovered by Columbus, the B.V.I. were first colonized by the Dutch in 1648, then annexed by Britain in 1672. Plantations were established during the 18th century's sugar boom and fortifications were erected at strategic points to protect the islands from seaborne attacks. In the hills surrounding **Road Town** are the ruins of forts built by the Royal Engineers in 1794 – Fort George on Fort Hill and Fort Charlotte on Harrigan's Hill. Another fort west of Road Town at Pockwood Pond, called the Dungeon, contains a set of stairs leading to an underground cell.

Other vestiges from colonial times include the remains of a stone windmill in Mount Healthy National Park, and a round tower at Fort Recovery on Tortola's West End – believed to be built by Tortola's earliest Dutch settlers. Salt Island contains evaporation ponds that are still panned for salt just as they were two centuries ago, and at the south end

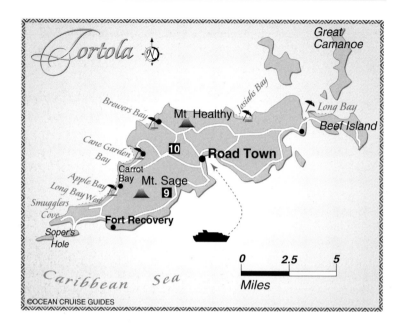

of Virgin Gorda is an abandoned copper mine worked by Cornish miners between 1838 and 1867 – the year in which the HMS Rhone sank off Salt Island during a hurricane. This wreck is now one of the Caribbean's most popular dive sites and the centerpiece of Rhone National Marine Park.

The first national parks were established in the 1960s, when the Rockefellers gave three sites to the B.V.I. government: Devil's Bay and Spring Bay on Virgin Gorda, and Sage Mountain on Tortola. Reforestation and the re-introduction of original vegetation in **Sage Mountain National Park** have returned this 92-acre parcel of land to its original habitat. At 1,780 feet, Sage Mountain is the highest point in all of the Virgin Islands. Views from its hiking trails are dramatic and, although the mountaintop receives only 100 inches of rain a year, its vegetation is similar to a rainforest with tree ferns and bromeliads thriving in the ocean mist that's carried upwards by the wind.

Other natural attractions include **The Baths** – beached granite boulders forming a series of pools and grottoes on Virgin Gorda. **Green Cay**, ringed with white sand beaches, is your classic 'desert isle' and has been featured in various commercials. The islands' marine life includes tropical fish, eagle rays and nurse sharks. In winter, humpback whales arrive in local waters to breed.

The B.V.I. are volcanic in origin, except for the low-lying coral and limestone atoll of **Anegada** which lies about 15 miles to the northwest. Its highest point is 28 feet above sea level, and the island is ringed with extensive beaches and reefs that have claimed more than 300 ships.

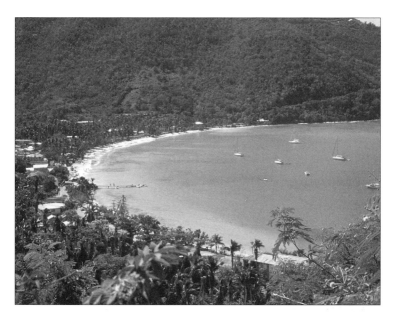

Cane Garden Bay is one of many beautiful beaches on Tortola.

Animals outnumber people on this island of about 200 residents. Wild goats, donkeys and iguanas all live here, as does a colony of flamingos for which a bird sanctuary has been established at one of the island's salt ponds. This protected nesting ground is also used by herons, ospreys and terns.

Piracy and plantations have been replaced with tourism and offshore banking as the major industries in the B.V.I. A politically stable British crown colony, the territory is ruled by a governor who is appointed by the Crown and by an elected chief minister and government. Tourism was introduced to the islands in the mid-1960s when Laurance Rockefeller built a resort at Little Dix Bay on Virgin Gorda. This was followed by the opening of The Moorings in 1969, which marked the beginning of the local charter yacht business. The future development of tourism is being planned carefully to preserve the islands' natural beauty.

Road Town, Tortola

Tortola, named for the turtle dove, is the largest island of the B.V.I. chain. Most of the island's 17,000 inhabitants live in Road Town, the colony's capital, administrative center and main harbor. The cruise pier is located at the north end of town on Wickhams Cay. Nearby is the **ℹ Tourist Information Office** and the Cable & Wireless Public Office, on Waterfront Drive near Nibbs Road, which sells Caribbean phone cards and other long-distance services. Road Town is a charming port of shuttered wooden houses, brightly painted and trimmed with fretwork.

GETTING AROUND

The B.V.I. Taxi Association is located at Wickhams Cay and its fleet includes open-air safari buses and air-conditioned vans. Rates are unmetered and some sample fares are: Road Town to Cane Garden Bay, $15 for 1-3 passengers, $20 for 4 passengers; Two-Hour Island Tour, $45 for 1-3 passengers, $60 for 4 passengers. A Budget Rent-A-Car office is located in the **1** Mill Mall near the pier.

Passenger ferries connect Tortola with Virgin Gorda, Peter Island and Jost Van Dyke. The ferry dock is opposite the town center and ferries depart two or three times daily. The 1/2 hour ride from Road Town to Virgin Gorda is about $10 one way. For an up-to-date schedule, visit the Tourist Information Office.

Shopping & Dining – The **2** **open-air market** on Wickhams Cay includes the B.V.I. House of Crafts where locally made tropical clothing and souvenirs can be bought. Main and Waterfront are the primary shopping streets. Main used to run along the waterfront before a land fill expanded the town site. Its quaint shops sell Caribbean arts and crafts, spices and preserves, wines and spirits, and cotton clothing.

A taste of colonial Britian can be enjoyed in Road Town's pubs and famous Pusser's Co. Store.

Pusser's Co. Store is located on Waterfront Drive and its famous Royal Navy Rum is sold here along with unique nautical gifts and sports clothing. Adjoining the store is Pusser's Pub where an English-style pub lunch can be enjoyed. Next door is Tavern in the Town, another British-style pub that's open for lunch. The North Shore Shell Museum at Carrot Bay is a good place to buy shell art and other local crafts.

Beaches – Tortola's best beaches are concentrated on the northwest coastline. **Cane Garden Bay** is a beautiful, crescent-shaped beach with watersports, restaurants and bars. To the south is **Long Bay**, a mile-long stretch of white sand. **Apple Bay** is the 'surfing beach' and location of Bomba's Shack, a popular beach bar. **Brewers Bay** has two beach bars and good snorkeling, as does **Smugglers Cove**, a small sandy beach at the northwest end of the island. **Josiahs Bay** is a dramatic beach on the north shore, and **Long Bay** on Beef Island offers seclusion and sheltered waters.

Dive & Snorkel Sites – There are two dozen established dive sites in the B.V.I.'s sheltered waters, a number of which can be enjoyed by snorkelers. **Rhone National Marine Park** was established to preserve the wreck of the *Rhone*, a 310-foot mail ship that went down in a hurricane off Salt Island in 1867 (see map on page 224). Its broken hull, encrusted in coral, lies 20 to 80 feet beneath the water's surface and is frequented by schools of tropical fish such as the queen angelfish and the parrotfish. Underwater footage in the movie *The Deep* was filmed at this famous wreck, which can be viewed by

Sailing yachts lie at anchor in idyllic Cane Garden Bay, Tortola.

snorkelers. Blonde Rock – a pinnacle between Salt Island and Dead Chest – has ledges that descend from 15 to 60 feet, the top one crowned with fire coral. Dead Chest Island is also part of the park and Painted Walls, off the island's southern point, consists of four long gullies covered with corals and sponges in depths of 20 to 30 feet.

Good snorkeling on Tortola can be had at Smugglers Cove on the island's western tip and at Brewers Bay on its north coast. On Virgin Gorda, The Baths and Spring Bay are excellent snorkeling sites. The Caves on Norman Island are ideal for snorkeling, as is nearby Angelfish Reef where divers will find excellent visibility at 90 feet. Santa Monica Rock, a pinnacle about a mile south of the island, is a good spot to see eagle rays and other open-ocean fish in depths of 10 to 100 feet.

LOCAL ATTRACTIONS

Most of Road Town's historic sites are on Main Street. The **3 Virgin Islands Folk Museum**, housed in a traditional West Indian building, contains artifacts from the islands' Taino and plantation eras, as well as items from the wreck of the *Rhone*. A few doors down from the museum is the **4 Post Office**, built in 1866 with stone walls and Gothic arches. Across the street is **5 Sir Olva George's Plaza**, a shady spot that once served as a busy market place.

Farther north on Main is **6 Britannic Hall**, an interesting structure perched atop a massive boulder, which houses a private business. Also on Main are St. George's Anglican Church, rebuilt following the hurricane of 1819, and the Methodist Church, built after the hurricane of 1924. In between the two churches is HM Prison where the infamous

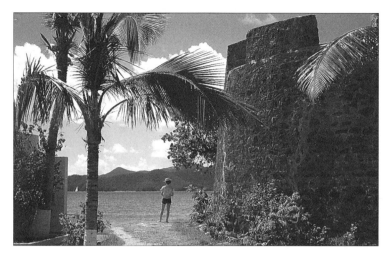

(Above) A 17th-century round tower, built by early Dutch settlers, still stands at Fort Recovery. (Below) Main Street, Road Town.

William Arthur Hodge was executed for murdering a slave. The Sunday Morning Well on Upper Main Street is marked with a plaque commemorating it as the site where the Proclamation of Emancipation was read in 1834.

The **7** **J.R. O'Neal Botanic Gardens**, created by the B.V.I. National Parks Trust, are located northwest of the town center and contain nearly three acres of indigenous and exotic tropical plants. Landscaped paths lead past flowering hibiscus and bougainvillea, a lily pond and a waterfall.

8 **Government House**, overlooking Road Harbor, is south of the ferry docks on Waterfront Drive. A bit further along is **Queen Elizabeth Park**. Part of the B.V.I. national park system, this small waterfront park contains shrubs, flowers and rows of white cedars.

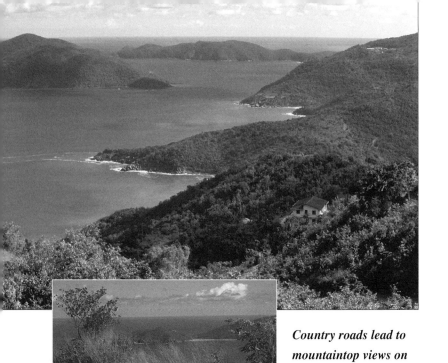

Country roads lead to mountaintop views on the pastoral island of Tortola.

ISLAND ATTRACTIONS (SEE MAP ON PAGE 226)

The architect William Thornton, who designed the Capitol in Washington, was born on Tortola in 1759. He trained as a physician in London and practised medicine on Tortola before emigrating to the United States in 1787. The ruins of his family plantation estate can be seen at **9 Pleasant Valley**.

The **10 Briercliffe-Davis Observatory**, established in 1984 atop Tortola's mountain ridge, provides panoramic views of the B.V.I. and U.S. Virgin Islands. Located along Ridge Road, a half-mile north of the Cane Garden Bay turn-off, it is part of a complex containing the Skyworld restaurant and bar, and a gift shop selling local artwork.

Callwood Rum Distillery at Cane Garden Bay is housed in a stone building from the plantation era. Copper boiling vats, an old still and a cane crusher remain in use, and bottles of Arundel Rum line the shelves.

Sopers Hole at the West End is where Dutch settlers first landed in 1648. A sheltered harbor with several restaurants and shops, it is today a major anchorage and location of Tortola's main ferry terminal.

Beef Island, at the eastern end of Tortola, used to be a buccaneer hang-out and is now the location of the B.V.I.'s international airport. Beef Island is connected to Tortola by the Territory's only toll bridge – a one-lane structure dedicated by Queen Elizabeth in 1966.

Virgin Gorda

Virgin Gorda (the fat virgin), was named by Columbus who may have anchored off the island in 1493. Today about 2,500 people live on the island, which consists of three distinct sections.

The northern third rings **North Sound**, a beautiful blue lagoon of protected coral reefs and white beaches. Yachts anchor here and the shore facilities include a number of resorts, dive operators and the famous Bitter End Yacht Club. The island's middle section is mountainous and crowned by **Gorda Peak** which, at 1,370 feet, rises in the middle of Gorda Peak National Park.

The southern third of the island is flat, its western shore lined with lovely beaches. The ferry from Road Town pulls into **St. Thomas Bay**, just north of the Yacht Harbor which is home to luxury yachts and charter fleets, as well as a shopping center which includes a dive shop, bar and restaurant. South of here is Little Fort National Park where a wildlife sanctuary and ruins of a Spanish fortress are located.

Further south is Virgin Gorda's famous landmark – **The Baths**. The beach here is dominated by unique rock formations containing sea caves and shallow pools of seawater connected by passageways. Geologists remain puzzled by the origin of these enormous granite boulders which could be the result of glacial action.

Virgin Gorda's most popular beaches, for both swimming and snorkeling, are The Baths and neighboring Spring Bay. Trunk Bay, a wide sandy beach, can be reached by a rough path from Spring Bay.

Giant boulders dot the sands of The Baths on Virgin Gorda.

CHAPTER TEN

ST. MAARTEN / ST. MARTIN

It's been called the island with a split personality, but both sides are friendly. The Netherlands and France have peacefully shared this semi- arid island since 1648 when a border was established dividing it in two. Variations of a popular legend explain why the French ended up with 20 square miles versus the Dutch share of 17 square miles. A foot race, so the story goes, was held between a Frenchman and a Dutchman, who walked in opposite directions around the shoreline until they met again and a line was drawn across the island between these two points. The Frenchman was drinking either wine or brandy, while the Dutchman was indulging in gin or perhaps beer. One version of the legend has the Frenchman abstaining, but this seems unlikely. Whatever their respective choices of beverage, the Frenchman walked faster than the Dutchman. Some say the critical factor was not the drink but the fetching French maiden deployed to delay the Dutchman.

Foot races aside, the Dutch were no doubt happy with their share of the island because the Great Salt Pond, with its high-quality salt, was what they wanted and what they got. The island was called Sualouiga (Salt Land) by the island's original inhabitants, the Arawaks. A seafaring people from South America, their ancient artifacts are still being discovered by local archaeologists. Columbus was the first European to sight and name the island in 1493, although some historians believe it was another island he saw.

The Spanish were seeking gold and they paid St. Maarten little attention. The Dutch and French, however, saw great worth in the island's salt flats. The Dutch West India Company needed a secure source of salt for preserving fish and in the mid-1620s some Dutch traders landed on St. Maarten's south shore. About the same time, a handful of French families settled on the island's north side and a peaceful co-existence prevailed until a Spanish fleet landed 1,300 soldiers on the island in 1633. The Dutch company's 80-man garrison was quickly overcome and a force of Spanish soldiers held the island for the next 15 years, fending off a Dutch attack in 1644 led by Curacao governor Peter Stuyvesant, who lost a leg in the battle and soon afterwards was appointed governor of New Amsterdam (later New York City).

In 1648, Spain withdrew and the remaining Dutch and French inhabitants returned to their peaceful co-existence, dividing the island along a customary boundary (or perhaps one determined by that legendary

A beachside view of Great Bay, the cruise port for St. Maarten.

foot race). A hilly island, St. Maarten was cultivated with sugar plantations during the 18th century, along with cattle ranches. Britain seized it
and other Dutch colonies after Napoleon invaded Holland in 1795, then
returned the island in 1815.

When France ended slavery on St. Martin in 1848, slaves on the
Dutch side simply took their freedom. Official emancipation came in
1863 and the plantation system disappeared, with planters unable to pay
wages and still make a profit. The freed slaves and white settlers grew
subsistence crops in the arid climate and sought seasonal work on other
islands. The island lacks an adequate water supply and a desalination
plant now provides fresh water for today's influx of tourists and an
exploding population which now exceeds 60,000 residents.

St. Maarten was one of the first Caribbean islands to open up to
tourism, which has boomed since the early 1970s. An extensively
developed island with an infrastructure to accommodate the thousands
of tourists who come here each year, St. Maarten calls itself the
Friendly Island. There are no border checks, just a monument commemorating the 300th anniversary (1648-1948) of the two nations'
peaceful sharing of the island. Both sides have retained their colonial
ties – St. Martin is an overseas region of France and a prefecture of
Guadeloupe, while St. Maarten is part of the Netherlands Antilles, an
autonomous part of the Kingdom of the Netherlands. Capitalizing on its
strong links to Europe, the island has forged its own identity in which
French and Dutch influences have combined with West Indian heritage
to create a vibrant Creole culture. It's a high-energy island offering cos-
mopolitan flair with a calypso beat.

Today it's a toss-up which country got the better half of the island.
Philipsburg, the Dutch capital, is where most of the cruise ships moor.

Marigot, on the French side, offers sidewalk cafes and elegant shops.

Marigot, the French capital, is where cruise passengers go to sample French boutiques and bistros. The Dutch side has gambling casinos and a golf course; the French side has Fort Louis and topless sunbathing. Both capitals are free ports and the entire island contains beach-lined bays which attract tourists in such numbers that the road leading from Philipsburg to Marigot is often clogged with bumper-to-bumper traffic. The **Princess Juliana International Airport** is one of the busiest in the West Indies and the island is one of the Caribbean's most popular ports of call, offering great shopping, dozens of beaches, and an impressive array of shore excursions. Yet, in spite of the island's high level of development, it's still possible to find a quiet stretch of sand on which to enjoy the island's ever-present sunshine.

GETTING AROUND

The cruise pier, which opened in 2001, is located at **Pointe Blanche**, about a mile from Philipsburg. It's possible to walk into town, take a taxi ($4 per person each way) or use **Bobby's Marina** tender service, which runs between the terminal and the town pier at a cost of $5 for the entire day. On busy port days, some cruise ships anchor in **Great Bay** and tender their passengers ashore to the town pier which is adjacent to **1 Cyrus Wathney Square** where a Tourist Information Bureau **i** and taxi stand are located.

Philipsburg is easy to explore on foot with its two main streets – Front and Back (Vorstraat and Achterstraat) – running parallel with the waterfront. Front Street, lined with duty-free shops, features West Indian-style buildings trimmed with gingerbread fretwork. Back Street, the former site of salt warehouses, is connected with Front Street by a series of interesting alleyways called *steegjes*.

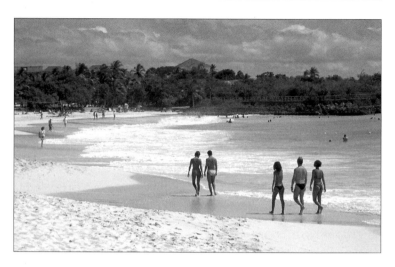

Long Bay, on the Dutch side, is one the longest and quietest beaches on the island.

The cheapest way to travel directly between **Philipsburg** and **Marigot** is by public bus. These vans pick up passengers on Back Street and drop off in downtown Marigot. The fare is only $2 each way and the buses run regularly throughout the day.

Taxis are unmetered and a few sample one-way fares from Philipsburg (1-4 per taxi) are: to Marigot $14, to Maho Beach $12, to Dawn Beach $15, to Orient Beach $18.

There are numerous car rental agencies in both St. Maarten and St. Martin, however the main roads are often congested and there have been reports of rental car break-ins by thieves looking for valuables (especially vulnerable are vehicles parked by beaches).

Dutch and French are the official languages but English is widely spoken – especially in the shops.

Shopping – The official currencies are the Netherlands Antilles florin and the French franc, but U.S. dollars are accepted throughout the island. With about 500 duty-free shops and savings of up to 50%, the island is a great place to shop for such goods as French perfume, Irish linen and designer fashions. Good buys are available in cameras, electronics, watches, jewelry, china, crystal, leather shoes and handbags, and Finnish stoneware. Bargains in liquor include fine cognac and St. Maarten's own guavaberry liqueur.

Beaches – On St. Maarten/St. Martin, there's a beach (37 in total) to suit everyone's taste, whether it's resort facilities, coral reefs or sandy solitude that you're seeking. All beaches have public access and those designated 'topless' and 'clothing optional' are on the French side.

Fine beaches on the Dutch side include **Great Bay**, just a few steps from Front Street. Nearby is **Little Bay**, a small but lovely beach backed by a number of resorts. **Maho Bay** has sparkling white sand and a surf that is sometimes rough. Facilities are available at the Maho Beach Hotel. The mile-long beach at **Mullet Bay** also has resort facilities. The island's only golf course is located beside this beach.

Cupecoy Bay's beach of powdery white sand is backed by sandstone cliffs and caves. A dramatic setting, there are no change facilities or watersports here, and there is topless bathing at the far end.

More beautiful beaches await on the French side. Those near Marigot include **Red Bay**, with snack facilities and good snorkeling at its eastern end. **Long Bay** is one of the island's largest beaches and is fairly quiet with little resort development. Topless bathers frequent this beach, and the neighboring beach at **Plum Bay** can be reached by walking west around Canonnier Point. Plum Point is a good snorkeling spot.

At the north end of the island is **Orient Bay** – one of St. Martin's busiest beaches, offering restaurants, snack bars, watersports and a non-stop water taxi to **Green Key Island**. Beach chairs, umbrellas, catamarans and windsurfers can all be rented here and those who like sunbathing in the buff can do so in front of the Club Orient Hotel.

For visitors with children, the beaches at **Anse Marcel** (north end) and **Coconut Grove** (east side) are quiet and shady. The one at Coconut Grove has change facilities, refreshments, chairs and sailboard rentals.

Dive & Snorkel Sites – At the island's north end, Flat Island, Pinel Island (reached by boat from Cul de Sac) and Orient Bay/Green Key are part of a **Regional Underwater Reserve** and offer excellent snorkeling. Also within the reserve is **Grand Cayes**, a unique diving site on the coral reef barrier. On the east side, Dawn Beach has some of the island's best snorkeling along its offshore reefs, and refreshments are available here.

Dive shops are located at various hotels, including Mullet Bay Resort. Some fascinating wrecks are within easy reach, such as the British ship HMS *Proselyte* which sank in 1801 about one mile off the eastern entrance to Great Bay.

An 18th-century courthouse overlooks the town square of Philipsburg.

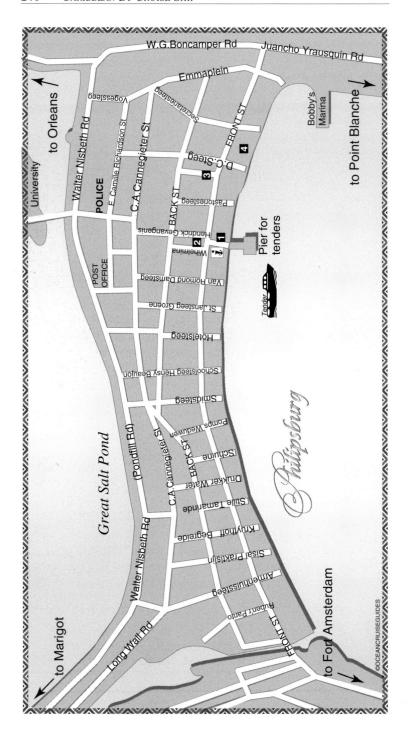

Near the western entrance point, off Fort Amsterdam, a 17th-century warship is resting on Man-O-War Reef, its scattered cannons still visible.

Golf – An 18-hole course is located at Mullet Bay Resort on the Dutch side.

LOCAL SIGHTS

2 The **Courthouse** overlooks the square on Front Street. Built in the 1790s, it has at various times housed a barracks, prison cells, secretariat and post office, in addition to its courtroom. The original wood-and-stone building was repaired following hurricane damage in 1819. Its most recent restoration was completed in 1969, and the building is now occupied by the Court of First Instance.

Entered off Front and Back Streets, **3** **Old Street Mall** is a colorful shopping alley featuring several dozen shops, boutiques and restaurants. Nearby, at the east end of Front Street, is **4** **Pasanggrahan Royal Guest House**.

Pasanggrahan Royal Guest House has hosted Dutch royalty.

The oldest and most authentic colonial style inn on St. Maarten, it used to be the **Governor's home** and was a royal residence for Dutch Queen Juliana during World War II when, as a princess fleeing the Nazi invasion of her homeland, she stayed there while en route to Canada.

ISLAND ATTRACTIONS

The ruins of Fort Amsterdam stand on Great Bay's western point, and directly north atop Fort Hill are the remains of Fort William. The St. Maarten Zoological and Botanical Garden, which focuses on education and contains baboons and St. Kitts monkeys, is located just north of Great Salt Pond.

The winding road from Philipsburg to Marigot provides scenic views of yacht-filled Simpson Bay Lagoon as it ascends the hilly terrain. An observation platform on top of **Cole Bay Hill** offers sweeping views of neighboring islands, including Anguilla and St. Barts. The Cole Bay Hill Cemetery contains the grave of Scottish adventurer John Philips, for whom Philipsburg is named.

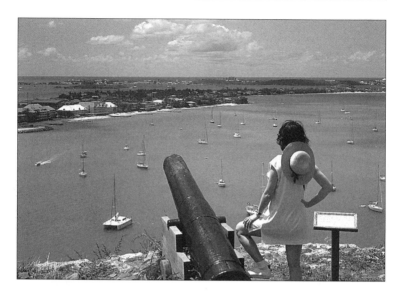

Fort St. Louis stands atop a hill overlooking Marigot Bay.

Paradise Peak is the island's highest point at 1,500 feet above sea level and a number of hiking trails lead in all directions from this point. It can be reached by a secondary road from Rambaud, which is located on the main road leading north of Marigot to **Grande Case** – a fishing village renowned for its gourmet restaurants and restored creole houses. This waterfront village is also the location of the Seaworld Explorer, a semi-submersible glass-bottom boat that provides narrated tours of the coral reefs around Creole Rock. The northern tip of the island, around **Anse Marcel**, consists of secluded coves and scenic hiking trails. The island's oldest French settlement of **Orleans** is located on the island's east side.

Marigot

A pretty port of French colonial buildings and elegant shops, the Marigot harborfront is a pleasant place to stroll along the water's edge and gaze at anchored sailboats or relax at an outdoor cafe beneath the shade of colorful awnings and umbrellas. Marigot's **Tourist Information Center** *i* is located near the waterfront, at the north end of Rue De La Republique. Beside it is a taxi stand and opposite is an open-air market where vendors sell their wares beneath multi-colored canopies. Perched above this festive scene is **Fort St. Louis**, its hilltop ruins reached by stairs leading from the Sous-Prefecture parking lot. With its sweeping view over Marigot Bay and the lagoon, this spot is a wonderful place to indulge in a picnic after wandering about the site. Built in 1767 during the reign of Louis XVI, the fort was armed with 15 cannons.

Two 12-meter yachts tack toward Philipsburg, their deckhands enjoying one of the Caribbean's most popular shore excursions.

Boat Excursions – St. Maarten offers visitors a good selection of boating excursions, including lively sightseeing cruises with unlimited rum punch and private-island beach stops for a chance to swim, snorkel and sunbathe.

A highly popular boating attraction is the 'America's Cup' Sailing Regatta out of Philipsburg. No sailing experience is necessary to sign on as 'deckhand' in this friendly regatta that takes place outside Great Bay onboard original 12-meter yachts that were raced in the 1987 America's Cup in Fremantle, Australia. The boats, about 70 feet in length, are manned with an experienced skipper and crew who assign each deckhand a task and explain its execution. A few practice tacks and jibes are made on the way to the race course, and then it's time to leap into action and experience the exhilaration of world-class yacht racing.

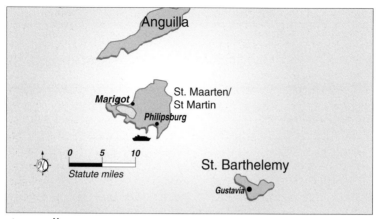

Anguilla

Anguilla is a short ferry ride from St. Martin but it's a world apart in terms of atmosphere. Northernmost of the Leeward Islands, this British territory of 10,000 residents is a true island hideaway, favored by celebrities, with miles of white powdery beaches and luxury resort accommodations.

While Anguilla's main attractions are the beaches and coral gardens, a unique feature on the island is the Fountain – a cavern containing several fresh-water pools, a fountain and a dozen or so petroglyphs as well as a 16-foot stalagmite that was carved by Taino Indians. Archaeologists believe this dome-shaped cavern was a major Amerindian center for worship.

St. Barts

Named St-Barthelemy by Christopher Columbus and once governed by Sweden, the island everyone calls St. Barts is unabashedly French and very chic. It lies 15 miles southeast of St. Maarten and is part of the French overseas *departement* of Guadeloupe. The island's capital is Gustavia, its sheltered natural harbor often filled with sailing craft and luxury yachts, its streets of northern European style homes overlooked by the ruins of forts that once defended this tiny island.

During colonial times, in the mid 1600s, the island was settled by Huguenots from Brittany and Normandy. In 1784, France's Louis XVI ceded the island to King Gustav III of Sweden in return for duty-free trading rights in Gothenburg. Gustavia was soon declared a free port and the island, benefiting from Sweden's neutrality, prospered until struck by hurricanes and a great fire in Gustavia in 1852.

In 1877, France bought the island back for 320,000 francs and to this day the island's French culture remains strong. Residents, about 5,000 in number, speak a French patois sprinkled with English and Swedish words, and women can still be seen wearing starched white caps like those of their Norman ancestors. The population is predominantly white, for the semi-arid island never supported a plantation economy, and in the past, local commerce was based on trade and fishing. That all changed when the jet set discovered this island hideaway, and tourism is now its major industry.

The Rockefeller, Ford and Rothschild families all have vacation homes on St. Barts, and this 8-1/2-square mile island is dotted with luxury resorts. Its varied shoreline of pristine coves and idyllic beaches includes Anse du Gouverneur, accessible only on foot and considered one of the finest in the West Indies, and Saint-Jean, the island's most photographed beach with its two crescents of pale sand separated by a rocky promontory. The remote beach at Columbier on the island's north shore is where David Rockefeller built a vacation home, and Grand Cul-de-Sac Bay, a favorite with wind-surfers, has two beaches – one embracing the tranquil waters of a sheltered bay, the other facing the ocean.

Beach hopping can be done by rented mini-moke and beach buggy, or by taxi. A taxi stand is located in Gustavia where local attractions include duty-free shops and the town's two historic churches – the Roman Catholic French church and the Anglican Swedish church. Fort Oscar, built in the 17th century, stands at the tip of a peninsula and is occupied by the Ministry of Armed Forces. The ruins of Fort Carl stand in the heights of Gustavia and provide a spectacular view of the harbor. Fort Gustave also provides panoramic views of Gustavia and neighboring islands.

Other island attractions include the Wall House Museum & Library, housed in a Swedish colonial building, and the Inter Oceans shell museum which is located in Corossol, one of the island's oldest villages.

French is the official language on St. Barts and the franc its official currency, but English is widely spoken and prices are often quoted in U.S. dollars.

Gustavia, on the tiny French island of St. Barts, is a popular port of call for sailing yachts and small luxury cruise ships.

Driving the open roads of St. Kitts.

Atlantic Ocean

Caribbean Sea

The Narrows
NEVIS

Black Rocks

St. Pauls

Sandy Point

Mt. Liamuiga

Brimstone Hill
Fortress

Romney Manor

Southeast Range

OLD ROAD

Middle Island

Old Road Town

Challengers

Bloody Point

Bloody Bay

Monkey Hill

Airport

Basseterre

Cruise Ship Dock

Conaree Beach

Half Moon Bay

North Frigate Bay

North Friar's Bay

South Frigate Bay

South Friar's Bay

Great Salt Pond

Sandy Bay

Cockleshell Bay

Banana Bay

Major's Bay

St. Kitts

Miles
0 10 20

N

©OCEAN CRUISE GUIDES

CHAPTER ELEVEN

ST. KITTS

T he verdant mountains of St. Kitts are a beautiful sight for cruise passengers as their ship draws close to this island of patchwork fields and sandy beaches. Its pastoral charm belies the bloody battles that took place on the island called Liamuiga – fertile land – by its early Carib inhabitants. So valued was St. Kitts for its sugarcane, the British eventually built a massive fortress on **Brimstone Hill,** which became known as the 'Gibraltar of the West Indies'.

A massive fortification of volcanic rock and limestone mortar, the fortress took more than a century to build using slave labor. When completed in 1794, its walls encompassed a citadel, bastions, barracks, officers quarters, storehouses, cookhouses and a hospital. Both impregnable and impressive, the Brimstone Hill Fortress looms nearly a thousand feet above the surrounding countryside with sweeping views of the coastline and other islands. Its name refers to the odor of sulphur that seeps from nearby volcanic vents. The fortress itself stands atop an upthrust of solidified lava covered by limestone.

St. Kitts and its neighboring island of Nevis are the upper slopes and cones of volcanoes resting on a submarine rock base. **Mount Liamuiga,** the highest peak on St. Kitts at 3,793 feet, was last active in 1692. Nevis Peak, a single volcano in the center of Nevis Island, rises to 3,232 feet. The two islands are separated by a two-mile-wide channel called the Narrows, its shallow sea floor covered with coral reefs.

The lower slopes of St. Kitts are cultivated right down to the coast, except on the island's south end where the vegetation is thorny scrub and dry forest. This relatively undeveloped area is inhabited with Green Vervet monkeys, often seen scampering across the road. They were brought to St. Kitts by the French who, along with the British, drew supplies of salt and building timber from the island in the late 1600s. A hundred years earlier, the island had been named St. Christopher by Columbus, in honor of his patron saint, but it became known as St. Kitts and the name was officially changed in 1988.

In 1605 England took possession of St. Kitts and in 1623 the island's first white settlers arrived, led by **Sir Thomas Warner**, a Suffolk gentleman who planned to grow tobacco here with the financial support of a syndicate of British merchants. He drove off a small group of hostile Carib natives, cleared the land and established the first permanent British settlement in the West Indies, only to have a hurricane destroy

Brimstone Hill Fortress, built of volcanic rock and limestone mortar, took over a century to complete.

his first crop of tobacco. But Warner and his followers persevered and a new crop was planted the next year. They soon had company in the form of French pirates, their damaged ship putting in to what is now Basseterre for repairs. The French, led by Belain d'Esnambuc, decided to stay and plant tobacco too.

The British and French joined forces to massacre some avenging Caribs and wipe them from the island. They then divided the island, which is 23 miles long and up to seven miles across. The central mountainous region went to the English; the north and south ends went to the French. But the living was far from easy, and frequent quarrels flared between the British and French farmers, many of whom died of diseases such as yellow fever and malaria. In 1628, a wealthy British planter led a group of settlers to Nevis, and by 1632 others had left St. Kitts to settle on Montserrat and Antigua. The French also used St. Kitts as a staging area for the settlement of their other islands, such as Guadeloupe, Martinique and St. Martin.

Mother colony of the West Indies for both the British and the French, St. Kitts was battled over for the next century and a half until the 1783 Treaty of Versailles recognized it as a British possession. In 1871, St. Kitts and Nevis were incorporated in the colony of Leeward Islands, and in 1983 they became, along with a small coral island called Sombrero that lies about 35 miles northwest of Anguilla, an independent state within the British Commonwealth.

The fertile soil on St. Kitts supported three centuries of sugarcane crops and showed no signs of exhaustion until the 20th century, when modern methods of cultivation initially doubled the yield per acre, followed by a marked decrease. Total output has been halved in the last twenty years, but agriculture is still the island's major export with the entire sugarcane crop of St. Kitts and Nevis processed at a refinery in Basseterre. Nearly 40 miles of narrow-gauge railway encircles St. Kitts, built between 1912 and 1925 to transport wagon loads of cane from the plantations to the refinery.

Basseterre

About 36,000 people live on St. Kitts and the chief town is Basseterre (pronounced *bass-terr*), originally founded by the French but developed by the English from 1706 onwards. The town suffered widespread destruction from an earthquake in 1843 and was rebuilt in 1867 following a great fire that destroyed most of the town. Another earthquake struck in 1974, followed by hurricanes in 1979, 1980 and 1988. The town's deep-water harbor, 2-1/2 miles south of the town center, opened in 1981. A newer pier is currently under construction in the center of town but progress has been hampered by recent hurricanes.

A tourism information booth **i** is located on the cruise pier, right beside some pay telephones. A tourist office is located on the downtown waterfront overlooking the Treasury Pier, at Bay Road and Fort Street. Next door is the Treasury Building and beside that is a post office (just west of the Pelican Mall).

American money is widely accepted although the official currency is the Eastern Caribbean dollar, worth approximately $2.70 EC per $1 US (or approximately $1 EC per 40¢ US).

GETTING AROUND

St. Kitts has good roads and beautiful scenery, so touring the island by taxi, rental car or organized shore excursion is a pleasurable way to spend your time in port. English is the official language and residents also speak a local patois.

Arranging for a **taxi** at the cruise pier is a well-organized procedure with drivers lining up outside a cordoned-off area while a dispatcher deals with disembarking passengers seeking a cab. Upon stepping ashore, you simply tell the dispatcher where you would like to go and he will tell you what the fare is and direct you to a driver. The set fare is per car, one to four persons. Approximate **fares** from cruise port: Downtown Basseterre (one-way) $8; Romney Manor (return) $26.00; Brimstone Hill (return) $32; Frigate Bay (one-way) $11; Friars Beach (one-way) $13; Tour of South East Peninsula $40; Island Tour $60. On round-trip fares, a 15-minute wait at each destination is included. After that, a small waiting fee is charged.

A cruise ship pulls into Basseterre on the island of St. Kitts.

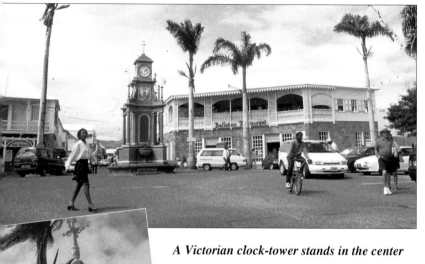

***A Victorian clock-tower stands in the center
of the Circus, Basseterre's main traffic circle.***

There are several **car rental agencies** in
Basseterre, including Avis and TDC in
Independence Square. A local driving license
(obtained by presenting your current license
and $20 at the Police Station) is required.
Driving is on the left-hand side of the road.
The one main highway circling the island is
well maintained with good signage, making
it easy to get around.

Shopping – St. Kitts is famous for its
locally produced clothing made of beautiful
batik and tie-dyed cotton. Other local crafts include hand-
embroidered items, straw goods and ceramics. Duty-free items
sold here include perfumes, jewelry, crystal and porcelain.

Shopping areas in Basseterre are found along Bay Road, Liverpool
Row and Fort Street. The Circus is where Island Hopper sells Caribelle
Batik's famous dresses, caftans, wraps and wall murals. The Caribelle
Batik studio, where these exquisite fashions are designed and made, is
located at Romney Manor (northwest of Basseterre). Duty-free shopping can be found on Liverpool Row and at the Pelican Shopping Mall
on the downtown waterfront. A philatelic bureau selling colorful collectors issues of postage stamps is also located in this mall.

Local art, including the renowned Carnival Clown series by Rose
Cameron Smith, can be bought in The Spencer Cameron Gallery on
North Independence Square. The Plantation Picture House, home to
Kate Spencer's studio and gallery, is at the northwest end of the island
near Rawlins Plantation.

A colorful **public market** is located on Bay Road, a few blocks west of the Treasury Pier, and local merchants also set up tables on the cruise pier when a ship is in port.

Beaches – Several attractive beaches are situated at the island's southern end. South Frigate Bay has resort facilities and watersports equipment rental, including snorkeling gear. Considered the island's best beach by locals, South Friars Bay is a quiet, undeveloped beach with good snorkeling. At the southern tip lie more remote beaches at Cockleshell Bay and Banana Bay, with an excellent view across the Narrows of Nevis. Dramatic beaches with surf on the Atlantic side include North Frigate Bay and Conaree Beach.

Diving & Snorkeling – The Caribbean side of the island has protected waters and extensive reefs that begin in shallow water and drop off to depths of 100 feet or more. Dive sites on St. Kitts include Bloody Bay Reef, laced with small caves filled with purple anemones and yellow sea fans, and the Grid Iron, an undersea shelf in the Narrows which is covered with shallow-water corals, sea fans and sponges. Snorkeling can be enjoyed at many of the island's beaches, especially those on the Caribbean side, such as South Frigate Bay and South Friars Bay.

Golf – There are two courses on St. Kitts – the Golden Rock Golf Club near the airport north of Basseterre, and the Royal St. Kitts Golf Course at Frigate Bay. The latter is an 18-hole championship course bordered by the Atlantic Ocean and the Caribbean Sea. Designed by the Golf Course Architectural Group, this par-72 course is both challenging and scenic, its fairways and greens adorned with ponds, palm trees and tropical flowers.

Fine beaches near Basseterre include those at South Frigate Bay and South Friars Bay.

St. George's Church

Cayon St

POLICE

Independence Square

Church Street

Central St

Fort Street

Hart Street

George St

Princess St

Bank St

The Circus

Liverpool Row

Bay Rd

Treasury Pier

P.O.

Pelican Mall

Bay Rd

to Cruise Pier (2 1/2 miles)

Ferry Pier (to Nevis)

Port Zante (under construction)

BASSETERRE

Basseterre Bay

©OCEAN CRUISE GUIDES

LOCAL ATTRACTIONS

The **Circus**, in the heart of Basseterre, is a traffic circle modeled after London's famous Piccadilly Circus. In the center of this busy hub stands **Berkeley Memorial**, a Victorian clock-tower monument commemorating a former president of the **General Legislative Council.**

Bank Street leads off The Circus to **Independence Square** (originally called Pall Mall Square) which was built in 1790 for slave auctions and council meetings. This open square, lined with colonial buildings, consists of eight paths converging on a central fountain, its pattern resembling the Union Jack when seen from the air. Facing the square on its east side is the Roman Catholic **Church of the Immaculate Conception**, and at its southeast corner is the Court House with a public library upstairs.

Independence Square and Church of the Immaculate Conception.

St. George's Anglican Church, an impressive brownstone structure surrounded by lawns and flowering shrubs on Cayon Street, was originally called Notre Dame when built by the French in 1670. Burned to the ground by the British in 1706, it was rebuilt four years later and named for England's patron saint. Two fires and an earthquake between 1763 and 1843 resulted in the church being rebuilt three more times, followed by its most recent restoration in 1869.

ISLAND ATTRACTIONS

Bloody Point at the mouth of Stone Fort River is the former site of a Carib village. Within the walls of the river's narrow canyon, 2,000 Carib Indians were massacred by the British and French in 1626. The Caribs, unhappy with the increasing number of Europeans settling their island, had been planning their own attack when they were trapped here and slaughtered. The river is said to have run red with their blood. Local taxi drivers will stop at Bloody Point if asked and young children with pet monkeys often wait here for camera-toting tourists. Carib carvings (petroglyphs) can be seen on the canyon walls, which are about a half hour hike from Bloody Point.

(Above) St. George's Anglican Church. (Below) Treasury Building.

Old Road Town is where Thomas Warner landed on St. Kitts in 1623 and established the first permanent British settlement in the West Indies. It was the island's capital until 1727. Nearby, at what is now Wingfield Estate, are Carib petroglyphs and pictographs sketched on boulders.

Romney Manor, site of a 17th-century plantation with sugar mill and great house ruins, is now home to Caribelle Batik, where local artisans practice the Indonesian art of batik to

The citadel at Brimstone Hill fortress, 'Gibraltar of the West Indies'.

produce high-quality fabrics and fashions of striking designs and colors. The lovely grounds feature an enormous 350-year-old saman (rain) tree and five acres of flowers, shrubbery and terraced lawns.

Thomas Warner's tomb is located in the churchyard of St. Thomas Church in Middle Island.

The second-largest fortress in the Caribbean, **Brimstone Hill** was inaugurated as a national park by Queen Elizabeth in 1985 and declared a UNESCO World Heritage Site in 2000. The impressive fortifications contain a visitor center at the base of the restored citadel, atop which 24-pounder cannons overlook the sea and surrounding countryside. The sweeping view includes the island of St. Eustatius to the northwest.

Beyond Brimstone Hill, at the northwest end of St. Kitts, are scenic sugarcane plantations and estates. At **Black Rocks**, on the north coast, you can view black cliffs and boulders formed by lava flowing from Mount Liamuiga and eroded by a pounding sea.

The island's **Southeast Peninsula** is easily accessible by modern highway from Basseterre. The Frigate Bay area contains several luxury resorts, sandy beaches and a golf course. At the far end of the peninsula, nestled among the cone-shaped hills, is the Great Salt Pond. This undeveloped area of breathtaking vistas and pristine beaches is also the place to spot wild monkeys in the low scrub that lines the quiet roads.

Nevis

Dominated by a single central mountain peak, the small island of Nevis (pronounced *Nee-vis*), is steeped in Old World charm. It was called Nieves (Spanish for snow) by Columbus because cloud-covered Nevis Peak reminded him of a snow-capped mountain. The main port of Charlestown is where most of the island's 9,000 residents live and is connected to Basseterre by passenger ferry.

Charlestown was once a fashionable health spa destination for the wealthy who stayed at the grand Bath Hotel and Spring House, built in

Nevis Peak rises above the links at the Four Seasons Resort Nevis.

1778. The resort's bath houses were positioned on a fault over a hot spring, and a soak in the thermal mineral water brought relief from rheumatism and gout. Today's visitors can still take a mineral bath and tour the reconstructed hotel, much of its original structure destroyed by a 1950 earthquake.

Other historic attractions in Charlestown include a cotton ginney (still used during the March/April picking season) and the **Alexander Hamilton House**, birthplace of the American statesman and aide to Washington. The Hamilton Museum, housed in a Georgian-style building, contains papers by Hamilton and other archival documents. Nevis's other famous figure is Horatio Nelson, the British naval hero who, as a young captain stationed in the West Indies, met and married in 1787 a local woman named Francis Nesbitt. A record of their marriage (and Alexander Hamilton's birth) is registered at St. John's Church in Fig Tree Village. There's also a **Nelson Museum** in Morning Star, and Nelson's Spring is where he took on water for his ships before sailing to North America during the American War of Independence. Other attractions on Nevis include its restored plantation estates, the golden sands of Pinney's Beach, and an 18-hole championship golf course at the Four Seasons Resort Nevis, one of the Caribbean's top-rated resorts.

St. Eustatius

The small Dutch island of St. Eustatius, commonly called Statia, was known as the 'Golden Rock' during colonial times when, as the headquarters of the Netherlands West Indies Company, its population grew to almost 20,000 and trade in rum, sugar and tobacco was brisk. The island also served as a transhipment port for supplies to the American colonies during the American War of Independence. A salute fired by an American warship on November 16, 1776, was replied to by Fort Oranjestad, thus making the Netherlands the first foreign power to recognize America's new flag, the Stars and Stripes. The fort, perched on a crag above the sea, was built in 1636 and restored in 1976. The town of Oranjestad contains a number of historic sites, including one of the oldest synagogues in the Western Hemisphere and a number of restored 18th-century houses, such as the one Admiral Rodney used as his headquarters when he captured the island for Britain in 1781.

Peaceful times now prevail on Statia, its population a mere 2,000. The island's scenic beauty can be enjoyed on nature trails that crisscross the island, including one that leads through tropical rainforest to the crater of an extinct volcanic peak called The Quill. For snorkelers and scuba divers, the island's surrounding waters are dotted with ship wrecks, coral reefs and rare fish.

Saba

The tiny volcanic island of Saba (pronounced *Say-ba*) is part of the Netherlands Antilles and is a unique piece of Caribbean geography. There are no beaches on Saba, which is the top of a dormant volcano, and its steep coastline consists of cliffs that plunge into the sea. Only five square miles in size, Saba's single road – called The Road – winds across the island and connects a handful of villages of red-roofed houses nestled at the base of green slopes.

The waters surrounding Saba contain a microcosm of sea life due to the continual currents flowing past the island's shores. A marine park completely encircles the island and features groove channels filled with juvenile tropical fish, underwater tunnels, barrel sponges and soft corals. Nearby is a range of underwater sea mounts, their peaks 80 feet beneath the surface. Thirty permanent moorings have been installed in Saba Marine Park to accommodate dive boats while protecting the coral. The island's decompression chamber at the Fort Bay Pier was donated by the royal Dutch Navy, and local dive operators help with many of the park's projects, which include the ongoing collection of data and sharing of marine information.

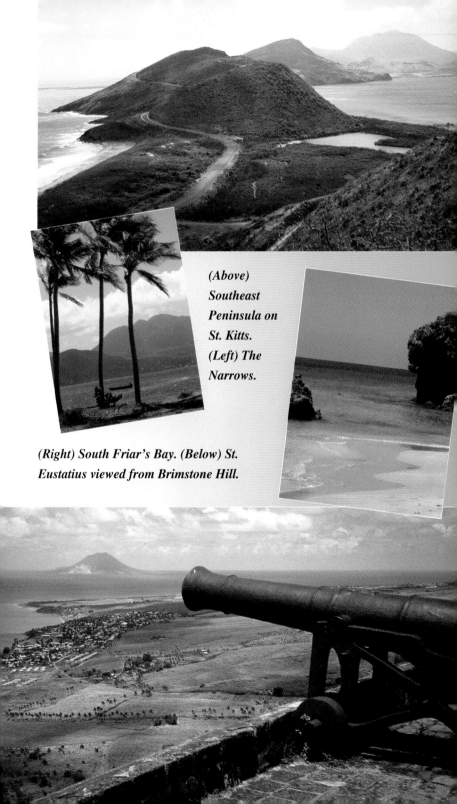

(Above) Southeast Peninsula on St. Kitts. (Left) The Narrows.

(Right) South Friar's Bay. (Below) St. Eustatius viewed from Brimstone Hill.

CHAPTER TWELVE

ANTIGUA

Antigua's beautiful bays and harbors have been providing shelter to seagoing vessels since the days of Columbus. English Harbour was already a popular hurricane haven when the Royal Navy began using it in 1725 as a dockyard. One of the finest natural harbors in the world with its narrow entrance and surrounding hillsides, English Harbour soon became Britain's major naval port in the West Indies. Fortifications were built on hilltops overlooking this and other harbors on the island, and ships would regularly pull in for repairs and provisions, or to ride out a storm during the hurricane season. This busy dockyard reached its zenith in the late 18th century when 26-year-old Horatio Nelson was headquartered here as commander of the Northern Division of the Leeward Island Station.

The sailing tradition continues today with Antigua's annual **Sailing Week** in April. One of the world's largest ocean racing events, attracting over 200 yachts from nearly 40 countries, this regatta has been called a 'sailor's Woodstock' for the fun-loving spirit of its competitors. The racing is serious but away from the course the rum punch flows and the dockside events are pure frivolity. A certain decorum does prevail, however, when the winning prizes are presented from the Old Officer's Quarters Balcony in Nelson's Dockyard, after which the Royal Antiguan Police Band 'Beats the Retreat'. The festivities conclude with the Lord Nelson Ball, a formal-dress affair complete with fireworks display.

Such is Antigua, an island conducive to languid lazing on beautiful beaches, but with a hint of British crispness in the accents of its people whose friendliness is tempered with a touch of reserve. The local school children wear uniforms, and cricket is popular here with international matches played at the Recreation Ground in St. John's. The bat used by Antigua-born Viv Richards, famous captain of the West Indies cricket team, is on display at the local museum.

Antigua is also a recluse for British royalty and rock stars, with the Queen herself once taking a dip in the sea at one of many secluded beaches. Princess Margaret and Lord Snowden honeymooned on Antigua and Princess Diana twice vacationed at the exclusive K Club on Antigua's sister island of Barbuda. Eric Clapton has a home near English Harbour, and Michael Jordan, Whitney Houston and Elton John have all vacationed on Antigua, its powdery white beaches stretching past some of the Caribbean's most elegant resorts.

Darkwood Beach, on the west coast of Antigua, is one of numerous beautiful beaches lining the island's shores.

Antigua (pronounced An-tee-ga) was named in 1493 by Columbus for Santa Maria de la Antigua, a miracle-working saint of the Seville Cathedral in Spain. The island's earliest signs of habitation date back to 1775 BC, and settlement by the Arawaks, who migrated here from South America, began in about 35 AD. The island's lack of natural springs discouraged European settlement until, in 1632, some hardy English farmers arrived from St. Kitts, claimed the island for the British crown and planted crops of tobacco, indigo and ginger. The island remained under British rule for the next three and a half centuries, apart from a brief occupation by the French in 1666.

In 1674, Sir Christopher Codrington arrived from Barbados and, with an army of slaves, established the island's first large sugar plantation, naming it **Betty's Hope** for his daughter. The plantation's success encouraged others and within 25 years the island's landscape was transformed. Its natural vegetation was cleared to grow sugarcane, and more than 150 sugar mills dotted the countryside. The slave laborers plotted an insurrection in 1736 but the slave trade didn't end until 1808, followed by the abolition of slavery in 1834. The boom market in sugar collapsed but, despite the demise of plantation estates on Antigua, the production of sugar remained the island's major industry well into the 20th century, until surpassed by tourism.

Antigua, its neighboring island of **Barbuda** and the tiny uninhabited island of **Redonda**, 20 miles to the west, gained their partial independence from Great Britain in 1967 and have been independent since 1981. The islands' population of 70,000 is mostly of African origin with a small community of Europeans, Americans and Canadians living here. English is the official language.

Heritage Quay and St. Mary's Street lead up the hillside from the cruise pier.

St. John's is the capital and although this historic trading port has been ravaged by earthquakes, hurricanes and fires over the centuries, its colonial past endures in the British street names and restored harborfront warehouses. Rising above the narrow streets and hip-roofed buildings are the twin spires of St. John's Cathedral – easily visible as your ship pulls into port and docks at the town's doorstep.

GETTING AROUND

Cruise passengers step ashore at Heritage Quay, a duty-free shopping complex where a **tourist information booth** 🛈 and public telephones are located. The post office is beside Heritage Quay on High Street. On busy port days some ships moor at St. John's Docks, located on the harbor's north side, about one mile from town.

Taxi fares are regulated but you should agree on the price in advance. Sample **fares** (for the whole taxi, one-way) from Heritage Quay to: Dickenson Bay $8; Deep Bay/Ramada Renaissance $10; Hawksbill Beach Resort $14; English Harbour $20.

Local **car rental** agencies include Avis, Budget and Hertz, and the daily rental rate is about $50. Driving is on the left side of the road and a temporary license ($20) is required. Many of the roads are unmarked, unpaved and in need of repairs.

The **shore excursions** organized by the cruise lines usually include an island drive to Shirley Heights and Nelson's Dockyard, a Jolly Roger Pirate Cruise along the northwest coast, and a catamaran cruise featuring a stop at a secluded beach for snorkeling, swimming and sunbathing.

Official currency is the Eastern Caribbean (EC) dollar which is tied to the U.S. dollar at approximately $2.70 EC to $1 US (or $1 EC to 40¢ US), but American currency is accepted everywhere.

Shopping – Batik island cotton, hand-painted clothing and tropical jewelry are among the Caribbean keepsakes sold in Antigua. Duty-free shopping is available at **Heritage Quay,** with dozens of international and local stores, and at adjacent **Redcliffe Quay,** where 19th-century warehouses have been carefully restored and transformed into a shopping district of inviting boutiques and courtyard cafes. More shops are located on **St. Mary's Street**, including Caribelle Batik, and on High and Long Streets. A colorful produce market is located at the junction of Valley and All Saints Roads and is a good place to buy some local pineapple – highly touted for its delicious sweetness.

Out-of-town shopping opportunities include **The Art Center** at Nelson's Dockyard, which features the island's largest collection of local art. Local handicrafts are also sold at Dow's Hill Interpretation Center and Shirley Heights Lookout. **Harmony Hall**, on the east side of the island, is a complex built around an old sugar mill which houses an art gallery featuring works by local artists. At **Sea View Farm**, a traditional pottery-making village in the middle of the island, residents still make and sell pinched pots from the local clay.

Beaches – Antiguans claim their island has 365 beaches – one for every day of the year. Watersports equipment and lounge chairs can be rented at most of the beach-front resorts, many of which are located along the island's west side. **Dickenson Bay**, at the northwest end, is the island's most popular beach with its resort facilities, dive shop and glass-bottom boat tours. **Deep Bay**, due west of St. John's and the location of a Ramada Renaissance resort, is also popular with cruise visitors. Directly south of Deep Bay the beaches become progressively quieter. Galley Bay is good for windsurfing and **Hawksbill Beach Resort** is located adjacent to four beach-lined coves, the southernmost one used by nude sunbathers.

Secluded and beautiful beaches lie south of St. John's, such as **Darkwood Beach**, popular with locals on the weekend but usually quiet during the week, and **Carlisle Bay** where an exclusive resort hotel stands atop Curtain Bluff at one end of this inviting stretch of sand.

On the Atlantic side, **Half Moon Bay** is considered by many Antiguans to be their most beautiful beach with its circular shape and ocean surf that can range from crashing waves to gentle swells. **Long Bay Beach**, also on the Atlantic side, is just around the point from Devil's Bridge, an eroded arch of limestone.

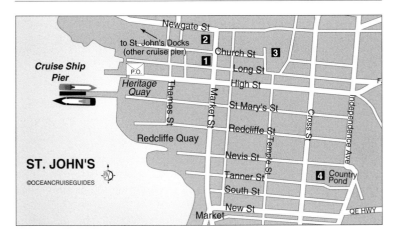

Dive & Snorkel Sites – Barrier reefs surround much of the island and wrecks are plentiful, including three in **Deep Bay**, with the *Andes* lying just off the beach in less than 30 feet. **Cape Shirley** is a premier dive site, with coral reefs, ledges and overhangs. **Cades Reef**, off the southwest coast, is a popular dive site and an underwater park. For advanced divers, the ledge of Sunken Rock is a popular site on the south coast. Dive shops are located around the island and include those at Dickenson Bay, Nelson's Dockyard and Club Antigua on Lignumvitae Bay.

Golf – The 18-hole course at The Cedar Valley Golf Club, a few minutes from St. John's, is a 6100-yard, par-70 course and home to the Antigua Open each March. Another 18-hole course is located at Jolly Harbour Marina Club, and the 9-hole course at Half Moon Bay has lovely sea views.

LOCAL ATTRACTIONS

The **1** **Museum of Antigua and Barbuda** is housed in the Old Court House, Antigua's oldest building, which was built in 1747 from stone quarried on some of Antigua's satellite islands. The museum is located at the corner of Long and Market Streets, and contains hands-on exhibits designed with children in mind, including a life-sized Arawak house. Nearby is the **2** **Police Station**, built in 1772 with a fence railing made from musket barrels, some with bayonets still attached.

St. John's Anglican Cathedral

(Left) Antigua and Barbuda Museum. (Below) English Harbour, location of Nelson's Dockyard, is one of the most sheltered anchorages in the Caribbean.

The twin baroque spires of the **3** **Anglican Cathedral of St. John the Divine** stand 70 feet high and are a town landmark. The third church built on this site, it is made of freestone with an interior encased in pitch pine to protect the structure from ruin during an earthquake or hurricane. The first church was built here in 1681 and the second one was destroyed by an earthquake in 1843. Five years later the present structure was completed and locals refer to it as 'big church'. The pillars of the south gate are topped with white-painted figures representing St. John the Divine and St. John the Baptist, and are said to have been taken from a French ship.

The **4** **Country Pond**, at the top of Tanner Street, was constructed in the mid-1700s by early settlers. Its name is likely a corruption of 'Congo Pond' because this and other ponds on the island were built by contract workers from the Congo. Its purpose was to collect water during heavy rainfalls, with the overflow running into a drainage ditch that

(Above) Nelson's Dockyard is a showcase of 18th-century Georgian architecture. (Right) A guide shows one of the capstans used to careen ships when repairing their hulls.

divides Tanner Street and runs down to the waterfront. During prolonged droughts, as the Pond's water level dropped, it could be accessed by steps built along its western wall.

ISLAND ATTRACTIONS

5 Nelson's Dockyard at English Harbour is the premier attraction on Antigua. The island's first national park, this 18th-century naval dockyard maintained a continuous squadron of British ships in the Caribbean and contains beautiful examples of Georgian architecture now housing a museum, two inns, boutiques, restaurants, several businesses and a major marina. Established at its present site in 1743, the dockyard came under the command of Horatio Nelson from 1784 to 1787. Its historic buildings include the Admiral's House, which now houses a museum; The Copper and Lumber Store (now a hotel and restaurant); the Engineer's Office (now the Admiral's Inn Hotel & Restaurant); the Officer's Quarters Building where officers lived during the hurricane season (now housing an art gallery, craft shop and other businesses); and the site of the Capstan House, where the walls no longer remain but the capstans used to careen the ships have been restored. Also intact are the Boat House Pillars that once supported a sail loft and the 200-year-old Sandbox Tree which stands beside the Admiral's House. The dockyard, closed by the Royal Navy in 1889, was reconstructed in the 1950s and officially reopened in 1961. Many of the businesses operating here now serve the local sailing community, a reflection of the dockyard's original function.

6 **Dow's Hill Interpretation Center**, situated on a ridge overlooking English Harbour, is an educational complex in which visitors can watch a 15-minute light and sound show, imaginatively presented, that depicts six different periods of Antigua's history. Lookout Trail, a nature walk connecting English Harbour with Shirley Heights, runs past the Center.

7 **Clarence House**, the official country residence of the island's Governor General, was built in 1787 as a residence for Prince William

LORD NELSON

Horatio Nelson, Britain's celebrated naval hero, was a man of great leadership abilities who inspired devotion and exceptional service in his men. Yet, while serving his only peacetime commission in the West Indies from 1784 to 1787, the young captain was anything but popular with the merchants of Antigua. As leader of the Leeward Islands Squadron, Nelson strictly enforced the Navigation Act, which prevented trade with American ships. This enraged the local merchants who threatened legal action over lost business. Nelson, to avoid arrest, confined himself to his ship for eight weeks. This was no great sacrifice for he regarded the island as 'barbarous' and the dockyard that today bears his name as 'vile'. In fact, he always slept aboard his ship while in English Harbour – a common practice among naval officers of the day who wished to avoid the mosquito-carried diseases of yellow fever and malaria.

A plantation owner on the nearby island of Nevis posted Nelson's bail, and when he went ashore at Nevis to thank his benefactor, Nelson met his future wife, a young widow named Fanny Nesbit. At their wedding in 1787, the bride was given away by Nelson's friend and fellow naval captain, Prince William Henry, who eventually became England's King William IV. As for Nelson, he returned to England with his wife and stepson, and pursued a brilliant naval career that ended with his famous victory at the Battle of Trafalgar in 1805. His marriage to Fanny came undone when he fell in love with Lady Emma Hamilton in 1798, but the notoriety of this liaison did not tarnish his reputation with the British public and his legendary status endures to this day.

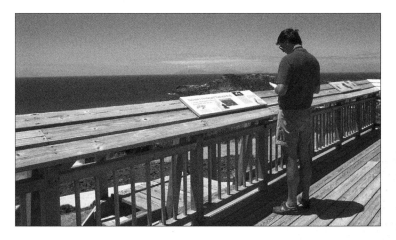

The Dow's Hill Interpretation Center includes a viewing platform overlooking English Harbour.

Henry while stationed in Antigua as a captain of the Royal Navy. This Georgian country house overlooks Nelson's Dockyard and, following the Prince's departure, was used as a residence for senior naval officers.

8 Shirley Heights, a fortified ridge of hills above the town of English Harbour, is one of the most famous views in the Caribbean. With its panoramic perspective, it was the principal lookout for enemy ships approaching English Harbour and is today a popular photo opportunity for visitors. Its restaurant facilities and refreshing breezes make it the ideal spot for the island's regular Sunday barbecue, popular with both locals and tourists, and featuring plenty of rum punch and steel band and reggae music. The heights are named after one of the island's early governors, Sir Thomas Shirley.

(Above) Shirley Heights Lookout. (Bottom) Tyrells Catholic Church.

Natural attractions on Antigua include **Boggy Peak**, the island's highest point at 1,360 feet, and **Fig Tree Drive** – four miles of hilly road that winds from Carlisle Bay to Liberta past groves of fruit trees. These include the mango, coconut and fig, which is the Antiguan name for banana. At the east end of Fig Tree Drive is eye-catching **9 Tyrells Catholic Church**, made of pink coral, and south of here, on the way to English Harbour, is the town of **Liberta** which was one of the first to be settled by freed slaves.

At the northeast end of Antigua at Indian Town Point stands a natural limestone arch called **10 Devil's Bridge**. Carved by the sea, this rock formation is a dramatic sight when a surf is running.

11 Betty's Hope, located southwest of Devil's Bridge, is a recently restored historical site. The original sugar plantation was founded here in the mid-1600s and its cotton house storeroom has been converted into a small museum. One of its twin windmills has been restored to a fully operational wind-powered sugar mill.

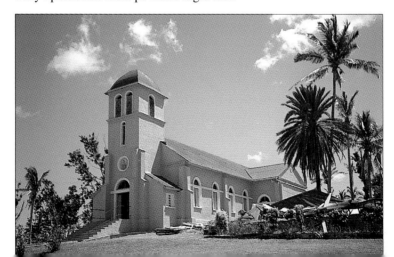

Barbuda

Sparsely populated Barbuda is a flat coral island lying 30 miles north of Antigua. Dominated by a large lagoon on its western side, the island's handful of upscale resorts are located on the south coast where beautiful pink coral beaches lie between Palmetto Point and Coco Point. The Martello Tower, a stone fort near Palmetto Point, is 56 feet tall with a view of almost the entire island.

The Frigate Bird Sanctuary, in the northwest area of the island, is a breeding ground for various indigenous species, including thousands of frigate birds that nest here in the tops of mangrove bushes.

Montserrat

The green and mountainous island of Montserrat, named by Columbus and claimed by the British, was known as the Caribbean's 'Emerald Isle' until part of it was devastated by a series of volcanic eruptions that began in 1995 and climaxed in June 1997 when the abandoned capital of Plymouth was destroyed. About half of the island's 11,000 residents had already evacuated the island, and those remaining now live on the north end of the island, outside of the off-limits zone which lies in ash-covered ruins. Peaceful, friendly and uncommercial, Montserrat is struggling to rebuild both its infrastructure and its tourism industry. Hidden, beach-lined coves lie at the base of steep mountains, and a hike up Garibaldi Hill provides panoramic views of the volcano's destruction. The island also has a bird sanctuary at Fox's Bay and a 9-hole golf course. Most of its beaches are of dark volcanic sand while the island's most beautiful white sand beach is found at secluded Rendezvous Bay.

A view of Chances Peak on Montserrat, before volcanic eruptions began blanketing much of this verdant island in ash.

Antigua

Guadeloupe Passage

the
French Antilles

Guadeloupe

La Desirade

Pointe-a-Pitre

Soufriere

Basse-Terre

Les Saintes

Marie–Galante

Dominica Passage

Caribbean

Dominica

Roseau

Sea

St. Pierre, Martinique

Martinique

Mt. Pelee

St. Pierre

Fort-de-France

©OCEANCRUISEGUIDES

CHAPTER THIRTEEN

GUADELOUPE &

MARTINIQUE

Guadeloupe and Martinique, the major islands of the French West Indies, have a great deal in common besides active volcanoes, lush rainforests and beautiful beaches. Former colonies of France, they both became *departements* in 1946 and and are now full-fledged regions with representation in the French government. These islanders, as citizens of France, can enjoy a bit of French culture while retaining customs of their African and East Indian ancestors. The result is a vibrant Creole culture, and one that visitors can experience first-hand on the crowded streets of Fort-de-France and Pointe-a-Pitre.

Parisian-style shops stand next to public markets selling piles of papayas and breadfruit, the aroma of freshly baked baguettes mixing with the pungent spices used in Creole cooking, while boutiques featuring imported porcelain and crystal compete with street vendors selling hand-painted wood carvings. Busy as the port towns are with their traffic-clogged streets and narrow sidewalks, the main squares are an oasis from the heat and bustle, with lawns that sweep past historic monuments and palm-shaded benches.

English-speaking visitors are encouraged to try a few words of French with the locals who, when conversing with each other, speak a Creole dialect based on West African grammatical structures and French vocabulary. A smile and a gesture are often all that's needed to communicate, especially if you're interested in purchasing something, and most shopkeepers can speak at least a smattering of English. The islands' official currency has been the French franc, replaced by the euro in June 2002, but American currency is widely accepted.

The economies of Guadeloupe and Martinique are based on food exports – bananas, pineapple, sugar and rum – and tourism is steadily increasing, but unemployment is widespread and there is a heavy reliance on subsidies from France. Funds used to flow the other way when these islands were major sugar producers and prized colonies of France.

The French connection began in 1635, when settlers from France landed on the two islands. Those arriving at Guadeloupe spent the next five years repelling attacks by the resident Caribs, while those on Martinique built Fort Saint-Pierre on its west coast, sharing the island for 20 years with the local Caribs before driving them away. Within a century both islands were covered with sugar plantations employing

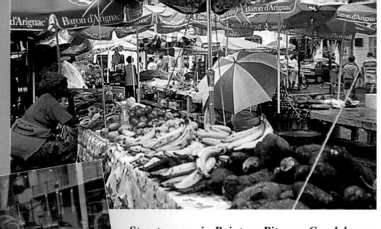

Street scenes in Pointe-a-Pitre on Guadeloupe include traditional West Indian markets and upscale shops featuring fine porcelain.

tens of thousands of African slaves. Meanwhile, the French repelled attacks by the British who eventually conquered Guadeloupe during the Seven Years War and held it for four years. This change of ownership did not, however, slow sugar production, and about 25,000 more slaves were imported and additional windmills were built under British occupation. In 1763, a bargain was struck with the Treaty of Paris in which Britain returned Guadeloupe to the French in exchange for Canada.

This allocation of New World colonies was short lived, for the American War of Independence began in 1776. Continued fighting ensued between the British and the pro-revolutionary French, including a famous naval battle off Les Saintes in 1782 in which a fleet of French warships was defeated by the British under Admiral Rodney. Turmoil continued with the outbreak of the French Revolution and the subsequent abolishment of slavery by the new Convention.

A mini-French Revolution was staged on Guadeloupe when Victor Hugues, commissaire of the Convention, arrived from France in 1794 and, after defeating the British, proceeded to guillotine the local plantation owners. This action made their counterparts on Martinique understandably nervous and they welcomed British occupation of their island until 1802, when it was returned to France under the Treaty of Amiens. At this point, slavery was reinstated in the French West Indies by Napoleon Bonaparte whose Creole wife, Josephine, was born on Martinique.

Nelson's annihilation of Napoleon's fleet at the Battle of Trafalgar in 1805 all but eliminated the French West Indian planters' lifeline to France. There was also, in keeping with the romantic spirit of the French, a hero by the name of Victor Schoelcher – son of a Parisian porcelain merchant – who campaigned for 15 years to free the slaves of the French West Indies. When the French Republic was proclaimed in Paris in 1848, Schoelcher drafted a decree that freed the 160,000 slaves of Guadeloupe and Martinique. Following the emancipation of slavery, contract workers from India took up the slack, but the era of plantation prosperity had ended. France's sugar islands, for two centuries a prolific source of 'white gold', were now bastions of black freedom.

Guadeloupe

Named by Columbus in 1493 for a monastery in Spain, Guadeloupe consists of two main islands – Basse-Terre and Grande-Terre – which are separated by a narrow saltwater channel. Basse-Terre, the western island, is mountainous and volcanic in origin, while the eastern island is chalky and flat. The nearby smaller islands of Marie-Galante, Les Saintes and La Desirade are part of Guadeloupe, which, as an overseas department of France, also administers the distant dependencies of St. Barthelemy and St. Martin.

Basse-Terre, situated on the island of the same name, is the capital of Guadeloupe. Pointe-A-Pitre on Grande-Terre is Guadeloupe's major port and commercial hub, its modern cruise facility located right downtown. Adjacent to the cruise pier is the **1** **Centre St. John Perse**, an air-conditioned complex designed in the French West Indies style. Here you will find a number of shops and restaurants as well as a currency exchange, car rental agency and public telephones.

GETTING AROUND

Most taxi drivers can speak English and are eager for business. The approximate one-way fares from Pointe-a-Pitre to the beaches east of town are, per vehicle (holding one to four persons): $20 to Gossier; $30 to Caravelle Beach; and $50 to St. Francois. A two-hour tour to Ste. Rose or Vernou is $20 per person, and a 3-hour tour to the Carbet Falls, based on four to six persons per vehicle, is $30 each. Guadeloupe has a network of modern highways and its car rental companies include Avis, Budget, Hertz and Thrifty. Ship-organized excursions often include a tour of Basse-Terre to view its lush rainforest and mountain waterfalls.

Shopping – 'Made in France' luxury items are good buys, sold at French domestic prices, and these include scarves, perfume, porcelain, crystal and liquor. Foreigners are entitled to a 20% discount on purchases made with traveller's checks or a major credit card. In **Pointe-a-Pitre**, the shops are concentrated at Centre St. John Perse, and on the main shopping streets of Rue Frebault, Rue Schoelcher and Rue de Nozieres. For local wares, the **2** public market on Rue Frebault features hand-painted wood carvings, jewelry and spices. In **Basse-Terre**, the principal shopping streets are rue Maurice Marie-Claire, rue du Cours Nolivos and rue du Docteur Cabre. An outdoor market is located on Boulevard du General de Gaulle opposite the Conseil General.

POINTE-A-PITRE

©OCEANCRUISEGUIDES

Beaches – The most accessible of Guadeloupe's beaches lie east of Pointe-a-Pitre. Closest is **Gosier**, where many of the island's resorts are situated along a white sand beach. Watersports equipment, change facilities and beach chairs are available to non-guests for a small fee. **Caravelle Beach**, outside Sainte-Anne, is the island's longest stretch of powdery white sand and, protected by reefs, is ideal for snorkeling. Watersports equipment can be rented at the Club Med. The **Raisins-Clairs Beach** at Saint-Francois is another lovely beach where sail boards and other watersports equipment can be rented at the Meridien Hotel. **Pointe Des Chateaux**, at the island's eastern tip, is a rugged section of coastline with wave-pounded boulders and beaches, including Beach of Tarare which attracts skinny dippers. On **Basse-Terre**, many of the beaches have dark sand. One of its best beaches is **La Plage de Grande-Anse** – a stretch of golden sand near Deshaies on the northwest coast.

Snorkel & Dive Sites – Pigeon Island, off the west coast of Basse-Terre, was described by Jacques Cousteau as "one of the world's 10 best diving spots." Glass-bottom boats and snorkeling trips can be taken to the underwater reserve at Pigeon Island from Malendure Beach. The snorkeling is also good at **Caravelle Beach** on Grande-Terre's south coast.

Golf – An 18-hole golf course, designed by Robert Trent-Jones, is located at the Meridien St. Francois. At 6,755 yards with a par-71, the course is fairly challenging.

LOCAL ATTRACTIONS

Pointe-a-Pitre was named for a Dutch fisherman and was first developed by the British in 1759, when they held Guadeloupe during the Seven Years War. The town was damaged by an earthquake in 1843, followed by a fire in 1899. Hurricanes have also wreaked devastation, including David and Frederick in 1979.

A number of attractions are in the vicinity of the cruise port, and a walk along the waterfront will take you past a bustling produce market to the **3 Tourism Office** which is housed in a colonnaded colonial building overlooking **4 Place de la Victoire** (Victory Square) – an expansive square lined on three sides with French colonial architecture and shaded with flamboyant trees and other tropical vegetation. Commemorating Victor Hugues's 1794 defeat of the British, this square is where he guillotined the island's aristocracy. Today the square is an inviting place to linger and visit one of the sidewalk cafes tucked beneath the brightly colored awnings on Rue Bebian.

A block west of Rue Bebian is the **5 Cathedral of St. Pierre and St. Paul**, built in 1847. Fresh flowers are sold at a stand in front of the church.

The **6 Schoelcher Museum** on rue Peynier is housed in a beautiful colonial building, its rose-colored facade decorated with relief stonework and ornate ironwork. Inside are exhibits dedicated to Victor Schoelcher, a key figure in the movement to abolish slavery.

The **7 St. John Perse Museum**, a colonial-style house on Rue de Nozieres, is dedicated to the great poet and diplomat who was born Alexis Saint-Leger Leger in Guadeloupe in 1887. He served in France's foreign office and, as an opponent of Nazi appeasement, he became one of Europe's foremost diplomats. His reputation grew as a poet following his self-imposed exile to the U.S. in 1940. Using the pseudonym St. John Perse, he was awarded the Nobel Prize in Literature in 1960.

Island Attractions: Some of Guadeloupe's most scenic attractions are on the island of Basse-Terre. These include the **8 National Park** which covers 74,000 acres of rainforest and includes 186 miles of trails. To the south is **9 Carbet Waterfalls**, its three separate cascades spilling 400 feet. The **10 Soufriere volcano**, surrounded by rainforest and banana plantations, is still active, with puffs of steam rising from its summit.

(Below) Cathedral of St. Pierre and St. Paul. (Right) Pointe-a-Pitre's Tourism Office overlooking Victory Square.

Basse-Terre is Guadeloupe's secondary cruise port, its historic architecture including the Cathedral of our Lady of Guadeloupe, the Conseil General, Palais de Justice and the Prefecture. Nearby is massive Fort Louis Delgres, dating back to 1650 and the site of numerous battles between the French and British.

Iles des Saintes, a cluster of islands off Guadeloupe's south coast, is a port of call for the smaller cruise ships. They often anchor in the spectacular harbor of Terre-de-Haute where a village of the same name is nestled at the base of a mountain, its streets of gingerbread houses easily explored on foot. A bus or taxi ride away is Fort Napoleon, with its barracks, drawbridge, art gallery and exotic garden. Nearby are underwater grottoes, coral beds and numerous beach-lined coves.

(Left) Isles des Saintes.
(Below) Caravelle Beach, outside Saint-Anne.

A cruise ship docks at Fort-de-France's downtown pier. (Right) The port's yacht-filled harbor.

Martinique

Martinique – beautiful, sophisticated and slightly snobbish – has long been a flower in the lapel of France. The Caribs originally called her Madinina – 'Island of Flowers' – and Columbus, who first laid eyes on Martinique in 1493, was so moved by her beauty when he came ashore in 1502, he described the island as "the most fertile, most delightful and most charming land in the world." But it was the French who eventually conquered Martinique and established the island's first capital of St-Pierre on the west coast.

Called the 'Paris of the West Indies', the town's 30,000 residents were so enamored by their surroundings they ignored warning signs that the nearby volcano – **Mount Pelee** – was about to erupt. The local wildlife evacuated the area before the town was smothered in ash and stones on the morning of May 8, 1902. Only one person survived – he was inside a prison cell at the time, the walls of which protected him from the hail of ash and burning gases. As the sole survivor of this catastrophic explosion, he became a sideshow with Barnum's Circus, complete with a replica of his prison cell.

Following the destruction of St-Pierre, the island's new capital became Fort-de-France, where about a third of Martinique's 360,000 residents now live. Often compared to the French Quarter of New Orleans with its narrow streets and iron grille balconies, Fort-de-France is a fascinating port to explore on foot.

GETTING AROUND

For passengers disembarking at the pier east of downtown, it's a 15- to 20-minute walk or an $8 cab ride into town. Passengers disembarking at the western pier are a 5-minute walk from the main shopping streets and attractions. The round-trip ferry ride from the Fort-de-France waterfront to the beaches at Pointe du Bout is about $6.

Unless you're fluent in French, you may want to tour the island with an organized **shore excursion**. The roads here are good, although steep and winding, and driving is on the right, so **renting a car** is an option if you're not intimidated by the French road signs and speedy drivers. Local rental agencies include Avis, Budget and Hertz, and the average daily cost is $60.

Taxis can be hired beside the cruise piers, along the downtown waterfront and beside Savannah Park. Many of the drivers speak basic English but they tend to strike a hard bargain, so indicate on a map exactly where you want to go, the stops you would like to make along the way, and write down the price agreed upon so there is no misunderstanding and renewed bargaining at the end of the tour. A round trip from Fort-de-France to St. Pierre with a half-dozen stops, including Morne-Rouge and Balata, costs about $100 (based on one to four persons sharing a taxi).

The cruise line shore excursions usually feature tours to St. Pierre, Balata and a butterfly farm, with opportunities to see the abundant flora of a tropical rainforest. Boat excursions include a catamaran cruise to a beach-lined cove and an opportunity to view a coral reef along the way.

Tourist Information is provided at various locations, including the cruise piers. A post office is at Rue de la Liberte and Rue Blenac.

Shopping – Best buys are in French-made luxury items, including perfume, jewelry, designer fashions, cosmetics, leather goods, watches, crystal, china and porcelain, with savings as high as 40% thanks in part to the 20% tax refund available to foreigners who pay by credit card or traveller's check. Local items of note include rum, fruit-flavored liqueurs and jams, wickerwork and handicrafts of bamboo, shell and madras cotton. Rue Victor Hugo is a major shopping street, with more shops located in the blocks between it and Rue Victor Severe. A handicraft market is located in **Savannah Park**.

Beaches – A 20-minute ferry ride from Fort-de-France provides access to some excellent beaches. The blue ferry goes to **Plage Pointe du Bout** where a there's a marina and luxury resorts. The red ferry goes to **Plage Anse Mitan**, a public beach of white sand with superb snorkeling, and to quieter **Plage Anse a l'Ane**, with picnic tables and a hotel/bar nearby. Either ferry costs about $6, return trip. More beautiful beaches lie along the island's south coast at **Diamant** and near **St. Anne** (about 30 miles from Fort-de-France), but reaching these beaches entails an expensive cab ride.

Several fine beaches south of Fort-de-France can be reached by a 20-minute ferry ride.

Dive & Snorkel Sites – There are good reefs for snorkeling around **Pointe du Bout** and off **Anse Mitan**. Two dive operations are located at Pointe du Bout.

Golf – The Golf Country Club is located one mile south of Pointe du Bout near the birthplace of Empress Josephine. A par-71 course designed by Robert Trent-Jones, its rolling hills offer scenic sea views.

LOCAL ATTRACTIONS

Originally a parade ground, **1 Place de La Savane (Savannah Park)** is 12 acres of lawns, stately palms and statues. It contains a children's playground and is a lively place during Carnival. A bronze statue of Pierre Belain D'Esnambuc (who led the first party of settlers to Martinique) faces the ferry pier, and a white marble statue of Empress Josephine, a gift from Napoleon III in 1859, stands near the park's northwest corner. The statue was beheaded in 1991 as a rather gruesome reminder that native-born Josephine, of Creole ancestry, was the Emperor's consort when he restored slavery in the French West Indies a decade after the Republic had abolished it.

The construction of **2 Fort Saint-Louis** took three centuries to complete, starting in the 1600s. Standing on a point of land overlooking the harbor, it is surrounded on three sides by water.

The **3 Museum of Archaeology** is located beside Savannah Park and its exhibits of pre-Columbian art include pottery and ceramic pieces that date back 1,700 years.

The ornate facade of the Schoelcher Library.

The **4** **Schoelcher Library**, designed by the 19th-century architect Henri Pick (a contemporary of Gustave Eiffel), was shipped in pieces from France and completed in 1893. Restored between 1980 and 1982, this magnificent multi-colored chrome structure, with a Byzantine glasswork dome, is registered as a historical monument of France. It's named for Victor Schoelcher – humanitarian, writer and book collector – who believed that freedom for slaves would be in vain without their receiving an education, and so donated his own library of 9,000 volumes to Martinique in 1883 to provide free access to knowledge. These books were destroyed in the huge fire of 1890, but Schoelcher's good intentions survive in the library now bearing his name.

The Prefecture (police station) on Rue Victor Severe (facing the library) is the former Government House and beside it is a colonial-style villa now housing an exhibition gallery. A few blocks down the street is the **5** **Old City Hall**, now a theatre, built in 1912. French President Charles De Gaulle gave a speech from its balcony in 1964.

Fort-de-France's Old City Hall (left) and the Court of Justice (right).

Nearby is the **6 Court of Justice**, built between 1906 and 1907, when iron and glass were widely used as building materials. A statue of Victor Schoelcher stands out front in a garden setting of greenery and benches. Three blocks over is the **7 Saint-Louis Cathedral**, inaugurated in 1895 and designed by Henri Pick to resist fire, hurricanes and earthquakes (see photo on page 87).

ISLAND ATTRACTIONS

A few miles north of Fort-de-France, at Balata, is the **Sacred Heart Basilica**, an exact but smaller replica of Montmartre Basilica in Paris (see photo, page 87). It was built in 1915 to accommodate the influx of worshippers to the Fort-de-France area following the eruption of Mount Pelee in 1902. The **Balata Tropical & Botanical Park** features plants and flowers from around the world and offers splendid views of Fort-de-France and the peaks of Carbet.

The inland route between Fort-de-France and St. Pierre winds past volcanic peaks and verdant rainforests. **Le Morne Rouge**, a pleasant resort town at the north end of this scenic drive, provides good views of Mount Pelee, as does **St. Pierre**, where a museum recalls that fateful day in 1902 when the mountain looming to the north brought death and destruction to this coastal community. South of St. Pierre along the coast is **Anse Turin**, where the French painter Paul Gauguin lived in 1887, and **Le Carbet**, where Columbus is believed to have landed.

South of Fort-de-France, near Les Trois Ilets, is the **Pagerie Museum**, a stone house commemorating the birthplace of the Empress Josephine, born in 1763 as Marie Josephe Rose Tascher de La Pageriein. Her first husband was guillotined during the French Revolution, in 1794, but she escaped with a brief imprisonment, and in 1796 she married Napoleon Bonaparte. In 1804, as consort of Napoleon I, she became Empress of France and her two children by her first marriage became titled heads of Europe. However, her union with Napoleon produced no heir and he had the marriage annulled in 1809 so he could marry the daughter of the Austrian emperor. Josephine, who had played a prominent role in the French court's social life, lived in retirement until her death in 1814.

©OCEAN CRUISE GUIDES

Dominica

Anse Du Male

Atlantic Ocean

Douglas Bay

Cabrits National Park

Cruise Dock

Prince Rupert Bay

Portsmouth

Northern Forest Reserve

Dublanc

8

Morne Diablotin

Carib Reserve

Central Forest Reserve

7

N

0 5 10

Miles

Canefield Airport

Morne Trois Pitons National Park

4

3

1

5

Woodbridge Bay Cruise Port

2

6

Caribbean

Roseau

Castle Comfort

Champagne Beach

Soufriere Bay

Sea

Grand Bay

Scotts Head

Scotts Head Village

Roseau, Dominica

CHAPTER FOURTEEN

DOMINICA & ST. LUCIA

When comparing Dominica and St. Lucia, it's a toss up which is more ruggedly beautiful. Both consist of volcanic peaks, dense tropical forests and fertile valleys filled with banana plantations. Each was coveted by the British and French who battled one another and the local Caribs for ownership. Neither nation fully succeeded, for the mountainous interiors of these islands discouraged colonization and provided cover for resisting Caribs and runaway slaves.

About 3,000 descendants of the early Caribs now live on a 3,700-acre territory of Dominica, their final enclave in a region they once dominated. The inhabitants of both islands are today mostly of African descent and, although both islands entered the 20th century as British colonies with English the official language, the unofficial culture is French. The common language is a Creole dialect like that used on Martinique and Guadeloupe, the dominant religion is Roman Catholic and the place names are frequently French. Still, the surname of many an islander reflects a British past, as does their love of cricket.

It's the natural beauty of these two islands, however, that most encourages comparison, their similar vegetation including plants and animals that are South or Central American in origin. Each island is a naturalist's dream with towering mountains, verdant valleys, rushing rivers and cascading waterfalls. The people who live on these lush islands are among the friendliest in the Caribbean and they proudly welcome visitors to their islands of untamed beauty.

Dominica

Pronounced Dom-in-eek-a, this island of 78,000 inhabitants was named by Columbus when he sailed past on a Sunday in 1493. One of the least developed of the West Indies, Dominica rightly calls itself the 'Nature Island of the Caribbean'. Large areas of virgin forest remain more or less intact, and are now protected within parks and reserves. Dominica has 20 major rivers and two freshwater lakes, both located in the National Park, and the government is committed to protecting this precious watershed. Water is currently shipped to St. Maarten, and bulk water could become a chief export. Meanwhile, bananas are a major export, as well as citrus fruits and coconut oil.

The island was badly hit by Hurricanes David and Frederick in 1979, with David causing 37 deaths and leaving 80% of the population homeless. The island's social history has also been stormy. The Caribs refused to give up their island without a fight and, in 1748, the British and French, both thwarted in their attempts at conquest, agreed to leave the island to its warlike inhabitants. But neither power could resist trying to conquer this fertile island, and France finally ceded it to Britain, but not before burning the capital of Roseau. The Commonwealth of Dominica gained independence from Britain in 1978, and its first election was held in 1980.

GETTING AROUND

Roseau, located at the mouth of the Roseau River on Dominica's southwest coast, is the island's capital and chief port, with a population of about 20,000. A cruise pier is located on the town center's waterfront and another pier, the **Woodbridge Bay Deep Water Harbor,** is about a mile north of the town center. A shuttle runs between the two locations and to nearby beaches. A **Tourist Information Office** at both cruise piers provides general information and prices for visitors looking to hire a taxi/tour operator. Dominica's third cruise ship pier at **Prince Rupert Bay**, near Portsmouth, was inaugurated in 1992 and is unique in that passengers disembark directly into a national park. The terminal building has displays and presentations to introduce passengers to the area's attractions.

Local **taxi** drivers are friendly, informed guides and their hourly sightseeing rate is about $20 an hour per car (1-4 passengers). Some sample **fares** from the Woodbridge pier to: Botanical Gardens – $2; Trafalgar Falls – $15 per person round trip; and Morne Trois Piton

(Right) Prince Rupert Bay.
(Below) A view of Rouseau and its downtown cruise pier. (Next Page) Scotts Head Beach

National Park – $20 per person round trip. Several car rental firms operate on Dominica, including Avis and Budget. Driving is on the left side of the road and a local driver's permit is required at a cost of EC $50 (approx $20 US).

Ship-organized **shore excursions** often feature island drives to the Botanical Gardens, Morne Bruce, Trafalgar Falls and the Emerald Pool. Longer tours take in the Northern Forest Reserve and the Carib Territory, terminating at Cabrits National Park where passengers are picked up by the ship.

Local currency is the EC Dollar (approximately EC$2.70 per US$1) but American currency is accepted. An entrance fee ($2) is charged by Dominica National Parks at its nature sites.

Shopping – Local handicrafts are sold at the cruise piers. Items to look for include straw crafts, pottery, hand-painted candles, wood carvings, handmade cigars and coconut-oil-based soaps, as well as unique Carib crafts such as tri-color baskets woven of larouma reeds. Authentic Carib weave baskets and hats are sold throughout the Carib Reserve and at various shops in Roseau, including Tropicrafts at the corner of Queen Mary Street and Turkey Lane. Cotton House Batiks at 8 Kings Lane sells original hand-painted clothing, as does the Artwear Gallery at 54 King George Street. The NDF Small Business Complex at 9 Great Marlborough Street houses a collection of craft shops selling batiks, jewelry and other handcrafted items.

Beaches – Most of Dominica's beaches consist of dark to silver-gray volcanic sand, although a few are honey-colored. Two of the best, both golden brown in color, are found north of Portsmouth, at Prince Rupert Bay and nearby Douglas Bay. Good beaches near Roseau include the one at Scotts Head.

Dive & Snorkel Sites – Dominica is a premier dive destination, its west coast lined with numerous underwater sites. Some of the best lie near or within the Scotts Head/Soufriere Bay Marine Reserve, at the south end of the island. A submerged volcanic crater forms this bay, which contains vertical drops from 800 to 1,500 feet within a half mile of shore. Snorkeling can be enjoyed at Champagne Reef, where walls of tiny bubbles rise continually from undersea vents that are releasing hot gases. Coral reefs and drop-offs also lie within Cabrits National Park. A half-dozen dive operators are located on Dominica, including two in Castle Comfort (just south of Roseau) and one at Soufriere.

👁 LOCAL ATTRACTIONS

The **1** Dominica Museum is a good introduction to Roseau's historic buildings, which are clustered near the harborfront on Victoria Street, including the 18th-century **2** Fort Young (now a hotel) and a number of Georgian-style buildings, namely the **3** Public Library, **4** Government House and the **5** Court House (located a few blocks away on Bay Front). Also in the vicinity is **6** St. George's Church, a 19th-century Anglican church, and the impressive **7** Cathedral of Our Lady of Fair Haven, the island's principal Roman Catholic church. The town's main attraction is the **Botanical Gardens**, 40 acres of landscaped gardens nestled at the base of Morne Bruce hill on land once cultivated with sugarcane. The planning and planting of the Gardens began in 1890, and the many exotic and indigenous trees and

Roseau's waterfront features a stone seawall and colonial buildings.

shrubs that grow here are identified with a tab number or letter to which visitors can refer on a written guide. Also located here is the Aviary – a breeding facility for Dominica's endangered parrots, namely the Jaco and the Sisserou (Dominica's national bird). The Gardens were once a popular cricket ground and have been visited twice by Queen Elizabeth. Sometimes seen parked at the Botanical Gardens is the Sisserou Express, a bus painted with tropical flora and fauna that travels the roads of Dominica to raise local awareness of conservation issues. Equipped with video recorder, t.v. monitor and other visual aids, its exhibits are used to further environmental education among the island's pre-school children. A look-out at the top of **Morne Bruce** provides panoramic views of Roseau and the coastline.

ISLAND ATTRACTIONS

1 Trafalgar Falls, not far from Roseau, can be reached by a steep winding road that terminates within a 15-minute walk to the base of the falls. A path, lined with ferns and mosses, leads from the parking lot to Trafalgar Falls, which consists of two major falls where visitors can bathe in rocky pools. Plants in the area include nutmeg, coffee, cocoa and banana, and the songbirds that can be heard include the Mountain Whistler. The **2 Wotten Waven Sulphur Springs** are located across the valley from Trafalgar Falls.

Morne Trois Pitons National Park, named for a three-peaked mountain within the park, was established in 1975, its 16,000 acres of steep volcanic landscape filled with natural wonders. Water from **Freshwater Lake** feeds the Trafalgar Falls which flow into the Roseau River. A trail, which takes about three-quarters of an hour to hike, leads from Freshwater Lake to **4 Boeri Lake** – a crater 3,000 feet above sea level which is filled with fresh water. In the other direction is **5 Boiling Lake**, the largest of its kind in the world. It's cupped in a volcanic crater, the heat of which keeps the water bubbling. Nearby, on the flanks of Morne Watt, is the **6 Valley of Desolation** – a barren landscape where

One of two spectacular cascades at Trafalgar Falls.

smoking fumaroles and boiling sulphur springs indicate there are heated rocks lying just below the surface. The sights include pools of gray, bubbling mud and multi-colored streams, their water containing minerals from old volcanic activity. The **7 Emerald Pool**, at the north end of the park, is a grotto filled with water that is brilliant green in color and fed by a waterfall. This Garden of Eden setting, with its profusion of plants, flowers and ferns, is an easy 10-minute walk through woodlands from the main road.

The 22,000-acre **Northern Forest Reserve** contains Dominica's highest peak – Morne Diablotin – which rises to 4,747 feet. The reserve's vegetation runs the gamut of a mountain ecosystem, with secondary and rain forests at lower levels, a montane (mist) forest at higher altitudes, and an elfin woodland near the summit.

A tract of land bordering the northwest side of the reserve, often referred to as the **8 'Parrot Preserve'**, is a habitat for the indigenous and endangered Sisserou and Jaco Parrots. The **Syndicate Nature Trail**, less than a mile long and easy to walk, loops through the Parrot Preserve's stand of mature rain forest, where orchids and bromeliads grow. The bird life here, in addition to parrots, includes blue-headed hummingbirds and broad-winged hawks.

At the **Carib Reserve**, on the northeast side of the island, about 3,000 descendants of the Caribbean's original inhabitants engage in farming, fishing and their traditional basket making and canoe building.

PORTSMOUTH'S ATTRACTIONS

Dominica's second town, Portsmouth is situated on a natural harbor backed by mountains. It contains sheltered Prince Rupert Bay, once home to the Caribs and a former port of call for Spanish conquistadors heading to the South American mainland. **Cabrits National Park** is situated on a forested peninsula at the north end of Portsmouth Harbor. The park contains two peaks which can reached by hiking trails, and the restored ruins of historic Fort Shirley stand on the hillsides. The park's extensive marine area offers good snorkeling among corals and tropical fish, and rowboat rides are available on the Indian River which winds past mangroves south of Portsmouth.

St. Lucia

Saint Lucia (pronounced Loo-sha) is the Caribbean's poster island. Gracing many a brochure (and the cover of this book) is its famous landmark, the Pitons – twin volcanic peaks rising from the water's edge. Conical in shape and lushly vegetated, they are evocative of the South Pacific. St. Lucia also has a 'drive-in volcano', and its National Rain Forest, home to the jacquot (St. Lucia's parrot), is a tropical paradise of wild orchids and giant ferns.

It's believed Columbus's navigator, Juan de la Cosa, was the first European to discover St. Lucia in 1499. When the British first attempted to colonize the island, it was inhabited by Caribs with whom the British signed a treaty in 1660. This situation was short lived, for the French West India Company took control of the island in 1667. This too was short lived, and from 1674 to 1814 the French and the British fought over possession of St. Lucia, the island changing hands no less than 14 times.

Since 1979 St. Lucia has been an independent country within the British Commonwealth, and its population of 154,000 enjoys a stable parliamentary democracy. This tiny country is the birthplace of two Nobel Laureates – the late Sir W. Arthur Lewis (Nobel Prize in Economics in 1979) and the poet Derek Walcott who won the 1992 Nobel Prize in Literature.

Growing and exporting bananas and other tropical produce is a major industry in St. Lucia. An oil refinery and trans-shipment facilities are also located here, near the capital of Castries on the northwest coast.

(Above) The traditional West Indian town of Soufriere.

(Below) The spectacular Pitons rise above Soufriere Bay.

GETTING AROUND

Castries, named for a French colonial minister, is the island's main cruise port. **The Elizabeth II dock** is downtown at the commercial docks, and another pier is located at **Pointe Seraphine**, where the St. Lucia **Tourist Board** office is located. AT&T telephones are also located here and on Jeremie Street in downtown Castries.

The roads on St. Lucia are steep and winding, with many a hairpin turn, so booking a ship-organized shore excursion or hiring a taxi are the best ways to see the island. The Courtesy Taxi Co-Operative Society operates at the waterfront and its drivers are capable, courteous guides. They charge government-set rates for standard trips, and island tours (1-4 persons) are $20 (US) per hour. Some sample fares are:

From Elizabeth II Dock to: Bagshaw Studio – $6; Pigeon Island – $16; Marigot Bay – $16. **From Pointe Seraphine** to: Bagshaw Studio – $10; Caribelle Batik – $12; Pigeon Island (return) – $34; Marigot Bay – $20; Vigie Beach Hotel – $5. A water taxi ($1 each way) travels between the Castries cruise pier and Pointe Seraphine. The cab fare between these two points is $4.00.

Ship-organized shore excursions often include a scenic drive to Marigot Bay. A longer tour to the Sulphur Springs and Diamond Falls usually terminates at Soufriere where passengers are returned to their ship which pulls into Soufriere Bay to retrieve them.

Shopping – For duty-free shopping, visit the modern harborfront shopping complex at **Pointe Seraphine**, where the selection of shops includes an outlet of Bagshaw's famous tropical clothing, made of high-quality, hand-printed cotton. Bagshaw Studios is located at La Toc Bay, just north of the Sandals resort. Caribelle Batik, another famous name in Caribbean clothing, has a workshop and store at **Howelton House**, a Victorian Caribbean house located on Old Victoria Road, the Morne. Local crafts, such as baskets, wood carvings and pottery, are sold at the craft market at the head of the harbor on Jeremie Street. Official currency is the

Eastern Caribbean dollar (EC$2.70 to US$1.00) but American dollars are widely accepted.

Beaches – North of Castries is the main resort area where excellent beaches include **Vigie Beach** (1¹/2 miles from Castries) and **Reduit Beach** on Rodney Bay, where watersports equipment and bar facilities are available. South of Castries, a fine beach lies on **La Toc Bay**, where a Sandals resort is located, and at lovely **Marigot Bay** (see photo, page 23), where there are several bars and restaurants.

Dive & Snorkel Sites – Diving off the island's west side is excellent, with dive operations located at Marigot Bay and Anse Chastanet. A **Marine National Park** is located off **Anse Chastanet** near Soufriere Bay where a beach-entry dive or snorkeling excursion can be made to an underwater shelf that drops from 10 to 60 feet. Another good dive site is off **Anse Des Pitons** (below the Petit Piton) where a wall of coral drops to 200 feet, and at **Anse Cochan**, where a sunken freighter lies in 60 feet. Snorkeling and wall dives can be enjoyed at **Anse La Raye**.

Golf – There are two nine-hole courses on St. Lucia – one at **Sandals St. Lucia** on La Toc Bay, the other at **Cap Estate Golf Club** near the island's northern tip.

LOCAL ATTRACTIONS

There is limited colonial architecture in Castries due to a 1948 fire that destroyed most of the town's wooden buildings. **1 Derek Walcott Square** (formerly Columbus Square) is where a 400-year-old samaan tree stands in front of the **2 Cathedral of the Immaculate Conception**, built in 1897. On the other side of the square, on Bourbon Street, is the colonial-style **3 Central Library**. The wooden buildings lining Brazil Street on the square's south side were among the few to survive the last fire. They were built in the 19th century in the French fashion with gabled roofs and second-floor fretwork balconies overhanging the sidewalk. **4 Government House** is situated west of the downtown, along Government House Road, which snakes up a hillside called The Morne.

CASTRIES
©OCEANCRUISEGUIDES

French colonial buildings overlook Derek Walcott Square.

ISLAND ATTRACTIONS

Overlooking Castries is **Morne Fortune** (Hill of Good Luck), a key battleground during skirmishes between the English and the French. North of Castries, a short distance inland from Choc Bay, is the **Union** nature trail, interpretive center and small zoo with a pair of St. Lucian parrots. Near the island's northern tip is **Pigeon Island National Park**, the spectacular open-air setting for St. Lucia's annual Jazz Festival held in May. Visitors can wander among the ruins of Fort Rodney, or enjoy the beaches. Owned by the National Trust, the park's museum is housed in the former Officers Mess. Local history includes stories of the French pirate **Francois Leclerc** (called Jamb de Bois because of his wooden leg) who used a large cave on the north shore as a hideout. Britain's Admiral Rodney set sail from here in 1782 to defeat the French fleet off Guadeloupe in the famous Battle of Les Saintes.

South of Castries lies the lush, mountainous scenery so often associated with St. Lucia, including valleys filled with banana plantations and **Morne Gimie**, the island's highest peak at 3,117 feet. Beautiful **Marigot Bay** is where a British fleet once ambushed the French by camouflaging its ships with palm fronds. Today a fleet of pleasure yachts uses this sheltered bay as a base. Some scenes from the film *Dr. Doolittle*, starring Rex Harrison, were filmed at this idyllic location. South of here is the quiet fishing village of **Anse la Raye**.

(Left) Vigie Beach.

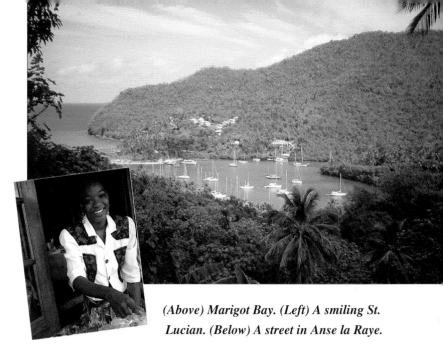

(Above) Marigot Bay. (Left) A smiling St. Lucian. (Below) A street in Anse la Raye.

Soufriere is St. Lucia's oldest town, established by the French in 1746. It lies at the base of the spectacular Pitons on the shores of Soufriere Bay. The town, with its old wooden buildings, colorful murals and a marketplace, is an authentic West Indian community. Nearby is **La Soufriere**, a dormant volcano that was about eight miles in diameter until it collapsed about 40,000 years ago. Entry is made on foot along the crater's west rim and guides take visitors on a steamy tour of the active **Sulphur Springs,** with its bubbling pools of ash. Also in this area are the **Diamond Falls** and **Mineral Baths**, originally developed by France's King Louis XVI when he had bathhouses built here for his troops. Today visitors can shower in the natural falls and soak in the mineral-rich baths.

Grenada
& St. Vincent / Grenadines

St. Vincent

Georgetown •

Kingstown ●

Bequia

Mustique

The Grenadines

Canouan

Mayreau

Union I.

Tobago Cays

Petit Martinique

Carriacou

Grenada

0   10   20

Miles

N

St. George's

Caribbean Sea

St. George's, Grenada

CHAPTER FIFTEEN

GRENADA

Should you step on deck one evening while your ship plies the waters of the Southern Caribbean, you may detect the sweet scent of nutmeg being carried by the warm breezes. The aroma of spices – cloves, cinnamon, ginger – is often detected when passing Grenada, the Caribbean's Spice Island. A third of the world's supply of nutmeg is grown and processed here, the ripened pericarps picked from sweet-smelling evergreen trees that were introduced to the island more than 200 years ago by a French sea captain.

Many exotic plants were brought to the West Indies during the era of European colonization, including the breadfruit tree that Captain Bligh went to great lengths to collect in Tahiti and transport to St. Vincent. The plants and trees that thrive on Grenada (pronounced Gra-nay-da) and St. Vincent come in all varieties, from flowering to medicinal. Residents grow most of their own fruits and vegetables, and it has been said that even a nail would grow in the rich soil of St. Vincent. Rugged and fertile, St. Vincent and Grenada lie at either end of the Grenadines, a string of beach-ringed isles frequented by yachts and small sailing ships. Most of this island chain belongs to St. Vincent, while the southern islands of Carriacou (pronounced Carry-coo), and Petit Martinique come under Grenada's jurisdiction.

European settlement of Grenada began in 1650 with the French purchasing some land from the resident Caribs in return for knives and baubles. The Caribs soon had a change of heart however and their rebellion was swiftly put down. When defeat was all but certain, the remaining Caribs – men, women and children – threw themselves over a cliff now called Le Morne de Sauteur (Leaper's Hill). With that enemy exterminated, the French then had to fend off the British who seized control of the island in 1762. The French regained Grenada in 1779 but a few years later, under the terms of the Treaty of Versailles, the island was once again Britain's.

The next violent clash was caused by mounting tensions between British settlers and the French planters who remained on Grenada. A free colored Grenadian named Fedon, who owned a large coffee and cocoa estate called Belvedere in the mountains north of St. George's, plotted an uprising inspired by the French Revolution's principles of liberty and equality. His estate became Camp Belvedere as the insurrection swept across the island and rebelling slaves set fire to crops and buildings. The British governor was taken prisoner and executed. For a time, the entire island was under a siege of terror during which British settlers found safety in fortified St. George's, the island's only stronghold until reinforcements arrived and eventually quashed the rebellion. As British troops closed in on Camp Belvedere, mountain warfare ensued with specially trained troops silently climbing under cover of darkness to the insurgents' armed camp, which they attacked at dawn. Fedon and his men fled but all were eventually captured, except for Fedon who, it's believed, escaped by small boat only to drown at sea.

Following emancipation in the mid-1800s, the island became a British Crown Colony and in 1974 it gained independence as a full member of the Commonwealth of Nations. This was followed by a bloodless coup in 1979 and the establishment of the People's Revolutionary Government under radical leftist Prime Minister Maurice Bishop. His close ties to Cuba and the U.S.S.R. strained relations with the U.S. and other Caribbean nations, and Grenada was once again gripped by turmoil when, during an internal coup in 1983, the army seized control. Prime Minister Bishop, ten of his cabinet colleagues and an undetermined number of civilians were executed.

Within weeks the U.S., at the request of other Caribbean nations, invaded the island and quickly restored law and order. The U.S. military, which received the overwhelming support of the Grenadian population, also rescued some American medical students who had been stranded on the island during the coup. A general election in late 1984 re-established democratic government.

The island capital is **St. George's** and its inner harbor, called The Carenage, is considered one of the prettiest in the Caribbean. Its historic harborfront warehouses are brightly painted, casting mirror images on

(Opposite page and above) St. George's inner harbor, called The Carenage, is one of the most picturesque in the Caribbean.

the water where fishing boats and schooners moor alongside the sea-wall, their lines tied to bollards made from cannons. The town's cobble-stone streets and walkways are lined with old churches and brick-and-stone warehouses, some roofed with red tiles brought as ballast by trading ships.

GETTING AROUND

Most cruise ships anchor in St. George's Bay and tender passengers ashore to the water taxi dock in the Carenage where a Tourist Information Center is conveniently located for disembarking passengers. A small cruise ship pier is located just south of the water taxi dock.

English is the official language of Grenada, its population 90,000, but a French-African patois is still used around the island, and many of the place names are in French.

The official currency is the Eastern Caribbean (EC) dollar (approximately $2.70 EC to $1.00 US) but American currency is accepted.

Card-operated phones are located at Grenada Telecommunications on the Carenage, and the card and coin phone booths located through-out the city are on the international direct dial system. A **ℹ Board of Tourism** office is located at the pier on the Carenage, and a post office is located just to the east.

Rental car firms operating on Grenada include Avis (Spice Isle Rentals) on Lagoon Road. Driving is on the left and a local driving per-mit ($12 US) can be obtained through most rental companies or at the

Fire Station on the Carenage. Some of the roads on Grenada are in need of repair and are quite rough and bumpy in places.

Local buses depart from Market Square and the Esplanade, the traditional ones painted bright colors with wooden seats. They cost between $1 EC and $5 EC (or 37¢ US up to $1.85 US), depending on the distance travelled.

Taxis holding one to four persons can be hired for $20 US per hour. Sample fares from the cruise pier to: downtown St. George's – $3; from St. George's to: Grand Anse Beach – $8-10; Point Salines $15. Water taxi fares are: Carenage to Grand Anse Beach – $4 (round-trip); across the harbor – $2.

Ship-organized **excursions** often include the 'Royal Drive' which traces the tour once given to Queen Elizabeth on an official visit. This tour takes in Fort Frederick, the Morne Jaloux Ridge, the south coast and Grand Anse Beach. Another popular drive is the one to Grand Etang National Park and Annandale Falls. Boat excursions often include a catamaran cruise with a beach stop.

Shopping – The **Spice Market** is located near the pier on the Carenage and is a good place to buy gift baskets filled with spices. Other local items to look for on Grenada include batik, wood carvings, pottery and rum, as well as jams and jellies made from nutmeg and guava. The **Carenage** is where a number of stores are located, selling Caribbean crafts and duty-free perfumes, china and crystal. (The Nutmeg, on the Carenage, is a recommended restaurant, popular with locals and visitors, serving homemade West Indian dishes.) Another good place to shop for duty-free goods and Caribbean handicrafts, including dolls, clothing and jewelry, is in **Grand Anse**.

Beaches – Just south of St. George's is **Grand Anse Bay** with two miles of beautiful white sand (see photo, page 23). The island's resort and watersports center, Grand Anse Beach is one of the best in the Caribbean and can be reached by water taxi from the Carenage. A quiet beach lies below **Point Salines**, where a reef near shore offers good snorkeling. At the island's north end, in **Levera National Park**, is beautiful **Bathway Beach**, protected from the Atlantic surf by a reef barrier.

Dive & Snorkel Sites – Grenada has plenty of reefs and wrecks to satisfy snorkelers, novice divers and advanced divers. A number of dive and snorkel operations are located at Grand Anse Beach. **Morne Rouge Beach**, beside Grand Anse Beach, is popular with snorkelers. An extensive reef lies south of Morne Rouge off **Point Salines**, its three main dive sites being The Hole, which starts in sand bars and descends 50 feet; the Valley of Whales, which contains hills of coral and canyon floors of sand; and Forests of Dean, where rays and octopus are often sighted. Snorkelers can explore the reef close to shore. North of St. George's the sites include **Molinere Reef**,

Grenada's famous Spice Market is located on The Carenage, near the tender dock.

which starts at 20 feet and is a good spot for snorkelers and novice divers. Other dive sites include the wall dive at Grand Mal Point; Channel Reef at the entrance to St. George's Harbor; and numerous wrecks, including the *Bianca C* – a cruise ship that caught fire in 1961 and which, after all the passengers were evacuated, sank in 100 feet of water.

Golf – The nine-hole course at the Grenada Golf & Country Club, near Grand Anse, is open to visitors and has scenic ocean views of both the Caribbean and Atlantic.

(Below) A quiet beach near Pt. Salines. (Opposite page) Historic buildings overlook St. George's Bay; scenic inlets dot the south coast.

LOCAL ATTRACTIONS

A walking tour of St. George's will take you past many historical buildings. The **National Library** has been at its present waterfront location, housed in a former warehouse, since 1892. The ❷ **National Museum**, housed in a brick warehouse built by the French in 1704, contains pre-Columbian exhibits including petroglyphs, and its gift shop carries books on the local history. Beside the museum is the Antilles Hotel, one of the oldest buildings in St. George's which was once a French barracks. ❸ **Simmons Alley**, a stepped pedestrian walkway, leads up to ❹ **St. George's Anglican Church**, built by the British in 1825 using stone and pink stucco.

The residential ❺ **Sedan Porches** were originally built open at each end so that people riding in sedan chairs could disembark without getting wet from the rain. The ❻ **Houses of Parliament** and its neighboring Registry, built in 1780, are good examples of early Georgian architecture.

The town's **7** **Roman Catholic Cathedral** stands high on the hillside with an unobstructed view down St. Johns Street to the water. Local produce is sold at colorful **8** **Market Square** which is also the site of parades and political rallies.

9 **St. Andrew's Presbyterian Kirk**, often called the Scot's Kirk, stands at the bottom of Church Street and was built in 1831 with help from the Freemasons.

10 **Fort George**, at the entrance to St. George's Harbor, was built by the French in 1705, with later additions by the British. Its ramparts provide commanding views of the Carenage, and within its walls are tunnels, staircases and narrow passageways. Grenada's former leftist Prime Minister Maurice Bishop was executed inside this fort, which is currently used as headquarters of the Royal Grenada Police.

ISLAND ATTRACTIONS

The restored remains of **Fort Frederick** stand on the tallest point of a ridge overlooking St. George's, providing visitors with panoramic views of the coast and surrounding countryside. Built by the British around 1791 to protect the rear flank of St. George's from attack, it is the central fort in a chain of defence along Richmond Hill which included Fort Matthew to the north and two other fortifications to the south, said to be connected by tunnels.

The **Annandale Falls** cascade into a freshwater pool surrounded by tropical gardens and paths. Swimming and refreshments can be enjoyed here.

Grand Etang National Park is located in the central, mountainous part of the island, its centerpiece a crater lake surrounded by 2,000-foot mountain peaks. An Information Center provides audiovisual presentations on the flora and fauna of the park's tropical rainforest.

Carmel Waterfall, the island's highest at 75 feet, was recently developed. A walking trail with hand rails, botanical labels and benches leads to this once-hidden waterfall.

Grenada's **spice plantations** are concentrated at the north end of the island and a nutmeg processing station is located outside **Gouyave** on the northwest coast. The 1994 opening of **Levera National Park**, on the rugged northeast coast, increased the island's protected area to 13% of its total land mass. Levera's pristine beaches and mangrove swamps provide habitat for sea turtles and a variety of birds. The islands of the Grenadines can be seen on the horizon, the two southernmost – Carriacou and Petit Martinique – forming a tri-island nation with Grenada.

Ground nutmeg is made from the fruit's inner seed.

St. Vincent's Leeward Coast – where rugged slopes and fertile valleys run down to a tranquil Caribbean Sea.

St. Vincent & The Grenadines

Affectionately known as the Garden Island, St. Vincent was called Hairoun or 'Land of the Blessed' by the original Ciboney inhabitants. This lush volcanic island was a Carib stronghold when Columbus sighted and named it for the feast day of the Spanish patron saint St. Vincent on January 22, 1493. But the island remained untouched by outsiders until 1675, when a Dutch slave ship foundered off the rugged east coast and the survivors, mostly slaves, were taken in by the local Caribs.

The British claimed the fertile island a few years later, but it was the French who established the first European settlement on the leeward coast in 1719. The island changed hands a dozen times until the Treaty of Paris in 1783 officially ceded it to the British, under whose rule it remained until 1979, when St. Vincent gained its independence.

The island's present population of about 100,000 is a melting pot of Caribs, Africans and immigrants from India, Portugal and the Middle East who came to the island following emancipation in 1838. This racial mix has nurtured the second-largest Carnival celebration in the Caribbean, after Trinidad's renowned gala, and this takes place the first week of July. In the hills outside the island's capital and port of Kingstown are the first Botanical Gardens established in the Western Hemisphere. A sucker from one of the original breadfruit trees unloaded here by Captain Bligh in 1793 still grows in the Gardens. At the north end of the island stands La Soufriere, an active volcano that last erupted in 1979.

(Above) A luxury sailing ship shares an anchorage with private yachts at Mustique. (Left) The poolside view at Princess Margaret's villa. (Below) The grounds of the famous Cotton House hotel.

Stretching south from St. Vincent, in a 60-mile arc, are the **Grenadines** – tiny islands ringed with white-sand beaches and coral reefs. Because of their small size and limited rainfall, the Grenadines remained uninhabited until the early 1800s when a band of French colonists established cotton plantations on two of them.

Bequia (pronounced beck-way) is the largest of the group (five miles long by two miles wide), with a population of 6,000. Its name is from the Carib word *becouya* – Island in the Clouds. The island became a busy whaling station in the mid-1800s when some seafaring Scots settled here. Port Elizabeth, in Admiralty Bay, is the center of island life, and the nearby beaches can be reached by water taxi.

The small, hilly island of **Mustique** was bought in 1958 by Colin Tennant, a Scottish heir whose title was Lord Glenconner. He paid 45,000 pounds sterling for the neglected island of about 100 inhabitants and spent an additional fortune reviving the local farming and fishing

industries. In 1960, Princess Margaret, Queen Elizabeth's younger sister, accepted a plot of land as a wedding gift and built a waterfront villa, thus prompting her wealthy and well-connected friends to buy and build on Mustique. Today the island is run as a private company, its 60-some homeowner-shareholders including Mick Jagger. The Cotton House, an old plantation house converted by Tennant into a luxury hotel, remains one of the most elegant accommodations available in the Caribbean. The island's private villas are rented out when the owners aren't there.

One of the oldest Catholic churches in the Windward Islands stands on the tiny islet of **Mayreau** (pronounced my-ro), atop the island's only hill. Built in the early 1800s by the St. Heliers family from France, the church functions as a Sunday gathering place for most of the island's 100 inhabitants. Sharing the hilltop is the island's school, and on the other side of the hill is **Salt Whistle Bay**, one of the finest beaches and anchorages in the island chain.

The four, deserted islets of **Tobago Cays**, surrounded by the huge Horseshoe Reef, have been declared a wildlife reserve. The brilliant white beaches and surrounding seas in shades of blue ranging from indigo to aquamarine, make this cluster of islands a tropical paradise for visitors arriving by sailing vessel.

Near the southern end of the chain is **Union Island**, with a population of 2,000. For decades it has been a port of entry for yachts plying the quiet waters of St. Vincent and the Grenadines, earning it the nickname 'Gateway to the Grenadines'.

(Above) Mayreau's idyllic Salt Whistle Bay.
(Left) The pristine islands of Tobago Cays.

CHAPTER SIXTEEN

BARBADOS

B arbados is perhaps the most British of the Caribbean islands. For more than three centuries the island was under continuous British rule, and its parliament, formed in 1639, is the third oldest in the English-speaking world (after Britain and Bermuda). An independent member of the British Commonwealth of Nations since 1966, Barbados is a stable democracy with a thriving economy and an impressive health care record. Cricket is the national sport, and the capital of Bridgetown has its own Trafalgar Square, complete with Nelson's Column.

The similarities to Olde England continue outside of Bridgetown, where a drive along narrow winding roads, past village greens and cricket fields, is a step back in time to the days of the British Empire when wealthy plantation owners lived in Georgian-style great houses built of coral stone, their thick walls a barrier to the tropical heat and brutality of slave labor.

There were no permanent inhabitants on Barbados when the first English ship visited its shores in 1625. Lying 100 miles east of the volcanic arc of Windward Islands, Barbados was at one time inhabited by Arawaks but the island escaped detection by migrating Caribs and, later, by Columbus. A coral island of ridges and hills, it began to form quite recently, geographically speaking. About 700,000 years ago, tectonic forces slowly pushed a section of seabed to the surface where this emerging coral cap was then fractured by two massive upheavals which left a ridge running down the island's west side and a 600-foot-cliff on the east coast. The clay and soil deposits lying on this uplifted coral were the result of silt build-up from the Orinoco River in what is now Venezuela; the volcanic dust responsible for the soil's fertility was carried in the stratosphere, over thousands of centuries, from the islands of St. Vincent and St. Lucia.

The island remained in isolation, visited mostly by birds. The seeds left in their droppings and the coconuts that washed up on beaches were the source of vegetation that slowly took root, including the Bearded Fig Tree for which the island was named Isla de los Barbados (Island of the Bearded) by a passing Portuguese explorer in the early 16th century. When British settlers arrived in 1627 and established Jamestown near present-day Holetown, they initially planted tobacco, then switched to sugarcane. African slaves were brought in to work the fields when indentured servants began avoiding Barbados, partly because its planters had a reputation as cruel masters who paid meager freedom dues, but mainly because it was a white man's graveyard.

Europeans had no immunity to tropical diseases, several of which were brought over by the Africans, and the majority of white settlers perished within their first year on the island. Those who survived, however, became extremely wealthy and Barbados dominated the sugar markets in England until the latter part of the 17th century. The island's easterly location (i.e. closer to England) and a coastline that was easily accessible from any point on the island, kept transport costs lower than on other islands. The island's location also helped preserve its British status, for the prevailing winds prevented enemy sailing ships from approaching the island's west side without tacking to and fro, making it difficult to stage a surprise attack.

The relative isolation of Barbados no doubt contributed to the independent streak of its early settlers. They resisted rule by outsiders, and this included Oliver Cromwell when he became Lord Protector of England. In defiance of **Britain's Navigation Acts**, Barbadians continued trading with Dutch shipping companies, which gave them better prices and service, and Cromwell had to send a fleet to "subdue the barbarous Barbadians." The blockade lasted several months, the stubborn Barbadians refusing to allow any of the English naval officers to land. Eventually a meeting took place in 'Ye Mermaid Tavern' and the articles of surrender gave the islanders a protected market for their sugar in England, even after the monarchy was restored.

Barbados continued shipping sugar almost to the end of the 18th century, and the island's plantation era endures in the many historic mansions that have been preserved through the efforts of Barbados National Trust, founded in 1961 by an expatriate Briton and a group of interested Barbadians. The miniature counterpart to the colonial great house is the chattel house. These tiny structures, a miniature version of the Georgian-style manor house, appeared after emancipation when freed slaves built themselves moveable wooden homes.

Following the end of the slave trade in 1832, communities began to center around each parish's local church and school. Education became widespread and today 97% of the island's population is literate. Only 21 by 14 miles in size, Barbados is densely populated with about a third of its quarter-million population living in the Bridgetown area. Yet, once you're away from the busy streets of Bridgetown, the island's natural beauty, healthy climate and sense of gentility exert their appeal. Protected powdery beaches line the west side of the island, in contrast to the rugged east coast where Atlantic swells roll ashore. Inland, the rolling country-side of parks and gardens exudes a pastoral charm, as do the villages where parish churches swell with singing on Sunday mornings.

Barbadian rum is among the finest and oldest in the world, the locally produced **Mount Gay** brand first distilled here in 1663 by Abel Gay. The island's ideal climate has long attracted visitors, one of its most famous being George Washington when, in 1751, he accompanied his ill half-brother who came for a change of air, as was fashionable at the time. Much has changed since the days of British colonialism but the island's summer festival, called Crop Over, still celebrates the end of the sugar harvest – an annual event in Barbados for the past three

(Opposite page) Morgan Lewis Mill is one of numerous heritage sites. (Below) Bridgetown's cruise port.

and a half centuries. Sugar remains an important export but tourism is well established, with more than 800,000 visitors arriving annually, half of these by cruise ship.

GETTING AROUND

The deep-water harbor, located about a mile north of **Bridgetown's** center, opened in 1961. It occupies Pelican Island, upon which pelicans once nested before it was joined to the mainland during the harbor's construction. The port's spacious complex contains a tourist information office and an assortment of shops carrying duty-free and locally made items.

Barbados is a very pleasant island to tour, whether by rental car, hired taxi or group excursion. The roads are in good condition, although they are generally narrow and winding, and visibility is sometimes restricted by bordering cane fields. Driving is on the left, roundabout lanes are common, and Bridgetown is best avoided during rush hour. A temporary license (available through local car rental firms) costs $5 US.

Rental cars and taxis can be hired just outside the shopping complex at the kiosks, and daily rental car rates are $55-$75.

Taxi rates (posted in the terminal building in Barbadian dollars) are fixed. Some sample fares, in US dollars, per cab, from the cruise port to: Bridgetown – $4; Hilton Hotel – $6; Crane Bay – $18; Sam Lord's Castle – $20; and Harrison's Cave – $15.

Ship-organized excursions usually include a countryside tour with popular stops being Gun Hill, St. John's Parish Church and one of the island's great houses. Also organized by most cruise lines is a visit to Harrison's Cave and a ride on the Atlantis Submarine.

The official currency is the Barbados dollar (worth approximately 50¢ US) but American and Canadian money is widely accepted.

Shopping – There is a good selection of duty-free shops at the cruise terminal, including branch stores of Cave Shepherd and Harrison's. Local arts and crafts are sold at **Pelican Village**, on the main highway leading into town. In Bridgetown, the duty-free shops are concentrated on **Broad Street** and its side streets, where good buys can be found in crystal, fine bone china, jewelry, perfumes and clothing. Harrisons, established in 1854, is considered the island's premier store. Local handicrafts, batik, ceramics and original paintings and prints can be bought at various galleries, including Verandah Art Gallery, 'Creative Expressions' in The Shops of the Ginger Bread House, Colours of de Caribbean and Mango Jam Gallery.

Mahogany woodcarvings and sculptures can be found at Best of Barbados Shops (with a location at the Cruise Ship Terminal) and Potter's House Gallery in Shop Hill. Contemporary and traditional pottery is sold at various rural potteries, including Chalky Mount and Castle Pottery in St. Peter, Earthworks Pottery at Shop Hill in St. Thomas, and Fairfield Pottery in St. Michael.

Beaches – The most sheltered beaches lie on the west coast, including **Mullins Beach** which offers glassy smooth water and good snorkeling, and **Paynes Bay** which is good for swimming and watersports. Restaurant facilities are available at both beaches. Just south of Bridgetown's central district is a crescent of white sand on **Carlisle Bay** which is popular with both locals and visitors and is backed by a small restaurant called The Boatyard. On the south coast, at Needhams Point, the grounds of the **Hilton Hotel** overlook a white sand beach.

On the southeast coast, a beach of sugary white sand and fairly big waves is located at **Crane Bay**. Another beautiful beach washed by surf is **Bottom Bay**, which lies at the base of a cliff north of **Sam Lord's Castle** and is reached by some steps, as is the fine beach right below Sam Lord's – a Georgian mansion built in 1820 by a 'gentleman pirate' and now part of a hotel resort. On the island's Atlantic coast, a dramatic sight is the pounding surf and eroded boulders at **Bathsheba Beach,** where signs warn that swimming is dangerous.

(Opposite page) Bridgetown's cruise terminal offers excellent shopping and services. (Below) Sam Lord's Castle is an island landmark.

(Above and left) Mullins Beach, on the sheltered west coast, is ideal for swimming and snorkeling. (Below) Beaches on the southeast coast are partially protected by Cobbler's Reef.

(Right) 'Red Roof Top' by award-winning Barbadian artist Neville Oluyemi Legall, whose works are sold at most of the island's galleries.

(Left) Atlantic swells roll ashore at Bathsheba Beach. (Below) Crane Bay offers fine white sand and some surf.

Dive & Snorkel Sites – The **Folkestone Underwater Park and Marine Reserve** is just north of Holetown. In addition to the park headquarters and interpretation center, the underwater park itself is divided into four zones – scientific, recreational, and a northern and southern watersports zone. The Recreational Zone contains a snorkel trail near shore and dive boats are available for trips to Dottin's Reef – part of a seven-mile stretch of intermittent banking reef about 1/3 mile offshore. South of the recreational zones, a 356-foot freighter has been sunk in 120 feet about a half mile from shore to form an artificial reef. Two dive shops are located in Holetown.

A number of wrecks lie on the bottom of **Carlisle Bay** where ships once anchored before the harbor was constructed; these include the *Berwyn* (scuttled in 1919), which is ideal for snorkelers.

Dive Boat Safari is located at the Hilton on **Needhams Point**, offering beach and boat dives for all levels of experience. Drift diving is popular on the south coast along the barrier reef that starts at depths of 60 feet and lies from a half mile to two miles offshore. Hawksbill turtles are commonly sighted there. Non-divers can view the island's underwater world to depths of 150 feet aboard an Atlantis Submarine or enjoy a snorkeler's perspective of the near-shore reefs on board the Atlantis Seatrec observation vessel, both based in Bridgetown.

Golf – The 18-hole course at **Sandy Lane Golf Club** is set in the upscale area of Sandy Lane Estate north of Bridgetown. A 6,533-yard, par-72 course, its signature hole is a 70-foot drop from tee to green. South of Bridgetown is the par-36, nine-hole course at **Club Rockley** which covers 2,736 yards.

LOCAL ATTRACTIONS

Founded in 1628, Bridgetown stands on the banks of the Constitution River, its wide mouth forming a harbor called the Careenage where boats moor alongside. Spanning the Careenage is the Chamberlain Bridge, its south end graced with the Independence Arch.

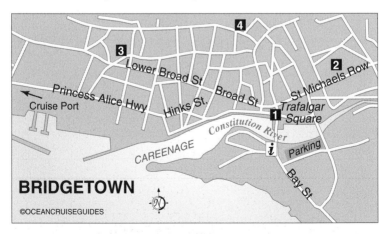

BRIDGETOWN
©OCEANCRUISEGUIDES

At the north end of the bridge is **1** **Trafalgar Square**, in the center of which stands a statue of Horatio Nelson which predates the one in London. The neo-Gothic Public Buildings on the north side of the square were erected in 1872 and they house the island's Parliament.

Other historic buildings in the downtown core include **2** **St. Michael's Cathedral** (rebuilt after it was destroyed by a hurricane in 1780), the 18th-century **3** **St. Mary's Church**, and the beautifully-restored **4** **Nidhe Israel Synagogue** which was originally built in 1654 and has won an American Express Preservation Award. Streets of interest include **Hinks Street**, with its old sugar warehouses, and **Broad Street** with its elegant shops and colonial buildings. A convenient parking lot is located between the two bridges on the south bank of the river.

ISLAND ATTRACTIONS

The Barbados National Trust preserves and operates a number of island attractions that have historic importance or natural beauty. These are indicated below with a star (*) and can be visited individually (a discount system is in place for those who visit more than one attraction). Ship-organized tours visit several National Trust properties (some of which are closed on Sundays and public holidays). In addition to those mentioned below, Trust properties include the Sir Frank Hutson Sugar Museum, Codrington College, Oughterson House & Barbados Zoo Park, and the elegant Francia Plantation House (near Gun Hill) which was built by a Frenchman for his bride at the turn of the century. In the historic Garrison area just south of Bridgetown are the **5** **Barbados Gallery of Art** and **The Barbados Museum*** which contains archaeological and historical exhibits as well as African and European decorative arts.

The Parliament Buildings and Trafalgar Square stand on the north side of Bridgetown's historic harbor, known as the Careenage.

(Above) Gun Hill Signal Station overlooks the Caribbean Sea.
(Opposite) A view of the Atlantic coast from Farley Hill National Park.

 6 The Mount Gay Rum Visitor's Center*, just north of Bridgetown, offers 45-minute tours which end with a sampling of the company's famous rum.

The authentic chattel houses at **7 Tyrol Cot Heritage Village*** are centered around an 1854 mansion, the former home of Sir Grantley and Lady Adams, and the village includes a popular market selling local arts and crafts.

In the 19th century, a series of signal stations were established by Britain's Royal Artillery along the island's high points to signal the approach of enemy ships or the safe arrival of cargo ships. The signal men communicated between stations using telescopes and flags. **8 Gun Hill Signal Station***, situated on the highland of St. George with a magnificent view of the west coast, was built in 1818 and restored by the Barbados National Trust in 1982. On the hill below the station, visible from the road when exiting the premises, is a British Military Lion that was carved by British soldiers.

At **9 Harrison's Cave*** trams take visitors on a spectacular subterranean ride past limestone stalactites and stalagmites that took millions of years to form. An underground stream of clear water runs through the cave, fed by rain that is filtered through 200 feet of coral before reaching a natural underground reservoir which is the island's supply of pure drinking water.

Harrison's Cave

Administered by the Barbados National Trust, **10 Welchman Hall Gully*** is an oasis of ornamental plants and trees nestled in a deep gully rimmed with cliffs. Located near Harrison's Cave, it was once part of a series of caves, the roofs of which collapsed to create the gully now filled with tropical plants and pathways. Its jungle setting is also a habitat for the Barbados Green Monkey which is frequently seen here in the early morning or late afternoon.

The 50-acre **11 Flower Forest** is a cross between a botanical garden and a nature trail. Located on a hillside of the Scotland District, its paths contain several seats, and walking sticks and umbrellas are provided. In addition to bar and restaurant facilities, the premises contain a Best of Barbados gift shop.

One of the oldest great houses in the Caribbean, **12 St. Nicholas Abbey*** is maintained by the National Trust. It was built by a British colonel around 1650 in the Jacobean style with Dutch gables and corner fireplaces – an unlikely feature for the tropics. Its second owner, Sir

St. Nicholas Abbey

Farley Hill was once the most opulent plantation estate on Barbados.

John Yeamans, colonized Carolina and became the third Governor of South Carolina. The current owner is Lieutenant Colonel Stephen Cave whose family has owned the estate since 1820. One of only three remaining great houses of its period in the Western Hemisphere, the ground floor is open for viewing and is furnished with English and Barbadian antiques. The wine cellar is now a gift shop.

A restored signal station is located at **13 Grenade Hall Forest & Signal Station*** in St. Peter. A panoramic view can be enjoyed from the signal station, and the surrounding forest contains coral pathways for viewing the various species of trees, vines and herbs, their present and past uses illustrated with a series of signs.

Established in 1985 on four acres of mahogany forest, the non-profit **14 Barbados Wildlife Reserve** includes a research center that focuses on conservation of the Barbados Green Monkey. The animals wander freely here and visitors are encouraged to take their time while walking quietly along the shady paths or pausing on a bench to wait and see which creatures appear.

At **15 Farley Hill National Park***, officially opened by Queen Elizabeth in 1966, visitors can wander the ruins of what was once the most opulent plantation estate on the island. Situated in the Scotland District at the north end of the island, the park's ridge-top location provides sweeping views of the surrounding countryside and the island's Atlantic coast. The mansion, built in stages in the 19th century, was gutted by fire in the late 1950s shortly after the filming of *Island In The Sun* starring Harry Belafonte. Its stone walls remain, as do the trimmed lawns and narrow lanes shaded by a corridor of palm trees. The park is a cool and breezy place to enjoy a picnic lunch, just as Sir Graham's royal guests – Prince Albert and Prince George (later George V) – did in 1879.

16 **Morgan Lewis Mill***, a Barbados National Trust Property in the rugged Scotland District, is the only complete sugar windmill surviving in the Caribbean. Built in the 18th century to grind sugarcane, hundreds of such mills used to dot the countryside when sugar was 'white gold' and Barbados was Britain's most valuable possession in the Americas.

The six acres of individual tropical gardens at **17** **Andromeda Botanic Gardens*** contain rare and unique species of plants.

One of the oldest and most picturesque churches on the island, **18** **St. John's Parish Church** stands atop an inland bluff overlooking the east coast. Originally built of wood, its stone replacement was destroyed by several hurricanes. The present structure dates from 1836 and the churchyard contains the tomb of Ferdinand Paleologus, who was the great-grandson of Thomas, brother of the last Byzantine Emperor. Ferdinand served in the army of the King of England before sailing to Barbados, where he was church warden from 1655 to 1656.

The original **19** **Villa Nova** was destroyed by a hurricane in 1831. Rebuilt in 1834 and now a luxury resort, its previous owners include British Prime Minister Sir Anthony Eden and the Earl of Avon, whose garden parties were attended by Lady Churchill and Queen Elizabeth.

20 **Sunbury Plantation House*** is a beautifully preserved great house built in the 1600s. Its original owners were the Chapmans, one of the first planter families on Barbados. The last owners, the Melvilles, lived here until 1985, although the residence was officially opened to visitors as a Heritage House in 1984. Carefully restored, the mansion is filled with mahogany antiques and all of its rooms are open for viewing. The grounds contain gardens, a gift shop, and a unique collection of horse-drawn carriages.

St. John's Parish Church overlooks the island's Atlantic coast.

Netherlands Antilles

Caribbean Sea

CURACAO

West Point

Christoffel National Park **14**

Soto

Daniël

Hato **15**

12
13

Piscadera Bay
Holiday Beach
Princess Beach
Underwater Marine Park

East Point

0   10   20
Miles

©OCEAN CRUISE GUIDES

ARUBA

Noord
Casibari ×
Arikok
San Nicolas
Oranjestad

California Lighthouse
Arashi
Underwater Park
Palm Beach
Eagle Beach

Tierra del Sol
Alto Vista Chapel
Natural Bridge
Casibari ×

Noord

Boca Prins ×
Arikok
× Guadirikiri Cave
San Nicolas

Colorado Pt. Lighthouse

Mangel Halto
Baby Beach

Oranjestad

CHAPTER SEVENTEEN

ARUBA, CURACAO & BONAIRE

T he Dutch islands of Aruba, Bonaire and Curacao (the ABCs) lie off the coast of Venezuela, outside of the hurricane belt. Unlike the other Lesser Antilles, they receive little rain in summer, their vegetation consisting of drought-resistant cacti and divi-divi trees bent by the steady trade winds. Their stark landscapes of wave-eroded rock formations and brilliant white beaches are in contrast to the colorful ports where Dutch gabled, pastel-painted buildings line the waterfront.

The islands' semi-arid climate, interrupted by a brief rainy spell each winter, is one reason they were deemed 'useless' by the early Spanish explorers. They were inhabited at the time by Caiquetios, a tribe of peaceful Arawak Indians who lived in villages and caves, the walls of which contain pictographs they left behind. Their food came mostly from the rich bounty of the sea, the surrounding waters filled with colorful coral gardens and an abundance of fish. Other foodstuffs were obtained from mainland tribes in exchange for salt, one of the few natural resources found on these barren islands.

Located within 40 miles of the Venezuela coast, the ABCs are actually part of the Andes chain of mountains which snakes up the western side of South America and branches into smaller ranges at the north end of the continent. Underwater volcanic activity helped form the islands,

Colorful Dutch colonial architecture houses shops and businesses in Aruba's main town of Oranjestad.

which consist of batholith rock as well as younger limestone which formed before uplifting slowly brought the islands to the sea's surface.

The treasure-seeking Spaniards were the first Europeans to discover the ABCs when, in 1499, a Spanish sea captain en route to South America left some of his scurvy-afflicted sailors on one of the islands to die. When he returned less than a year later, he found them all alive and well. Hence the name Curacao – based on the Portuguese word for 'the cure'. Yet, despite its promising name, Curacao did not impress the Spanish for it was a dry, prickly place with no apparent gold deposits. Even the Valencia orange trees brought from Spain produced a bitter, almost inedible fruit when planted here.

It took the resourceful Dutch to see the potential of Curacao and make it an integral part of their trading empire. They seized the island in 1634, transferring the few Spanish settlers and Arawak Indians to the mainland, and took possession of Aruba and Bonaire a year or so later. Some Arawaks lived on Aruba where they maintained the cattle and horses that roamed freely on the island.

The Dutch West India Company was initially attracted to Curacao as a source of salt and hardwood, but it soon became a base for raiding settlements on other islands and the coastal mainland. Its sheltered harbor was fortified on either side at the entrance and, under the governorship of Peter Stuyvesant from 1642 to 1647, Willemstad became an important world port. With the soil unable to support sugar cane or other cash crops, Curacao's survival depended on trade, which came in the form of slaves. Throughout the latter half of the 1600s and well into the 1700s, Curacao was an enormous slave depot for the Caribbean and South America.

Meanwhile, Aruba was maintained as a vast cattle ranch, and corn was grown on Bonaire to feed the slaves passing through Curacao, which also became a commercial meeting place for pirates, American rebels, Dutch merchants and Spaniards from the mainland. As for those bitter-tasting oranges brought from Spain, it was discovered that their sun-dried peels contained an etheric oil which became the

Fort Amsterdam was the center of the fortified town of Willemstad, Curacao.

basis for Curacao's famous liqueur. The ABCs remained for the most part Dutch, briefly besieged by the British in 1804, and occupied by British troops from 1807 to 1814.

Slavery was finally ended in 1863 and the islands had to develop new resources. Trade with Venezuela became the mainstay of Curacao's economy and was helped greatly when the Dutch government lifted all import taxes on goods from the Netherlands, which local merchants could then exchange at a profit for Venezuelan products. On Aruba and Bonaire, the aloe plant became an important crop, its gel used in numerous pharmaceuticals, and the pods of the divi-divi tree were also exported for use in leather tanning.

In 1824, alluvial deposits of gold were found on Aruba and the island's mines, which operated for nearly a century, yielded more than three million pounds of gold. When, following World War I, oil was discovered at Lake Maracaibo in Venezuela the oil companies, seeking a stable place to locate their refineries and storage facilities, chose the nearby Dutch islands. When the demand for oil slumped, the islands developed yet another untapped resource which continues today – tourism.

Blessed with natural appeal – beautiful beaches, turquoise waters, colorful coral reefs, and a climate that's sunny and dry – the islands have added duty-free shopping, waterfront casinos and championship golf courses to their growing list of attractions. Their residents, who descend from a mix of races and cultures, are a people known for their racial and religious tolerance. They are also multilingual, learning Dutch – the official language – at school, and are often fluent in English and Spanish, as well as their native tongue of Papiamento, which is a lilting blend of Spanish, Portuguese, Dutch, English and African dialects.

All three islands are part of the Kingdom of the Netherlands but Aruba is no longer part of the Netherlands Antilles, of which Curacao is the capital and Bonaire is a member, along with the Leeward Islands of St. Maarten, Saba and St. Eustatius. Aruba, seeking more autonomy in connection with its oil revenues, became a separate entity in 1986.

Aruba

Once a cacti-studded cattle ranch, Aruba is today a holiday paradise with miles of blinding white beaches and crystal-clear turquoise waters. The island's first inhabitants, the Caquetio Indians, had established themselves at the mouth of Venezuela's Aroa River until repeated attacks by the Carib Indians prompted them to leave. Some of the tribe members moved to the shores of Lake Maracaibo and still bear the name Arubaes. Others moved to the island now called Aruba.

The island's southwest coast has beach resorts, shopping malls and casinos; its rugged northeast coast is where wave action has carved coral cliffs into dramatic sea arches. In between lies a hilly desert of

A ship docks at the Oranjestad cruise terminal.

caves, cacti and scrub. Splashes of color are provided by flamboyant trees, in bloom from June through August, and gardens of homes which often contain a variety of tropical flowers. Wells tap into the island's water table but a huge saltwater distillation plant at Spanish Lagoon, once a hideout for pirates, is the island's main source of fresh water.

GETTING AROUND

The cruise ships dock in the heart of Oranjestad, within easy walking distance of the shops and other attractions. **Taxis** are unmetered and rates are fixed, based on a carload of up to four passengers, but be sure to establish a fare before departing. People returning from the beach in wet bathing suits are usually refused, so be sure to dry off and take a cover-up. US currency is accepted, but not large bills (i.e. $50 or $100). The minimum rate to any destination is $4, and the hired rate per hour is $30. Some sample fares (in US$) from the cruise terminal: Eagle Beach ($7); Noord ($9); Mangel Halto Beach ($14).

Most major American **car rental** companies operate on Aruba, in addition to several local companies. Avis has an office at the cruise ship terminal. A valid driver's license is all that's required to rent a car. The island is 19-1/2 miles long by six miles wide, the main roads are paved, and driving is on the right. It's hard to get lost, and the divi-divi trees – bent by the trade winds – all point toward the island's leeward side where Oranjestad is located.

The official currency is the Aruban Florin (AWG) but US dollars are readily accepted island wide, and major credit cards are accepted at most establishments. The bank rate of exchange is fixed at 1.77 Afl. to $1 US (stores exchange at AWG 1.75 to $1 US).

Beaches – A string of fine beaches lie along the coast northwest of the cruise terminal, starting with Druif Beach (about 2 miles

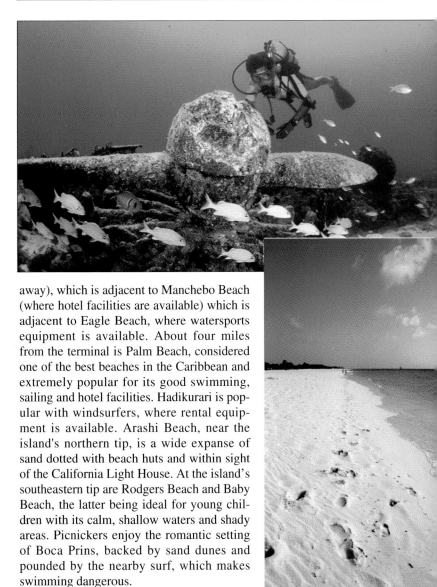

away), which is adjacent to Manchebo Beach (where hotel facilities are available) which is adjacent to Eagle Beach, where watersports equipment is available. About four miles from the terminal is Palm Beach, considered one of the best beaches in the Caribbean and extremely popular for its good swimming, sailing and hotel facilities. Hadikurari is popular with windsurfers, where rental equipment is available. Arashi Beach, near the island's northern tip, is a wide expanse of sand dotted with beach huts and within sight of the California Light House. At the island's southeastern tip are Rodgers Beach and Baby Beach, the latter being ideal for young children with its calm, shallow waters and shady areas. Picnickers enjoy the romantic setting of Boca Prins, backed by sand dunes and pounded by the nearby surf, which makes swimming dangerous.

Dive and Snorkel Sites – The shallow waters and abundance of fish off Malmok Beach (8 miles from the terminal) make it an ideal spot for snorkelers but there are no facilities nearby. Another good snorkeling beach is Manguel Halto beach, with its nearby barrier reef. Arashi Reef and the *Antilla*, a German freighter

Several dive sites and powdery sand beaches beckon on Aruba. (Above) Palm Beach.

destroyed during World War II, are popular dive sites, and can also be viewed by semi-submarine and submarine, both available through ship-organized shore excursions. Seaworld Explorer transports passengers by bus to the north end of the island where their semi-submarine is boarded, while Atlantis transports passengers to and from their sub site by ferry from Seaport Village Marina.

Golf – An 18-hole course designed by Robert Trents Jones Jr is situated at Tierra del Sol near the island's northwestern tip. This par-71 course with water on two sides, has stunning sea views and is dotted with giant cacti and clusters of natural grasses.

Shopping – Shopping malls are located at the harborfront, in town and stretching northwest along the coast. **1** **Seaport Village Mall**, a five-minute walk from the cruise terminal, is Aruba's largest shopping and entertainment complex with dozens of stores, boutiques and a casino. The nearby **2** **Seaport Marketplace** is also popular with its shaded central walkway and sidewalk cafes. Oranjestad's main shopping street is Caya G.F. Betico Croes, with chic boutiques and shops.

International items to look for include cachet cosmetics and perfumes, designer fashions, china, crystal, fine jewelry, watches and cameras. There are also good buys in embroidered tablecloths, Spanish porcelain, Danish silver and pewter, Dutch cheeses, Austrian figurines, Peruvian hand-knit sweaters, Brazilian semi-precious stones, Venezuelan shoes and handbags, Colombian emeralds and leather, and locally made aloe vera products. Clay pottery and other local artwork is sold at outdoor stands along the waterfront.

Local Sights – **3** **Fort Zoutman** is the oldest building in Oranjestad, erected in 1796 and named for a Dutch Rear Admiral. Added to the fort in 1868 was King Willem III Tower which served as a lighthouse and now houses a heritage museum.

ORANJESTAD

Car Rentals
Yacht Harbor
Cruise Ship Terminal
Governor's House
©OCEAN CRUISE GUIDES

4 **Queen Wilhelmina Park**, adjacent to the Seaport Marketplace, contains a marble statue of the former Dutch queen gazing toward the Governor's home. Wilhelminastraat contains interesting colonial architecture including the **5** **Protestant Church**, built in 1846. The **6** Archaeological Museum on Zoutmanstraat contains artifacts and pottery of the island's first Indian inhabitants.

Island Attractions – Santa Anna Church in Noord was built in the 1770s and its hand-carved oak altar, neo-gothic in design, won the exhibition award in Rome in 1870. The **Chapel of Alto Vista**, built by a Spanish missionary, is a place of pilgrimage situated on the north coast overlooking the sea. The interesting rock formations at **Casibari** can be climbed via some steps to the top for a view of the island and the Haystack. Aruba's famous landmark is the **Natural Bridge**, made of coral and carved by the sea on the island's windward coast. The arch is over 100 feet long and stands 23 feet above sea level.

Arikok National Park contains natural and man-made paths, a restored cunucu (countryside house), a traditional stone well and the Natural Pool, near Boca Keto, which is surrounded by rocks and filled with sea water. Several caves are situated along the north coast, including **Guadirikiri Cave**, its caverns containing stalactites and ancient drawings.

Curacao

Few Caribbean ports of call can surpass the arrival awaiting passengers at Curacao. Here the Queen Emma Pontoon Bridge swings open to allow ships to enter the canal-like entrance of St. Anna Bay and glide past the waterfront buildings of colonial Willemstad. A centuries-old capital, its channel-side streets are lined with gabled buildings which were painted a variety of colors in 1817 when the Governor complained that the sun's glare off the stark white buildings was giving him headaches.

Initially founded as Santa Anna by the Spanish, the port's name was changed to Willemstad when Holland took possession of the island in 1634. Settlement grew on both sides of the channel with the eastern side called Punda and the western side Otrabanda ('other side').

Ferry boats have long transported residents across the channel but in the late 1900s the American consul, Leonard Burlington Smith, suggested a pontoon foot bridge be built. Fixed at one end so it could open whenever a vessel had to pass, the bridge was completed in 1888. A toll charge was based on each person's ability to pay – those wearing shoes were charged 2¢ and those walking barefooted were free. It's said that the poor would borrow shoes to prove their ability to pay, while the rich would take off their shoes to save 2¢. Today there is no charge for either the bridge or the passenger ferries which run continuously throughout the day.

ARUBA & CURACAO

(Top) A cruise ship departs Oranjestad, Aruba. (Above, left) A souvenir stand on the Oranjestad waterfront. (Above) Natural Bridge, Aruba. (Left) A shopping street in Oranjestad.

(Top) The Seaport Marketplace in Oranjestad, Aruba. (Middle) The Penha Building in Willemstad, Curacao. (Bottom) Dutch-gabled buildings line the canal-like entrance to Willemstad.

GETTING AROUND

Dutch charm and duty-free shopping await the visitor to Willemstad. The official currency is the Netherlands Antilles guilder (NAfl) but U.S. dollars are widely accepted. The cruise ships dock on the Otrabanda side of the channel and passengers can make their way to the Punda side on foot over the pontoon bridge, via the free passenger ferry which docks at Mathey Wharf, or by taxi (about $8 US) over the Queen Julianna Bridge which spans the harbor at a height of 185 feet. Taxis are unmetered and the fee should be agreed upon before departing. Sample fares, per taxi, from the cruise pier: Holiday Beach – $10; Piscadera Bay – $12; Princess Beach – $15; island sightseeing – $30 per hour.

There are several **tourist information booths** along the Otrabanda waterfront, and the main office is located on the Punda side at the east end of Wilhelminaplein. A post office is directly east of the Central Market.

Organized ship excursions often include: a trolley train tour through the Punda section of Willemstad; an island tour with stops at the Curacao liqueur distillery and Curacao Seaquarium; a semi-submarine ride along coral reefs; and beach and snorkel excursions.

Beaches – Curacao's southern coast is indented with beach-lined bays and coves. Private beaches charge a small entrance fee, as do some of the hotel beaches. A popular hotel beach close to the cruise port is Holiday Beach. Farther west is the private beach at Blauwbaai (Blue Bay) – considered one of Curacao's best with its white sand, shady areas and change facilities. More hotel beaches are located at Piscadera Bay, including the Sonesta Hotel, Las Palmas and Curacao Caribbean. Fine beaches east of Willemstad include Princess Beach, where a hotel is located, and Seaquarium Beach and Santa Barbara Beach, both private beaches with change facilities and snack bars.

Dive & Snorkel Sites – Excellent snorkeling and diving are available all around the island with visibility of 60 to 80 feet, and sometimes up to 150 feet. The Curacao Underwater Park, ideal for both diving and snorkeling, protects 12-1/2 miles of unspoiled coral reef along which is an underwater nature trail and spectacular dive sites which include coral beds, sheer walls and shipwrecks. Klein Curacao, lying off East Point, is an uninhabited islet with beautiful beaches and good snorkeling and diving.

Golf – A nine-hole course with sand greens is open mornings at the Curacao Golf & Squash Club just north of the Willemstad Harbor.

Shopping – Duty-free bargains in Willemstad include brand-name jewelry, watches, European fashions, perfumes, crystal, china, electronics and cameras. Fine stores are located on Handelskade, Heerenstraat and Breedestraat, with more shops and boutiques located in the restored **3** **Waterfort Arches.** Local crafts are sold at the Central Market, located in a large circular building east of the **6** **Floating Market**, and at various shops in Punda such as Tropical Visions in the **5** **Penha Building**. Along the Otrobanda waterfront, facing the cruise pier, are a number of shops selling duty-free liquor and local handicrafts, including pottery at the Arawak Craft Factory opposite West Wharf.

LOCAL ATTRACTIONS

Located at the harbor entrance within the battlements of **1** **Waterfort** (built in 1634), and within hailing distance of ships entering the harbor, is the Van der Valk Plaza Hotel – one of only two hotels in the world that is covered by marine collision insurance. Still attached to the sea wall are iron rings once used to secure a chain that was stretched across the channel to prevent enemy ships from entering the harbor. During World War II, a steel net was stretched across the channel between Waterfort and **2** **Riffort** – built on the other side in 1838. Stretching east of Waterfort along the sea front are more old battlements, including the **3** **Waterfort Arches**, housing shops and restaurants.

4 **Fort Amsterdam** with its mustard-colored walls, was the center of the fortified town from 1648 to 1861. Today it's the seat of the Netherlands Antilles government. Its inner courtyard, entered through an arched walkway, is formed by the Governor's Palace (facing the water), the Fort Church Museum (opposite), and government offices on each side. In case of siege, the church was built with a cellar for provisions and an adjacent water cistern. A cannon ball fired in 1804 by English troops, led by Captain Bligh of Bounty fame, remains embedded in its front wall.

The much-photographed **5** **Penha Building**, golden yellow with white trim, stands at the corner near the east end of the pontoon bridge. One of Curacao's oldest examples of Dutch colonial architecture, the building was formerly a social club with a gallery overlooking the harbor. Other waterfront buildings along this block resemble the canal houses of Amsterdam, one of which houses Gallery '86 – a showcase for the works of well-known artists of the Caribbean and Netherlands.

At the other end of the block is the **6** **Floating Market** where Venezuelan boats loaded with fruit, vegetables and fish sell their wares. At the east end of the market is the **7** **Queen Wilhelmina Bridge** which spans the Waaigat and leads to the former residential district of **8** **Scharloo** where wealthy merchants built opulent homes, their architectural styles ranging from 18th-century colonial to Victorian.

In 1651, a dozen Jewish families from Amsterdam arrived in Willemstad and by the early 1700s the local Jewish community numbered 2,000. The **9** **Mikve Emanuel Synagogue**, built in 1732 and

The Queen Emma Pontoon Bridge connects the two sides of
Willemstad and can be accessed from the cruise docks.

similar in style to the old Portuguese one in Amsterdam, is today the oldest active synagogue in the Western Hemisphere. The Jewish Cultural Museum is entered off the synagogue's courtyard. Other museums in Punda include the **10** **Postal Museum**, housed in a 1693 building at the corner of Keukenstraat and Kuiperstraat, and the Numismatic Museum on Breedestraat.

The town's central park, **11** **Wilhelminaplein**, contains a statue of Queen Wilhelmina, as well as shaded benches and a playground. Opposite the park's east side is the former Jewish Reformed Synagogue Temple Emmanuel (the Temple Building) and City Gate, which marks the boundary of Willemstad when it was a fortified settlement.

Island Attractions – Outside of Willemstad the attractions include beautiful beaches, secluded coves, village churches and restored land houses which are former country estates situated on hilltops so the owner could watch his slaves and signal his neighbors if trouble developed. Popular attractions include the **12** **Curacao Liqueur Distillery**, located in the former colonial mansion of Chobolobo on the east side of Willemstad's harbor, and the **13** **Curacao Seaquarium** where visitors can view 400 species of sea life native to local waters, including various sharks and stingrays. Beside the aquarium is a full-facility beach of white sand.

At the north end of Curacao is **14** **Christoffel National Park**, a 4,500-acre nature reserve containing the island's highest point of Mount Christoffel (1,239 feet), Indian caves and trails. The prehistoric caves at **15** **Hato** were recently opened to the public, their limestone terraces containing fossilized coral that formed before tectonic uplifting brought the submerged island to the sea's surface.

The passenger ferry is another way to cross the channel running through the center of Willemstad.

Bonaire

Boomerang-shaped Bonaire is one of the best islands in the Caribbean for diving and snorkeling. The entire island is a protected marine park and its coral reefs are home to more than a thousand different species of aquatic creatures, including sea horses and turtles. There are 86 charted dive sites on the island, many of these located on the sheltered western side of the island, clustered north of Kralendijk and around the offshore islet of Klein Bonaire. Reefs and wrecks, beach dives and drop-offs – the variety of dive sites and the clarity of the water is spectacular. Conditions are also ideal for snorkelers, with little current and plenty of shallow water snorkeling sites.

The island capital of **Kralendijk**, meaning 'coral dike', is a quiet place where about 3,000 of the island's 15,000 residents live. Shops carrying duty-free and local items are found at the Harborside Shopping Mall and along the main street which runs parallel with the waterfront. Historic sights include Fort Oranje, two churches and a museum. Wild donkeys and goats roam free on this unspoiled island where the centuries-old industry of salt mining has been joined by oil bunkering and tourism.

Bonaire's famous underwater sites, all of which are protected within a marine park encompassing the island's entire coastline, include three vertical wall dives.

Pink Beach is ideal for swimming, snorkeling and scuba diving.

Bonaire's land-based attractions are as fascinating as its underwater world, for the island is home to one of the largest flamingo colonies in the Western Hemisphere. More than 15,000 flamingos nest in the island's salt pans and, in addition to two flamingo sanctuaries, a 13,500-acre game preserve (Washington-Slagbaai National Park) has been established at Bonaire's north end. Here iguanas and green-tailed lizards can be viewed in addition to flamingos and other birds such as yellow-winged parrots, often seen perched on the giant cacti that grow as high as 30 feet.

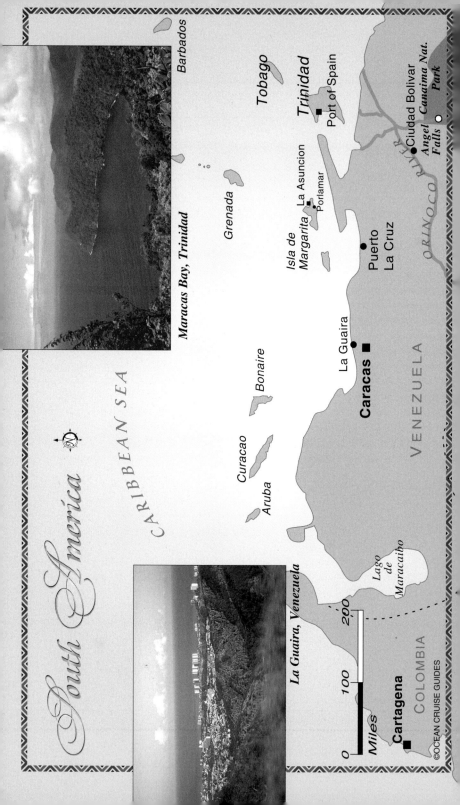

South America

CARIBBEAN SEA

Barbados

Tobago

Trinidad
Port of Spain ■

Ciudad Bolivar ●
Angel Canaima Nat.
Falls ○ Park

Grenada

ORINOCO RIVER

Isla de Margarita
La Asuncion ■
Porlamar ●

Puerto ●
La Cruz

Maracas Bay, Trinidad

Bonaire

La Guaira ●

Caracas ■

Curacao

VENEZUELA

Aruba

Lago de Maracaibo

La Guaira, Venezuela

200

200

100

Cartagena ■

Miles

0

COLOMBIA

©OCEAN CRUISE GUIDES

CHAPTER EIGHTEEN

VENEZUELA / TRINIDAD & TOBAGO

The sight of native villages set on stilts above the water prompted an early Spanish explorer, when exploring the northern coast of South America in 1499, to name the area Venezuela – 'little Venice'. Venezuela is, however, anything but little, with its 350,000 square miles of scenic wonders, including one of South America's longest rivers, the Orinoco, and spectacular Angel Falls – the highest uninterrupted waterfall in the world, its cascade plunging 3,200 feet. Venezuela's Caribbean coastline is nearly 1,800 miles long and its numerous offshore islands include Margarita, famous for pearl fishing.

Venezuela is also a country of great wealth. The lowlands around Lake Maracaibo are rich in oil deposits that, since 1918, have been developed by Dutch, British and American interests, with large amounts processed in the nearby Netherlands Antilles. Still, the majority of the country's 24 million inhabitants live in poverty, their shacks covering the surrounding hillsides of Caracas where colossal monuments and steel-and-glass skyscrapers attest to the city's historical greatness and continued growth.

Caracas, with some six million residents, is the capital of Venezuela. A modern city driven by oil money, it is situated on a high plateau. The surrounding mountain range is a spur of the Andes, and an earthquake destroyed much of the city in 1812, shortly after the country declared its independence from Spain under patriot leader Francisco de Miranda. This setback helped the royalist forces but South America's great liberator, Simon Bolivar, continued the revolutionary cause from his base in the lower Orinoco basin. In 1819, as the newly elected president of Venezuela, Bolivar led his revolutionary forces across the flooded Apure valley and over the bitterly cold Andes mountains to defeat a surprised Spanish army in north-central Colombia. A brilliant military strategist, Bolivar won further battles with Spanish forces, gaining independence for Venezuela and its neighboring territories, which then formed the federal republic of Greater Colombia.

In 1830, Venezuela became a separate state, and subsequent power struggles among the landholding class resulted in corrupt regimes ruling the country until 1947 when, for the first time, a president was elected by direct popular vote. This was followed by a military coup,

Caracas enjoys a magnificent setting atop a mountain plateau.

but democracy was restored in 1958. Inflation and unemployment are ongoing problems, and social unrest erupted into riots in 1989 when falling oil revenues prompted the government to make cuts in social services.

La Guaira is the port of access to Caracas, the two cities connected by a modern highway built during the 1950s military dictatorship of General Marcos Perez Jimenez. This highway hugs the mountainsides – its marble-lined tunnels burrowing through the coastal range – and provides spectacular valley views along the 45-minute drive. A colonial port, La Guaira's historic buildings include the 17th-century Customs House and the Casa Boulton, which houses a museum tracing the town's history since its founding in 1589. However, the majority of passengers visiting La Guaira promptly head to Caracas or outlying areas, such as Rancho Grande National Park, with its dense tropical

forests, and Colonia Tovar, an isolated village settled by German farmers in 1843. Further afield and reached by air is Canaima National Park, deep in the mountainous jungle where natural wonders include the Tepui mountains, some soaring 7,000 feet above a valley floor, from which multiple waterfalls spring, including famous Angel Falls.

A scenic mountain highway connects La Guaira and Caracas.

(Above) Bolivar Plaza, with statue of Bolivar in background. (Right) Hallway of Heroes.

City tours of **Caracas** include a visit to Bolivar Plaza, named for Venezuela's national hero who was born in Caracas to a wealthy Creole family. Amid the fountains and mosaic walkways stands a magnificent statue of Bolivar on horseback. At the opposite end of the tree-lined square is the Hallway of Heroes – towering statues of black stone that stand in two facing rows. Numerous government buildings surround the plaza, including the golden-domed Capitol with its famous Elliptical Hall and ceiling paintings that depict the final battle of the war of independence. The nearby Cathedral is a 19th-century reconstruction of the original built in 1595.

GETTING AROUND

The cruise lines offer a number of ship-organized excursions from La Guaira, including half-day and full-day city tours. For passengers wanting to tackle Caracas on their own, the round-trip taxi fare (per car) is about $70 US.

The official currency is the bolivar, with the U.S. dollar buying approximately 600 bolivars, although this exchange fluctuates. There are 100 centimos to the bolivar. Spanish is the official language but English is widely spoken.

Shopping – Good buys can be made in handcrafted leather goods, including coats and jackets, as well as handbags, wallets, shoes and belts. Venezuelan souvenirs to look for include hand-embroidered t-shirts, woolen throw rugs, gold jewelry and pearls from Margarita Island. Visitors whose city tour includes a stop at the Cristalart Glass Factory can choose from a wide variety of intricate ornaments and elegant vases that are crafted on site.

MARGARITA ISLAND

Only 25 miles from the mainland, Isla de Margarita has long been a vacation hot spot for Venezuelans drawn to the island's powdery beaches and duty-free shopping. Dotted with Spanish colonial forts and churches, Margarita was sighted by Columbus in 1498 and used as a base by the brutal Spanish rebel Lope de Aguirre in 1561. In the 1800s, Margarita's inhabitants supported Simon Bolivar and, following independence from Spain, the island – along with smaller neighboring islands – was made a state of Venezuela. La Asuncion is the capital and Porlamar is the economic center. Pearl fishing remains an important industry, as are fish canning and boat building on this island of about 300,000 residents. Construction of a fresh water pipe from the mainland has allowed the island to prosper, especially as a tourist resort.

A cruise terminal is slated to open in the near future at **Porlamar**; meanwhile ships anchor and tender their passengers ashore. Beaches line the island and can be reached by public buses or by taxis. Local attractions include a national park in which boat rides can be taken through an extensive mangrove swamp, and the historic buildings of La Asuncion, founded in 1565, which include a 16th-century cathedral. Also of interest is the Virgin of the Valley Sanctuary, located in a village near Porlamar. For shoppers, Porlamar is a duty free area offering designer clothing and electronic goods, as well as ceramics, tiles, sisal hats and wood carvings.

ORINOCO RIVER

The mighty Orinoco, about 1,600 miles long, carves its serpentine course through tropical rainforests and savannahs before terminating in a vast marshy delta where its many arms drain into the Atlantic Ocean. Rising in the Guiana Highlands of South Venezuela, the Orinoco is navigable for most of its length and is dredged to allow oceangoing ships to travel as far as Ciudad Bolivar, about 270 miles upstream.

Sir Walter Raleigh was one of a series of adventurers inspired by the legend of El Dorado (the Golden Man) to search for a mythical land of plenty along the northern coastline of South America. Drawn to the Guiana coast in 1595 in a fruitless search for gold, Raleigh returned to the region in 1617, leading an ill-fated expedition to the mouth of the Orinoco and sending five small vessels upriver while he waited, sick with fever, at Trinidad. No gold mine was discovered and Raleigh's eldest son was killed in a skirmish with some Spaniards. Raleigh, once a favorite of Queen Elizabeth I, returned home to face arrest and execution on earlier charges of treason under King James I.

Trinidad & Tobago

Trinidad and Tobago, lying off the coast of Venezuela, were once part of the South American subcontinent, with Trinidad becoming an island as recently as 10,000 years ago when the last Ice Age ended and sea levels rose. The variety of flora and fauna is matched by the diversity of cultures found in this two-island nation. Trinidad (named by Columbus for its three southeastern peaks) and Tobago (named for pipe tobacco by British settlers) were fought over and farmed by various nationalities, including the Spanish, Portuguese, Dutch, French and British.

Trinidad's capital, **Port of Spain**, is an amalgam of European, African and Indian heritage with churches, mosques, markets and museums built in a diversity of styles – Moorish, neo-Gothic, Italian Renaissance, Victorian and West Indian gingerbread to name a few. There's even a German castle resembling the medieval castles of the Rhine which, along with the official residences of the prime minister and governor general, overlooks Queen's Park Savannah – the site of glittering revelry during Trinidad's famous Carnival when the Parade of Bands proceeds up Frederick Street on the final day of street parties and calypso competitions.

In contrast to the pulsating beat of Trinidad is the unspoiled holiday island of Tobago, 21 miles away but a world apart. **Scarborough** is the island's main port and nearby is Pigeon Point with its glorious beaches and famous Buccoo Reef, where colorful coral gardens, popular with divers and snorkelers, can be viewed by glass-bottom boat.

The two islands, both of which prospered as producers of sugarcane during colonialism, were joined together under one government at the end of the 19th century and gained independence from Britain in 1962. Trinidad is the larger and more heavily populated of the two islands, with only 45,000 of a total 1.3 million inhabitants living on Tobago. Both islands boast lush rainforests, rare birds and brilliant butterflies, their colorful wings copied in the elaborate costumes of Trinidad's world-famous Carnival.

The Red House, in Port of Spain, houses the Parliament of Trinidad and Tobago.

For more information about the cruise lines and their ships, visit our web site: www.oceancruiseguides.com. (Note: The average space ratio per passenger is an indication of how spacious a ship will feel; the higher the number, the better.)

CARNIVAL CRUISE LINES: This mainstream cruise line, which started in the early 1970s, has mushroomed into the largest cruise corporation in the world, with Carnival Corporation owning numerous lines including Cunard and Holland America. The story of Carnival is a fascinating one. It began with the company acquiring one ship, the *Mardi Gras* (which ran aground on its first cruise), and progressed to the building of some of the most revolutionary ships of the 70s and 80s.

Carnival Destiny, 1996 – 101,000 tons

Carnival can take credit for changing the public's perception of cruising, from its being stuffy and formal to its being casual and fun. The ships' interiors reflect this outlook, with an enthusiastic use of color and contemporary themes. This exuberant approach attracts a high number of first-time cruisers and, with extensive facilities for children and teens, families. With a fleet of 17 ships, Carnival has one of the most varied selections of Caribbean itineraries, offering everything from 2- and 3-day cruises to the Bahamas to 7- and 8-day cruises into the southern Caribbean. Base ports are Miami and Port Canaveral, as well as Tampa, Galveston, New Orleans and San Juan, Puerto Rico. Officers are Italian. Average space ratio: 35. (Website: carnivalcruises.com)

Carnival Pride, 2001 – 84,000 tons

CELEBRITY CRUISES: Founded in 1990 as an offshoot of the Greek line Chandris Inc., Celebrity Cruises is now owned by Royal Caribbean International. A premium cruise line, Celebrity is noted for its gourmet cuisine, sophisticated service and a quality finish throughout its ships. Meticulously maintained, the ships are a pleasure to explore and Celebrity is one of the few premium lines to offer butler service for its passengers staying in suites. The children's facilities on most of the ships are generally good. Celebrity has nine ships in the Caribbean with stops at most of the popular ports. Base ports are

Galaxy, 1996 – 77,000 tons

Fort Lauderdale, San Juan, Miami and Tampa. Celebrity's private-island stop is Catalina Island off the coast of Dominican Republic. Officers are Greek. Average space ratio: 41

COSTA CRUISES: The Costa family of Genoa, Italy, has been in shipping since the 1800s. They introduced their first passenger ship in 1948, and today the Costa fleet is Europe's most popular cruise line. The company positions at least one ship in the Caribbean, sailing 7-day cruises out of Fort Lauderdale. Costa's 'Italian style' of cruising is upbeat with an international ambiance and authentic Italian and continental cuisine. Officers and crew are international. Average space ratio: 37. (Website: costacruises.com)

CRYSTAL CRUISES: Owned by NYK of Japan, this luxury line operates one ship on a handful of Caribbean itineraries out of Fort Lauderdale. Crystal features tailor-made shore excursions to suit individual preferences and the line's ships, which carry 960 passengers each, are finely appointed with spacious interiors and almost all outside cabins. Caribbean cruises range from 9 to 14 days. Officers are Scandinavian. Average space ratio: 52. (Website: crystalcruises.com)

Crystal Harmony, 1990 – 48,000 tons

DISNEY CRUISE LINE: Appealing to a broad family market and home ported in Port Canaveral, Disney Cruise Line can provide the ultimate land tour in the form of Walt Disney World in Orlando. Disney offers 3- and 4-day cruises to the Bahamas and 7-day loop cruises to the Eastern and Western Caribbean. The company has two 83,000-ton ships, *Disney Wonder* and *Disney Magic,* each carrying 1,750 passengers. The company's private island is Castaway Cay in the Bahamas. Officers are European. Average space ratio: 48. (Website: disneycruise.com)

Disney Magic, 1998 – 83,000 tons

HOLLAND AMERICA LINE: This company's connection with North America began in 1873 with regular service between New York and Rotterdam. Now based in Seattle, HAL began offering holiday cruises in the 1960s and has established a loyal following for its worldwide itineraries. A premium

Volendam, 2000 – 63,000 tons

cruise line, HAL currently has 10 ships, with six new ships planned over the next few years. The line's highly successful "S" class ships (*Statendam*, *Maasdam*, *Ryndam* and *Veendam*) are medium-sized (55,000 tons) and offer good amenities, including a full-wrap teak promenade deck, and are spacious, carrying 1,250 passengers in a refined, relaxing atmosphere. Holland America entered the megaship club in 2002 with the launch of *Zuiderdam*, an 85,000-ton ship with an impressive space ratio of 46. Holland America's Dutch officers and service staff of Indonesians and Filipinos have built a solid reputation of well-run, immaculate ships with a high level of friendly service. HAL ships cut a fine profile with their distinctive sheer and blue hull, and the ships' interiors contain extensive artwork to complement each ship's thematic decor. HAL offers a good range of 5- to 14-day cruises to most Caribbean ports from its home ports of Fort Lauderdale, Tampa and Port Canaveral. In 1997 HAL debuted its private island – Half Moon Cay – after purchasing the uninhabited Bahamian island of Little San Salvador and developing shoreside facilities for its passengers. Average space ratio: 41. (Website: hollandamerica.com)

Norwegian Dream, 1992 – 50,000 tons

NORWEGIAN CRUISE LINE: This company is considered one of the first lines to invent modern cruising when it introduced trips from Miami to the Bahamas in the mid-1960s. NCL also pioneered the concept of a private-island port of call when it purchased Great Stirrup Cay from the Bahamian government in 1977. The line appeals to young couples and families, with its excellent entertainment and sports activities. NCL's fleet of eight ships offer mostly 7-day voyages out of Miami and San Juan, but with 3- and 4-day cruises to the Bahamas, 5- to 10-day Western Caribbean cruises, and several 13- to 15-day cruises from New York and Boston, which include a stop at Bermuda. Officers are, of course, Norwegian. Average space ratio: 33. (Website: ncl.com)

Golden Princess, 2001 – 109,000 tons

PRINCESS CRUISES: Well known for its role in *The Love Boat* television show in the 1970s, this line has always been an innovator with its ships and itineraries. From the start, when *Princess Patricia* first steamed to the Mexican Riviera in 1965, Princess Cruises established a reputation for a high standard of service. Like other cruise industry leaders, Princess has experienced phenomenal growth in the last decade and has launched over half a dozen new ships since 1996. These new megaships have all the modern facilities cruise passengers have come to expect, including several swimming pools, health spa, tennis court, computer center and show lounges, as well as traditional favorites such as a full-wrap teak promenade deck and an intimate wood-panelled pub. A high percentage of staterooms on these new ships have a verandah, while the public areas are beautifully appointed with brass trim, tile work and marble flooring. Princess has succeeded in appealing to a broad market, from retired couples to young families, with ships that are well laid out with good amenities. Children's facilities are generally good with a spacious playroom and teen center, and youth counsellors on most ships. Most itineraries are 7- and 10-day loop cruises out of Fort Lauderdale but this premium line also uses San Juan as a home port for 7-day loop cruises to the southern Caribbean. Eastern and Western itineraries include a stop at Princess Cays, the company's private beach on the Bahamian out-island of Eleuthera. Officers are international. Average space ratio: 40. (Website: princess.com)

RADISSON SEVEN SEAS: This luxury line offers small-ship intimacy, spaciousness and fine cuisine. Caribbean itineraries are 4- to 8-day cruises out of San Juan to a mix of ports, often including one or two smaller, less-visited islands. Officers are European. Average space ratio: 54. (Website: rssc.com)

ROYAL CARIBBEAN INTERNATIONAL: One of the original cruise lines to set up shop in the Caribbean in the late 1960s, Royal Caribbean maintains a strong presence with a cruise product appealing to young couples (good entertainment and lots of activities) and to families (excellent children's facilities). This line is not afraid of innovation and was the first to introduce an 18-hole miniature golf course and, most recently, an onboard rock-climbing wall and ice rink. RCI's handsome, modern megaships offer spacious and impressive public areas, including a multi-deck atrium with glass elevators as well as the company's hallmark Viking Crown Lounge – a glass-wrapped observation lounge

Vision of the Seas, 1998 – 78,000 tons

Voyager of the Seas, 1999 – 138,000 tons

located on the highest deck to provide passengers with a panoramic view of the passing scenery. Family suites, a spacious playroom and a teen center make these ships ideal for passengers with children. RCI currently operates a dozen ships in the Caribbean, including some of the largest ships in the world. Its Voyager class ships, at 138,000 tons, are too large to transit the Panama Canal. RCI's Caribbean itineraries include 3- and 4-night cruises from Florida to the Bahamas and 7-day loop cruises to different parts of the Caribbean. The company also offers 10- and 11-night "Circle the Caribbean" itineraries which take in western and southern ports. The company has two private beach stops – Labadee on the north coast of Haiti and CocoCay, a Bahamian island that RCI acquired in 1988 (then called Little Stirrup Cay). Average space ratio: 37. (Website: royalcaribbean.com)

ROYAL OLYMPIC CRUISES: Formed in 1995 from the merging of two well-known Greek cruise lines, Royal Olympic's fleet consists of both mainstream and budget priced ships. At present, Royal Olympic offers "Mayaribbean Cruises" out of Houston to the Yucatan Peninsula, Belize and Honduras on its 25,00-ton *Olympia Voyager*. Officers are Greek. Average space ratio: 24. (Website: royalolympiccruises.com)

Star Clipper, 1992 – 3,000 tons

Seabourn Spirit, 1989 – 10,000 tons

STAR CLIPPERS: This line offers a unique product for those seeking a sailing adventure with plenty of comforts. With a reputation for good food and an authentic tall-ship experience, Star Clippers has recently added its third sailing ship, the 5,000-ton *Royal Clipper* (with no less than five masts) to its fleet. Itineraries are 7-day loop cruises using Barbados and St. Maarten as base port and cruising to many of the smaller, off-the-beaten-trail islands. Average space ratio: 20. (Website: starclippers.com)

SEABOURN CRUISE LINE: Widely considered the ultimate in luxury cruising, Seabourn operates a small fleet of mega-yachts, each carrying 208 passengers in outside suites, many of these with balconies. In addition to providing gourmet cuisine, white glove service, and spacious and elegant accommodations, Seabourn combines interesting itineraries with unique shore excursions. The line currently offers a limited number of Caribbean cruises (a 10-day and a 14-day itinerary) out of Fort Lauderdale. Officers are Norwegian. Average space ratio: 50. (Website: seabourn.com)

SILVERSEA: Consistently rated the Number One Small Ship Cruise Line by Conde Nast Traveler, this luxury line offers a 16-day Caribbean cruise from Fort Lauderdale to New Orleans, with stops at the popular ports of call as well as the smaller, quieter islands that are often bypassed by the large ships. Average space ratio: 60. (Website: silversea.com)

WINDJAMMER CRUISES: This fleet of small sailing vessels is one of the Caribbean cruise pioneers with four decades of experience. Windjammer has always positioned itself as a fun-time and romantic cruise product and has succeeded with a loyal, almost cultish, base of customers. Started in the early 1960s by Mike Burke with one small sailing ship, the line now has six ships working eastern and southern itineraries. Their one motor vessel, *Amazing Grace*, is the company's supply ship, and also carries passengers. Their ships often go to the smaller islands rarely visited by large cruise ships. Officers and crew are international. Average space ratio: 6. (Website: windjammer.com)

WINDSTAR CRUISES: This is a premium line of high-tech sailing ships, each accommodating about 150 passengers (except *Wind Surf* which carries 312 passengers). Noted for their fine cuisine and good service, Windstar ships appeal to cruisers seeking luxury in a casual setting as well as a bit of sailing adventure. The line offers several seven-day cruises from Barbados to an excellent array of the smaller islands, and from Fort Lauderdale to the Bahamas and the Virgin Islands. Average space ratio: 39. (Website: windstarcruises.com)

Wind Spirit, 1988 –
6,000 tons

If you require specific information about cruise lines, their ships or their itineraries, contact your local cruise specialist.

ABCs, 53, 320-335
Abolition Act, 60
Accra, 57
Adam Smith, 56
Admiral Rodney, 272, 292
Altun Ha, 155
Alligators, 94
American Revolution, 55, 178,272
Amiens, Treaty of 375
Anegada, 226
Angola, 57
Anguilla, 62, 244
Anna Maria Island, 133
Antigua, 17, 31, 40, 53, 55, 62, 73, 75, map 258, 258-269
Arawaks, 47, 48, 51, 165, 177, 235, 321, 322
Armstrong, Louis, 135
Aruba, 40, 53, 62, 320-327
Athol Island, 185
Audubon, John James, 119
Azores, 64
Aztec, 146
B
Bahamas., 10, 11, 12, 14, 20, 40, 47, 49, 51, 62, 65, 69, 74, 176-187
Bailey, Donavon, 79
Balata Tropical & Botanical Park, 281
Banco Chinchorro, 154
Barbados, 19, 23, 30, 35, 40, 53, 56, 57, 59, 61, 62, 67, 73, 75, 306-319
Bartolome de Las Casas, 51
Barbuda, 259, 260, 269
Basseterre (St. Kitts), 43, 249, 252, 253,
Basse-Terre (Guadeloupe) 273, 275
Battle of Les Sainte, 292
Bayside Marketplace, 115, 117
Bearded Fig Tree, 307
Beef Island, 232
Belize City, 154
Belize, 94, 143, 154
Bequia, 304
Bermuda, 43, 177

Betty's Hope, 260
Bianca C, 300
Bienville, Sieur de, 135, 139
Big Cypress Swamp, 109, 112
Birds, 94, 95
Biscayne National Park, 117
Bishop, Maurice, 63, 295
Blackwell, Chris, 79, 83
Bligh, Captain, 303
Blue Lagoon Island, 185
Blue Mountains, 165
Bonaire, 40, 52, 53, 57, 62, 95, 334, 335
Bonaparte, Napoleon and Josephine, 272, 281
Bonny, Anne, 67
Bonnet, Maj. Thomas, 67
Bourbon Street, 138
Bradenton, 133
Brazil, 61
Breadfruit, 303
Brewers Bay, 229, 230
Bridgetown, 67, 309-311, 314, 315
Brimstone Hill Fortress, 17, 52, 247, 248, 254
British Commonwealth, 289, 294
Bromeliads, 90
Brown, Pelican, 94
Browning, Elizabeth Barret , 173
Buccaneer Beach, 220
Bustamante, Sir Alexander, 168
C
Calica, 153
Caloosas, 110
Cancun, 147, 152
Cane Garden Bay, 229
Cape Canaveral, 111, 128
Carbet Falls, 275
Caribbean Sea, 10
Caribs, 47, 48, 157, 253, 271, 277, 283, 284, 288, 289, 295, 307, 323
Carnival, 74
Cartagena, 51, 191
Castries, 13

Cayman Islands, 28, 62, 156-163
Cayman Turtle Farm, 157
Cayman Wall, 162
Celebrity Cruises, 35
Central America, 49
Castries, 289, 290
Chances Peak, 269
Chankanaab Bay, 150
Chankanaab National Park, 150
Charles, Eugenia, 79
Charlotte Amalie, 30, 66, 68, 205, 207, 209
Chetumal, 153
Chichen Itza, 151
Chichimec, 146
Christiansted, 60, 207, 219, 220, 221
Christie, Linford, 79
Charlestown, 254
Ciboney, 47, 48
Cinnamon Bay, 216, 217
Clapton, Eric, 259
Clarence House, 266
Clemente, Roberto, 79
Cliff, Jimmy, 83
Coba, 152
Cockpits, The, 165
Cockscomb Basin Wildlife Sanctuary, 155
Coconut Grove, 239
Codrington, Sir Christopher, 260
Columbus, Christopher, 47, 48, 157, 165, 168, 177, 190, 205, 219, 269, 277, 283, 289, 307
Coral Gables, 114
Coral, reefs, 95
Cortes, Hernan, 146
Costa Maya, 153
Cousteau, Jaques, 143
Coward, Noel, 173
Cozumel, 12, 28, 34, 35, 143, 146, 147, 148-151
Crocodile, 92
Cromwell, Oliver, 308
Crooked Tree Wildlife Sanctuary, 155
Cruise Lines International Association (CLIA), 14
Cruise, Tom, 159

Cruz Bay, 216
Crystal Cay Marine Park, 181, 185
Crystal Cruises, 35
Cuba, 10, 34, 47, 49, 61, 62, 63, 110, 111, 165, 191, 192, 209, 296
Cupecoy Bay, 239
Curacao, 22, 35, 40, 52, 62, 235, 327-333
D
d'Ango, Jean, 64
Dade County, 45
Danish West India Company, 54, 206, 235
Devil's Bridge, 268
Diving, sites, snorkeling, 149, 151,162, 171, 181, 210, 217, 220, 229, 239, 251, 256, 263, 274, 29, 299, 314, 325, 331,
Dolphins, 103
Dominica, 53, 62
Dominican Republic, 10, 28
Dow's Hill Interpretation Center, 262, 266
Drake's Seat, 215
Drake, Sir Francis, 52, 64, 65, 191, 225
Dramamine, 25
Dutch West India Company, 52
E
Eastern Caribbean, 12
El Faro, 203
El Garrafon National Marine Park, 152
El Morro, 64, 65, 189, 191, 192
El Mundo Maya, 143
El Salvador, 143
El Yunque National Forest, 192, 203
Eleuthera, 177, 179
English Harbour, 259, 265-268
Estafan, Gloria, 79
Estate St. Peter Greathouse, 17, 215
Euro, the 271
Everglades National Park, 110, 117
Everglades, 17, 109
F

Faulkner, William, 135, 136
Firefly, 173
Fish, 99, 100
Fitzgerald, F. Scott, 136
Flagler, Henry, 111, 113, 179
Flamingo, bird, 95, 184
Flamingo, Bonaire sanctuary, 335
Fleming, Ian, 173
Flipper, 104
Florida Keys, 99, 117
Florida Straits, 51, 177
Florida, 10, 16, 34, 45, 108-133, 191
Foreign Slave Bill, 59
Fort Amsterdam, 241, 322, 332
Fort Charlotte, 184
Fort Fredereick, 302
Fort. Lauderdale, 11, 16, 123-128
Fort Myers, 133
Fort Napoleon, 276
Fort St. Louis, 242, 279
Fort Shirley, 288
Fort-de-France, 21, 280, 281
Frederiksted, 223
Freeport, 179, 186
French Antilles, 62, 270
French Quarter, 136
Frenchtown, 214
French West Indies Co., 289
Frigate, bird, 94
Frigate Bird Sanc., 269
G
Galatoire's, 138
Galveston, 11, 43, 140
Garden of the Groves, 186
Garrison Seaport, 35, 131
Gauguin, Paul 281
George Town, 159-162
Goldeneye, 173
Golf, 117, 127, 130, 162, 172, 175, 181, 186, 195, 211, 221, 241, 251, 255, 263, 274, 278, 291, 300, 314, 331
Grand Anse Beach, 23
Grand Case, 242

Grand Cayes, 239
Grand Cayman, 12, 35, 101, 156-163
Great Egret, 95
Greater Antilles, 10, 40, 47, 51, 58, 62, 65, 190
Green Cay, 221, 226
Green Key Island, 239
Green Vervet Monkey, 247
Grenada, 23, 40, 53, 62, 63, 73, 294-302
Grenadines, 62. 303-305
Guadeloupe, 40, 53, 55, 56, 62, 73, 244, 270-276
Guanahani, 177
Guatemala, 143
Gulf of Mexico, 141
Gulf Stream, 34
Gustavia, 244
H
Hackman, Gene, 159
Haiti, 10, 34, 53, 56, 58, 65, 120, 177
Hamilton, Alexander, 255
Hammond, Beres, 82
Harmony Hall, 262
Harrison's Cave, 316
Havana, 51, 64, 191
Hawksnest Bay, 21
Hell, 163
Hellman, Lillian, 136
Hemmingway, Ernest, 119
Hispaniola, 47, 49, 65, 165, 177, 190
Hol Chan, 155
Holetown, 308
Holland America Line, 32, 35
Homestead, 117
Honduras, 143, 155
Houston, 11, 140, 141
Houston, Sam, 141
Hugues, Victor, 272
Hurricanes, phenomena, 43-46
Hurricane, names: Andrew, Camille, George, Lenny, Marilyn, "The Great", 45-46
Hurricane David, 283
Hurricane Gilbert, 168

I
Iguana, 92
Intracoastal Waterway, 135
Isla Cancun, 147
Isla Mujeres, 147, 152
Isla Verde Beach, 195
Isles des Saintes, 275
J
Jagger, Mick, 305
Jaguars, 94
Jamaica, 12, 43, 55, 58, 60, 61, 62, 65, 73, 78, 158, 164-175
Jamaican Tourist Board, 175
John F. Kennedy Space Center, 16, 111, 128
Johnson Space Center, 140
Junkanoo, 74
K
Kennedy, Jacqueline, 143
Key Largo, 118
Key West, 12, 15, 16, 20, 110, 119-122
Keyes, Francis Parkinson, 139
Kincaid, Jamaica, 78
Kings, Louis XVI, 293, William IV, 266
Kingston, 165, 169
Kingstown, 303
Klein Bonaire, 22
Kralendijk, 334
L
La Desirade
La Soufriere, 42
Lafitte, Jean, 147
Lagos, 57
Lake Okeechobee, 109, 111
Lamani, 155
Las Cabezas de San Juan Nature Reserve, 203
Leaper's Hill, 295, 298
Le Carbet, 281
Leeward Group, 10
Legall, Neville Oluyemi, 313
Leon, Juan Ponce de, 110, 190, 191, 199, 201, 202

Lesser Antilles, 10, 12, 40, 42, 43, 45, 47, 51, 70, 219
Lewis, Sir Arthur, 79, 289
Liberia, 35
Limetree Beach, 210
Little Bay, 239
Little Cayman, 157
Liverpool, 58
Long Bay, 239
Louisiana Purchase, 135
Love Beach, 181
Lowe Art Museum, 114
Luanda, 57
Lucaya National Park, 186
Luquillo Beach, 195
M
Madeira Islands, 49
Magen's Bay Beach, 210
Maho Bay, 239
Mangrove, trees 98
Manatees, 104
Manley, Norman, 168
Mardi Gras, 134, 138
Marie Galante, 270, 273
Marigot Bay, 23, 292
Marigot, 21, 237, 242
Marley, Bob, 79, 82, 169
Maroons, 58
Martha Brae, 173
Martin, Ricky, 79
Martinique, 22, 42, 53, 56, 62, 73, 206, 277-281
Maya, 48, 143, 147
Mayreau, 305
Meclizine, 25
Merengue, music 83
Merida, 151
Mexico, 40, 51, 64, 147
Miami, 11, 16, 113-117
Middle Passage, 59
Mississippi River, 135
Mobile, 139
Monrovia, 35
Montego Bay, 173, 174
Montserrat, 42, 53, 62
Morgan, Sir Henry, 66, 71, 147, 168
Morningstar Beach, 210
Mount Gay, 309, 316
Mount Pelee, 42, 277

Mount Soufriere, 275
Moyne Report, 62
Mullet Bay Resort, 18
Mullet Bay, 239
Museo de Pablo Cassals, 202
Museums,
– Antigua and Barbuda, 263,
  – Cayman Island, 161
  – Dominica, 286
  – Grenada 301
  – Nelson 255
  – Pagerie, 281
  – Vizcaya 115
Mustique, 303, 304
N
Naipaul, Sir V.S., 78
National Hurricane Center, 15, 45, 46
National Oceanic and Atmospheric Administration (NOAA), 45, 46
National Space Hall of Fame, 141
Naussau, 20, 69, 74, 177, 178, 179, 180
Navigation Act, 55, 266. 308
Negril, 168
Nelson, Horatio, 266
Nelson's Dockyard, 17, 55, 262, 265
Netherlands Antilles, 320-335
New Orleans, 11, 16, 80, 135
New Providence Island, 177, 179
Nobel, Prize, 289
North Carolina, 68
North Sound, 233
O
O'Barry, Richard, 104
O'Daly, Thomas, 192
Ocho Rios, 35, 170, 171, 173
Orient Bay, 239
Orinoco, River, 307, 320
Orlando, 128
Orleans, 242
Orsted, A.S., 215
Oranjestad, 324-327
P

Palm Beach, 113
Palm, trees, 92
Palmer, Annie, 174
Panama Canal, 62, 64, 205
Panama, 35, 49, 66,168
Paradise Island, 181, 185
Pardise Peak, 242
Parrots, 95, 288
Passports, 24
Pedro St. James Castle, 163
Peru, 64
Philpsburg, 21, 28, 235
Pindling, Lynden Oscar, 179
Pirates, 64-69
Pitons, the, 289
Pitt, William, 59
Plum Bay, 239
Plymouth, 42
Pointe-A-Pitre, 273-275
Poitier, Sydney, 79
Port Antonio, 168
Port Canaveral, 11, 16, 128, 129
Port Everglades, 123, 124
Portsmouth, 288
Port Royal, 43, 165, 168
Portobelo, 51, 65, 66, 168
Prince Charles, 179
Princess Cruises, 35
Princess Diana, 259
Princess Margaret, 304
Professional Association of Diving Instructors (PADI), 18
Protestant Cay, 220
Puerto Rico, 61, 62, 72, 74, 110, 188-203
Pyle, Howard, 65
Q
Queen Anne's Revenge, 69
Queen Elizabeth, 158
Queen's Staircase, 183
Quetzalcoatl, 146
R
Rackam, 'Calico' Jack, 67
Rastafarianism, 169
Rays, 101

Read, Mary, 67
Redonda, 260
Reggae, 82, 169
Renta, Oscar de la, 79
Reynolds, Burt, 125
Rhone National Marine Park, 226, 229
Rice, Anne, 136
Richter Scale, 43
Rio Bueno, 168
Rivera, Luis Munoz, 189, 190
Road Town, 227-229
Roatan Island, 155
Rockefeller, Laurance, 215
Rogers, Capt. Woodes, 69, 178
Romney Manor, 253
Roseau, 284-287
Royal Caribbean International, 13, 35
Royal Navy Rum, 73
Rum, 71-73, 309
Runaway Bay, 171
S
Saba, 40, 62, 256
Sage Mountain National Park, 226
Salsa,83
San Fancisco Reef, 149
San Juan, 11, 12, 16, 43, 64, 65, 188-203
San Miguel, 148
San Salvador, 177, 179
Sanibel Island, 133
Santa Rosa Reef, 149
Santo Domingo, 191
Sarasota, 133
Victor Schoelcher, 272, 273
Scholten, Peter von, 61, 219, 221
Seabourn Cruise Lines, 13, 35
Seagrass, 98
Seaview Farm, 262
Seminoles, 111
Senegal, 57
Seven Mile Beach, 159
Seven Years War, 54, 110, 272
Sharks, 100, 101
Shark Ray Alley, 155
Shark Wall, 181

Sharpe, Sam, 60
Shipwrecks, 69
Shirley Heights, 267
Skytsborg, 68, 214
Slavery, 56-61
Smith, Rose, 250
Smugglers Cove, 229
Soca, 82
Sombrero Is., 248
South America, 58, 320
Southern Caribbean, 12
Spain, 64, 135
St .Augustine, 110, 113, 191
St. Barts, 53, 244, 273
St. Croix, 49, 53, 54, 50, 71, 73, 74, 205, 206, 207, 219
St. Eustatius, 62, 255
St. George's, 296-302
St. John, 54, 73, 205, 206, 207, 215
St. John's, 21, 31, 54, 261-264
St. Kitts/Nevis, 17, 19, 43, 52, 55, 63, 246-257
St. Lucia, 23, 54, 56, 62, 78, 283, 289-293
St. Maarten/St. Martin, 12, 18, 21, 28, 40, 52, 62, 234-245, 273
St. Martin, 62
St. Pierre, 42, 281
St. Thomas, 12, 13, 16, 21, 43, 54, 66, 74, 205, 206, 207, 209
St. Vincent, 42, 53, 54, 62, 303-305
Steelband, music, 81
Stingray City, 160, 163
Sugar, 70, 71
T
Tallahassee, 111
Tampa, 11, 16, 35, 129-132
Teach, Edward 'Blackbeard', 67, 68, 206
Thatch Cay, 210
The Baths, 233
Theroux, Paul, 78
Thornton, Dr William, 55
Tobago Cays, 305
Toltec, 146
Tortola, 2˜27, 230

Toussaint L'Ouverture, 56
Tragalgar, Battle of, 266, 272
Trafalgar Falls, 31, 284, 287
Trafalgar Square, 315
Treaty of Amiens, 272
Treaty of Madrid, 158
Treaty of Versailles, 248
Trinidad/Tobago, 40, 61, 62, 74, 78, 340-341
Tripplehorn, Jeanne, 159
Trunk Bay, 216, 233
Tugwell, Rexford, 190
Tulum, 20, 153
Tunnel Wall, 181
Turks/Caicos, 65, 179
Turtles, 102, 157, 163
Twain, Mark, 135
U
Union Island, 305
Uxmal, 151
V
Venezuela, 10, 12, 24. 307
Venice, 133
Veracruz, 51, 191
Virgin Gorda, 226, 230, 233
Virgin Islands - British, 53, 55, 62, 73, 205, 225
Virgin Islands - US, 12, 19, 40, 61, 62, 65, 73, 74, 205
Virgin Islands National Park, 215
W
Walcott, Derek, 78, 289
War of Jenkins Ear, 54
Warner, Thomas, 247, 254
Water, 283
Watling Island, 49
West Bay Beach, 155
West Indies, 10, 54, 55, 57, 63, 64, 78, 84, 93, 168, 191, 205, 219
West Wall, 162
Whales, 102, 103
Whim Plantation Museum, 223
Wilberforce, Wiliam, 59
Willemstad, 22,

327,330, 331
Williams, Tennesee, 135
Windstar, 14
Windward Group, 10
Windward Passage, 34
X
Xaymaca, 165
Xcaret, 153
Xel-Ha, 153
Y
Yaxchilan, 143
Ybor City, 130, 132
Yucatan Penn., 12, 20, 28,40, 93, 143, 146, 151
Z
Zaandam, 32
Zouk, music, 83

PHOTOGRAPHY

Barbados News Bureau, 316 (bottom).
Johnnie Black, 169.
George Brizan, 56.
Carnival Cruise Lines, 121.
Celebrity Cruises, 16 (top), 17 (top), 88 (top), 96 (bottom, right), 145 (top), 147, 148, 149, 152, 289 (bottom).
CORBIS, 89 (top), 112.
CORBIS, Tom Brakefield, 103.
Michael DeFreitas, 6, 9, 21 (right), 22 (top & bottom), 47, 48, 57, 69, 74, 76 (top & middle), 77 (second from top, right bottom), 80, 88 (bottom), 89 (bottom), 91 (bottom), 92, 93, 95 (top), 96 (bottom left), 97 (all three), 98, 99, 100, 101, 102, 157, 160, 163, 166 (bottom), 167 (top), 181, 185, 193 (top & bottom left), 195 (bottom), 196 (top), 197 (top), 200, 201 (top & bottom), 220 (top), 233, 255, 269, 276 (bottom right), 285, 297, 300 (bottom), 303, 304 (middle), 305 (top), 325 (top

& bottom), 328 (middle right), 334, 335, 336 (top right), 341.
Florida Division of Tourism, 130.
Holland America Line, 32, 159.
Fred Jensen, 12, 302, 310.
Bob Krist, 64, 197 (middle).
Mariano Advertising, 137 (bottom).
Mary Evans Picture Library, 52 (top), 59, 66.
NASA, 46.
Raymond Norris-Jones, 39, 166 (top).
Gordon Persson, 3, 142, 158, 167 (bottom).
Port Canaveral, 129.
Port Everglades, 123.
Port of Galveston, 140, 141.
Port of Miami, 109.
Port of New Orleans / Donn Young Photograph, 136.
Princess Cruises, 37 (bottom), 175, 188, 220 (bottom).
Puerto Rico Tourism Company, 190 (top).
George Rhodes, 104.
Rio Grande Press, Inc., 67 (top & bottom).
Royal Caribbean International, 13 (top), 33, 37 (top), 75, 239.
St. Croix Landmarks Society, 54, 58, 60, 61, 70, 71.
Michael Terranova, 137 (top).
VP Records, 82.
Windstar Cruises: Gerald Brimacombe, 5, 245. Bernard Gvilly, 304 (top). Harvey Lloyd, 14, 276 (bottom left), 304 (bottom), 305 (bottom).
All other photography by Anne Vipond.